Strengthening the family

Strengthening the family: Implications for international development

Marian F. Zeitlin, Ratna Megawangi,
Ellen M. Kramer, Nancy D. Colletta,
E.D. Babatunde, and David Garman

 United Nations
University Press

TOKYO · NEW YORK · PARIS

United Nations University Press
The United Nations University, 53-70, Jingumae 5-chome, Shibuya-ku, Tokyo 150, Japan
Tel: (03) 3499-2811   Fax: (03) 3406-7345
Telex: J25442   Cable: UNATUNIV TOKYO

UNU Office in North America
2 United Nations Plaza, Room DC2-1462, New York, NY 10017
Tel: (212) 963-6387   Fax: (212) 371-9454
Telex: 422311 UN UI

United Nations University Press is the publishing division of the United Nations University.

Typeset by Asco Trade Typesetting Limited, Hong Kong
Printed by Permanent Typesetting and Printing Co., Ltd., Hong Kong
Cover design by Paul Perlow Design, NY

UNUP-890
ISBN 92-808-0890-7
03500 P

Was ist das Schwerste von allem?
Was dir das Leichste dünket,
mit den Augen zu sehen,
Was vor den Augen dir liegt.

(What is the most difficult of all?
That which seems to you the easiest,
To see with one's eyes
What is lying before them.)

—Goethe, *Xenien Aus Dem Nachlass #45*

Contents

1

Introduction and purpose

Introduction

The impetus for this study grew out of the Positive Deviance in Nutrition Research Project, a five-year, three-country study for UNICEF New York and the WHO/UNICEF Joint Nutrition Support Programme, which investigated a wide range of factors contributing to good child growth and cognitive development under conditions of underdevelopment (Zeitlin, Ghassemi, and Mansour 1990; Zeitlin 1991). The main conclusion of this research was that good overall development of the child in poverty is a product of high-quality child care, taking place mainly at the level of the well-functioning family. Children thriving in poor communities were statistically most likely to live in families characterized by traditional fireside family values, devoted mothers and fathers, happy marriages, and warm cooperative bonds with siblings, grandparents, other relatives, and the broader community.

We use the terms "family social health" and "family social wellness" to designate these positive aspects of family functioning. We wished to capture the wellness concept and at the same time to emphasize that the family is a living entity and that the health of this entity in one generational cycle generates continued health in the next.

1

Goals

The goal of this research project was to identify the characteristics of healthy families in order to understand better how family social health improves the well-being of children and how family functioning interacts with national and international development. Therefore, the word "development" in the title refers not only to child development but also to social development more generally.

The following steps were taken to reach this goal:

1. Review family literature from sociology, anthropology, economics, psychology, and international development programmes such as international health, nutrition, and child development, focusing on definitions of family social wellness, correlates of family functioning, and relationships between family care in the present generation and developmental outcomes of the children.
2. Use findings from this literature to construct systems models of material and social resources, cultural values, family-level care, and developmental outcomes. While focusing specifically on children, we articulate generalizable analytic approaches that could be applied equally well to other family members, such as the elderly.
3. Use these models to explore further our positive deviance project conclusions with data sets from Indonesia and Nigeria, to investigate the strength of associations between "social health" at the family level and "overall development" at the child level, and to test the hypothesis that the same family measures that predict individual dimensions of child development also predict the other dimensions that contribute to the concept of "overall development."
4. Synthesize a cross-disciplinary paradigm of "family social health" or "family social wellness" in relation to national and international development – a paradigm relevant to both current and future family entities, represented by children.
5. Draw conclusions for further research on family functioning to support social policies and programmes.
6. Recommend policies and programme designs to improve family social health in the context of a sustainable, food-secure environment.

Project scope

We were unable to review in depth the vast literature on the family – over 5,000 listings in Harvard libraries alone; we therefore relied strategically on review volumes and inevitably left areas uncovered.

In this pass through our subject matter, we wished to reveal the most readily accessible conclusions about the social health of the family, to make these findings available for policy purposes, and to invite scholars specializing in the different branches of family and development studies to carry these ideas further.

To meet these requirements we reveal the fact that the smallest unit of analysis for sustainable development is not the household or the individual, but rather the biosocial family with its hereditary physical, social, and material endowments. It is the fundamental viability or, for want of a better term, "social health," of this cross-generational unit that we attempt to define and spotlight. We explore the language and logic used by the different disciplines to analyse and prescribe solutions to problems of family functioning. We relate these findings to a broad spectrum of development-assistance activities, as we seek to identify ways to strengthen the long-term viability or social health of families.

In-depth descriptions of two very different family types, the Javanese of Indonesia and the Yoruba of Nigeria, counterbalance the dominance in our cited literature of studies of Western – mainly North American Caucasian – families, as well as our lesser number of contrasting studies from Japan. We return repeatedly to the Yoruba and Indonesian cultures for details of family life that may contradict, validate, or expand generalizations from the Western literature.

Need for a family focus

Almost all development strategies now recognize the problems confronted by families. The Department of International Economic and Social Affairs, United Nations (1987) listed the problems faced by families in developing countries, including poverty, low levels of education, poor health and nutrition, inadequate housing and sanitation, and unsupervised and unwanted children. Yet until recently, in the design of development policies and programmes, families have remained an invisible layer sandwiched between the individual and the community.

As stated by the Agency for International Development (AID) in 1990, many development programmes have been designed and their impact measured with emphasis either on the individual level or on the national level. According to the United Nations (1987), the emphasis in development activities is almost always on individuals and only rarely on families as units. Policies and programmes have been

3

focused on individuals who comprise the family – children, mothers, the young, the ageing – whose interests and needs are related, but not identical, to those of the family. Thus, children's allowances are based on number of children; educational programmes are based on children in primary and secondary schools, and occasionally on vocational training for adults; and health programmes are based on prenatal care, postnatal care, and child health.

The broad range of issues that simultaneously affect family members, and that family members may perceive to be their most urgent problems, finds no forum in these fragmented, issue-specific initiatives. This void leads to lack of commitment and participation at the level of the family entity, which is the management unit that cares for family members. By materially rewarding an individual-centred approach to family problems, existing programmes may contribute to the breakdown of family functioning.

An additional need to focus on the family arises from recent rapid increases in female-headed households among the poor. This growing detachment of women and children from the earnings and the care of their men is linked to worsening conditions of the poor (Bruce and Lloyd 1992).

Definitions of the family and its functions

Families are groups related by kinship, residence, or close emotional attachments and they display four systemic features – intimate interdependence, selective boundary maintenance, ability to adapt to change and maintain their identity over time, and performance of the family tasks listed below (Mattessich and Hill 1987).

The tasks performed by families include physical maintenance, socialization and education, control of social and sexual behaviour, maintenance of family morale and of motivation to perform roles inside and outside the family, the acquisition of mature family members by the formation of sexual partnerships, the acquisition of new family members through procreation or adoption, and the launching of juvenile members from the family when mature (Mattessich and Hill 1987).

Definitions of the family must be flexible enough to accommodate a wide variety of family forms. According to Walker and Crocker (1988), a family system can be defined as any social unit with which an individual is intimately involved, and which is governed by "family rules." One key concept of the family system is recursive causality, in which family members reciprocally influence each other over time. Another concept is that the family is greater than the sum of its members.

Leaving room for alternate arrangements, we can assume that the majority of families centre on residential units containing parents and their children, a mother and her children, or a childless couple, with a number of grandparents, aunts, uncles, cousins, and other kin living at varying distances from the core group. We also need to note that the reduction of distances by communications technology and other post-modern changes makes it increasingly difficult to generalize about actual or desirable family forms or residential arrangements.

Potential multiplier effects for family interventions

To the extent that enhancement of family social health simultaneously improves multiple dimensions of child development, we expect multiplier effects from family-level inputs compared with the effects of the same inputs directed through vertical programmes for individual children (Schorr 1988).

Seeking development from within each culture

We seek to nurture the family in newly emerging technological societies in a manner that maintains continuity from the past to future, and that avoids mistakes made by the industrialized countries. This goal was a part of the Positive Deviance Project. Family, as the cradle of culture, cannot be approached generically.

In Africa, the goal of development from within has been explicit since the introduction of the terms "Negritude" or "African Personality" by Senghor and "African Socialism" by Nkrumah, starting in the 1940s and 1950s (Lloyd 1972, 267–287). Failure of some attempts by political movements to harness African traditional values in the service of socio-economic development has not changed the importance of this agenda, nor that of agendas of uniting Africans of different ethnic groups around their common values and continuing to look for models, such as the Japanese experience, for incorporating family and lineage values into newly emerging industries (Babatunde 1992, 222–240).

In Indonesia, the unity and the diversity of that country are manifested by *Pancasila*, Indonesia's national ideology. There were conflicts, during the struggle for an independent Indonesia, over the kind of basic principles upon which the future state would be founded: one group proposed Islam as the basis, while other groups favoured a secular state. On 1 June 1945, President Sukarno delivered a famous speech in which he proposed a compromise that the state would be neither an Islamic nor a secular state but a *Pancasila* state. From then on, 1 June has been celebrated as "the birth of *Pancasila*." Literally, *Pancasila* means "five principles," namely:

1. The Principle of One Lordship (One God);
2. A Just and Civilized Humanity;
3. The Unity of Indonesia;
4. The Principle of Peoplehood Which is Guarded by the Spirit of Wisdom in Representation;
5. Social Justice.

The appeal to believe in one God is a message of religious tolerance to citizens of all religions, from Islam to Christianity, to Hinduism, to Javanese Mysticism, and an appeal to worship God by practising their own religion. Indonesia has more than a hundred distinct ethnic groups with a wide array of languages, and *Pancasila* has sustained their unity in diversity based on the concept of "harmony and balance." Over the years, the present Indonesian Government has been seriously committed to national development, with economic development as the central focus. It has shown remarkable progress. At the same time, the Government has also conducted an intensive and pervasive educational programme on *Pancasila*, ranging from the primary school to the top management level, assuming that *Pancasila* will provide a needed moral basis for national development, even though this assumption has been questioned (Darmaputera 1988).

Organization and overview

Chapter 2, on Social Change and the Family, reviews the literature (sociological, anthropological, psychological) on changes that call into question traditional family values and supports while preparing children for new lifestyles. During the process commonly referred to as modernization, rational bureaucratic authority and impersonal markets gradually come to dominate social life. Ties to kin weaken, face-to-face interdependencies are reduced, and impersonal markets and agencies of the state increasingly mediate between individuals and between small families. The break from the past never is clean, as the old either persists or evolves into the new. Moreover, the order in which these changes occur and the forms they take vary greatly from one society to another (Dizard and Gadlin 1990).

We view family life among our Yoruba sample as highly susceptible, and our Javanese sample only moderately vulnerable, to disruption by secular change. Therefore, the discussion of the family in Nigeria and the Nigerian model consider these influences much more explicitly than do our chapters on Indonesia. As detailed in the chapter introducing the description of the Javanese family (ch. 6), Indonesian socio-economic development appears to follow an East Asian pattern best documented among the Japanese; in this pattern, traditional hierarchies and value systems, forms of respect, and dependencies developed in feudal eras appear to contribute positively to the industrialization process.

For Nigeria, on the other hand, problems attendant on rapid social change are elaborated by the authors cited in our chapter on the Yoruba family (ch. 7), and many of these appear to be concerns similar to those voiced by Dizard and Gadlin (1990) in the United States. In Africa, low self-esteem derived from perceived inequalities in wealth and technology increases the disruption of traditional social norms. Major cultural discontinuities, such as those that occurred for the immigrating population of the United States and during the colonial domination of Africa, throw populations into transitional states in which the formation of new cultural norms is particularly vulnerable to market forces. Barnlund (1989) points to the discontinuity of the American experience, compared with the long continuity of Japanese culture, as an explanation for the US obsession with individualism as contrasted with Japanese authoritarian hierarchies.

Powerful cultural differences pervade global trends. In promoting democracy, the United States must be wary of exporting aspects of American culture that are not essential to the democratic process. Much of what is distinctive in American values has been traced to the constant mobility of its early settlers, including good traits such as optimism, individualism, achievement orientation, and love of novelty, and negative aspects of superficiality, alienation, loneliness, and materialism (Slater 1980; Darling 1986). Chapter 2 explores these cultural differences.

Chapter 3, on economics, distils relevant findings from research methods using mathematical equations that are relatively inaccessible to non-economists. Mathematical game theory used by economists to study bargaining between husbands and wives, for example, cannot be applied by marriage counsellors. Yet economics increasingly supplies useful mathematical models for more general applications. Used to the rationality of the market, economists studying the family are in the midst of a fascinating process of redefining their concepts to accommodate cultural and psychological determinants of household behaviour. These adaptations hold out the promise of quantifying the effects of family change on economic development and human welfare.

Chapter 4, on psychological theories, spans thousands of documents, which we were forced to deal with mainly through review volumes and articles. Psychological studies of families as systems provide a broad inventory of concepts and measurements for use in cross-disciplinary synthesis of methods and findings.

Chapter 5, on development-assistance approaches, highlights the pioneering role of early childhood development programmes in working with families. This programme type strengthens the family's capacity to play its socialization and educational role, while protecting the family member at highest risk and strengthening, through the child, the foundation for the family's next generation.

Chapters 6 and 7, on Javanese and Yoruba family life, illustrate family concepts and family life in two well-known non-Western and less-industrialized cultures. Rather than focusing on social wellness of the family as an entity, we set forth each culture's own concepts of family life and values. Chapter 8 presents and tests empirical models using field data contextualized in the previous two chapters.

Chapter 9 draws upon the earlier chapters to produce a unified cross-disciplinary paradigm of the socially well family. Chapter 10 provides a list of policy and programme priorities that is limited to those approaches that improve family social health and the conditions of children, either through, or in parallel with, the conditions of the family.

References

Agency for International Development. 1990. "Family and Development: An A.I.D. Initiative, December 1990."

Babatunde, E.D. 1992. *A Critical Study of Bini and Yoruba Value Systems in Change: Culture, Religion and the Self.* Lewiston, New York: The Edwin Mellen Press.

Barnlund, D.C. 1989. *Public and Private Self in Japan and the United States: Communicative Styles of Two Cultures.* Tokyo: Intercultural Press (by arrangement with Simul Press).

Bruce, J., and C.B. Lloyd. 1992. "Beyond Female Headship: Family Research and Policy Issues for the 1990s." Presented at IFPRI–World Bank Conference on

Intrahousehold Resource Allocation: Policies and Research Methods, 12–14 February 1992, IFPRI, Washington, DC.

Darling, C.A. 1986. "Family Life Education." In: M.B. Sussman and S.K. Steinmetz, eds. *Handbook of Marriage and the Family*. New York: Plenum Press, pp. 815–833.

Darmaputera, E. 1988. *Pancasila and the Search for Identity and Modernity in Indonesian Society*. New York: E.J. Brill.

Dizard, J.E., and H. Gadlin. 1990. *The Minimal Family*. Amherst, Mass.: University of Amherst Press.

Lloyd, P.C. 1972. *Africa in Social Change: Changing Traditional Societies in the Modern World*. Baltimore, Md.: Penguin.

Mattessich, P., and R. Hill. 1987. "Life Cycle and Family Development." In: M.B. Sussman and S.K. Steinmetz, eds. *Handbook of Marriage and the Family*. New York: Plenum Press, pp. 437–469.

Schorr, L.B. 1988. *Within our Reach; Breaking the Cycle of Disadvantage*. New York: Anchor, Doubleday.

Slater, P. 1980. "Some Effects of Transience." In: E. Douvan, H. Weingarten, and J. Scheiber, eds. *American Families*. Dubuque, Ia.: Kendall/Hunt.

United Nations. 1987. *The Family: Strengthening the Family, Guidelines for the Design of Relevant Programmes*. New York: United Nations.

Walker, D.K., and R.W. Crocker. 1988. "Measuring Family Systems Outcomes." In: H.B. Weiss and F.H. Jacobs, eds. *Evaluating Family Programs*. New York: Aldine de Gruyter, pp. 153–176.

Zeitlin, M.F. 1991. "Nutritional Resilience in a Hostile Environment: Positive Deviance in Child Nutrition." *Nutrition Reviews* 49: 259–268.

———, H. Ghassemi, and M. Mansour. 1990. *Positive Deviance in Child Nutrition*. Tokyo: United Nations University Press.

2

Social change and the family

Sociological, anthropological, and historical perspectives

Pre-modern families

Early hunting-and-gathering societies appear to have lived first in small nomadic bands and later, in some locations, in larger, more settled, and hierarchically organized communities (Wenke 1984). Judging from groups of !Kung, Native Americans, Australian Aborigines, and others whose lifestyles have remained relatively intact into recorded history, small kin groups of hunter–gatherers tended to be cooperative and relatively egalitarian. Although marital partnerships were formed, hunter–gatherer bands valued compatibility among their members more highly than continuous co-residence with a single band, and individuals might fluidly move from one related band to another (Quale 1988). They have been idealized by ecologists for holding values of living in harmony with other life forms instead of striving to dominate and exploit them. However, the integration of such families into modern life tends to be a long and difficult process.

Most herders and pastoral nomads tend to have patriarchal families and a tendency toward polygyny (Schneider and Gough 1961; Maccoby 1966). Women's productive work tends to be limited to herding of small animals, dairying, and food processing and preparation (Quale 1988). Where exchange relationships must be set in place over widely dispersed territories, marriage partnerships may be strategically located, and the exchange of daughters in marriage may help to cement economic alliances. These families are difficult to integrate because their mobility interferes with the schooling of their children and the regular health care of their members.

Pure forms of nomadic family types may be the exception rather than the rule. The Dinka of the Sudan, for example, grow about one-third and gather and hunt two-thirds of the food types that they use (Zeitlin 1977). Dinka women and old men tend to be sedentary year-round, while young men are nomadic pastoralists for a part of the year (Deng 1972).

Societies engaged in traditional agriculture, crafts, and trade have been broadly divided into those practising communal land ownership and those practising private land ownership (Caldwell and Caldwell 1990). Most populations of Europe and Asia made the transition from communal to private land ownership from 4,000 to 5,000 years ago, in response to the accumulation of significant agricultural surpluses, or possibly wealth from other sources such as copper mines. In sub-Saharan Africa, isolated by the desert, and with growing conditions that did not favour the accumulation of surplus, communal land ownership remained predominant.

Polygyny, as a family form, is well suited to a shifting agricultural system using abundant low-yielding communal land farmed by labour-intensive technologies (Caldwell and Caldwell 1990). Each additional wife and her children permit the family to farm more territory and to achieve economies of scale in domestic labour and trade. The family unit, which is headed by the husband and the elders of his lineage, starts with one wife and adds more after accumulating the bride-wealth needed for each. The more wives and children, the larger and more affluent this unit can become. Sexual fidelity of the wives is not a top priority, and all children born to a man's wives are legally his. Societies with this family form appear to place the highest cultural and religious value on child-bearing. According to Quale (1988), it may not be reasonable to assume that all early agricultural societies fit this model, when agriculture evolved in rich localized topsoil deposits of annually flooding rivers.

Monogamous marriage, with strong cultural safeguards for the sexual fidelity of women, is important for the maintenance of traditional subsistence agriculture on privately owned farms. Family lands must be passed to male heirs whose paternity is beyond question. For greater security in land transmission, cross-cousin marriage may be preferred. Brothers whose children marry, reunite land and other possessions separated by inheritance. Such cousin marriage has been common in many cultures, with the highest current rate of about 60 per cent of all marriages claimed for Pakistan (DHSL/Institute of Population Studies 1992). It may also reduce property-related feuds common among societies of peasant farmers in the Middle East and elsewhere (Sweet 1970).

In spite of ethnographic variations, agrarian families are recognizable as a type. Throughout the world, these settled institutional families are organized around agricultural production, traditional crafts, or other family business ventures. They have large kinship networks and hierarchical authoritarian governance. These families are producers, employers, consumers, and social welfare agencies in one. Family management tends to be well developed. The highest family value is responsibility (Doherty 1992).

While the maximum kin that one person can keep track of fairly closely has been estimated at 50 (Quale 1988), the traditional hierarchical Yoruba lineage structure (ch. 7), housed from 20 to 2,000 lineage members together in a single walled compound, in which the immediate family units lived and worked in public view under the watchful eye of the compound head. Marriage in institutional families is a functional partnership rather than a romantic relationship. Children tend to be valued as apprentices and next-generation managers of the family lands and enterprises.

Historical and current records indicate, however, that both former and present-day institutional farming families do not usually live in large residential units. The most common dwelling arrangement still is mother, father, and their children; or mother, her children, and others. These small traditional units differ from modern families in part in their economic interdependence with nearby family and community members, and in part in their attitudes towards family life (Hareven 1987).

Evolution of the family

As they evolve, family and community structures adapt to the physical and social conditions of production (Wenke 1984). Similar evolutionary forces lead to changes in family dynamics and in child-rearing practices. Parents adjust their child-rearing behaviour to the risks that they perceive in the environment, the skills that they expect their children to acquire as adults, and the cultural and economic expectations that they have of their children (LeVine 1974; LeVine, Miller, and West 1988). There is a powerful interplay between a society's technology, family structure, and social values.

Yet technology is not a rigid cultural taskmaster. The same production technologies and ecological conditions accommodate variations in family organization, management style, and emotional climate. Within Indonesia, for example, the Javanese are known for their warmth toward young children (ch. 7), whereas the Alorese are reported to be low in child nurturance. In Coastal West Africa, the Yoruba and Ibo of Nigeria have contrasting patrilineal hierarchies, family settlement patterns, and gender roles. The Akan of Ghana are matrilineal by heritage. Americans and Japanese both are industrialized but differ culturally. Similar changes in technology stimulate family change in similar directions but from different starting points and along variable pathways.

The modern family

Early history

According to research by Stone (1977), the presence of the modern family in the West was first documented in England in the mid-1600s, at which time the élite gradually stopped sending their infants away to be wet-nursed and swaddling of infants declined; there was heightened regard for the infant as a person and the woman's role as a mother; there were new ideals of intimacy and privacy for the couple; and there was growing emphasis on love, personal attraction, and compatibility as the basis for mate selection. Within the next hundred years, these changes gradually became predominant; the young were choosing their own mates even if resorting to pregnancy before marriage was necessary to do so (Dizard and Gadlin 1990, 5–24).

The emphasis on emotional bonds between husband and wife set the modern family off from its predecessors (Stone 1977). The modern family is expected to be emotionally self-sufficient. Other relatives become peripheral, while the bonds among nuclear family members grow more intense and emotional (Burgess and Locke 1953; Dizard and Gadlin 1990, 5–24).

The modern nuclear family was shaped by three sentiments: romantic love between spouses rather than marriage arranged for reasons of property and social status; maternal love, or the idea that women have a maternal instinct and a need to care for young children; and domesticity, or the belief that relationships within the family are always more binding than are those outside it (Elkind 1992). As a family based on the personal satisfaction of its individual members, the modern family also has been termed the psychological family; its chief value is satisfaction (Doherty 1992).

Forces driving family transition

The modern family evolved in concert with industrialization, science, and technology. With the growth of specialized wage labour, economically productive work moved beyond the reach of the family compound. Individualized remuneration and liability led to a redefinition of kinship obligations. The family that was engaged in farming or crafts could be expanded because extra hands could produce extra food and other products. Its boundaries were elastic. The resources of the salaried family and the number of people who could be supported by its wage-earners were fixed. Living space in the neighbourhood of factories and other specialized worksites was expensive and non-expansible. Where neighbours were strangers, the modern family became a "haven in a heartless world" (Lasch 1977).

Even without significant industrial growth, the expansion of global markets, the mass media, the civil service, and other services such as health care, education, and transportation led to the formation of modern families in developing countries. Caldwell and Caldwell (1977) described this change in Nigeria and Ghana as "a movement toward monogamy, a strengthening of the conjugal bond over all others, a strengthening of the parent–child bond over all relationships external to the nuclear family, and ultimately an emphasis on what parents owe children rather than what children owe parents."

Falling birth rates and the death of the institutional family

Falling child death rates lead to falling birth rates, through the sequence of events known as the demographic transition (Caldwell and Caldwell 1990) that occurs under favourable socio-economic conditions. Wherever such fertility control is successful it brings not only fewer children but fewer extended family ties in subsequent generations of children, who have far fewer uncles, aunts, and cousins than their parents' generation. The arithmetic of the demographic transition is such that it is impossible to lower death rates to internationally acceptable levels and simultaneously to control population growth without reducing the number of children per family to an average of two (Zeitlin et al. 1982). With the lure of out-of-family employment, this small number of children is insufficient to sustain the farming or other business enterprises of the institutional family.

Positive links between socio-economic development and the modern family

Optimism and ideology

The modern family came into being with the surge of optimistic thinking that began in the Renaissance and continued through the Industrial Revolution. Human progress, universality of the newly discovered laws of science, and the consistency and regularity of the laws governing the universe were underlying assumptions of this era. Widespread agreement remains today that the modern nuclear family, with its two parents and two or three children, is the ideal end result of progress in the evolution of family forms (Elkind 1992).

Evidence for progress

The modern family's vital statistics are far better than those of the institutional family, and of all previous family forms. Quantum changes in income, mortality rates, life expectancy, nutritional status, educational opportunities, and other indicators of the quality of life occur in response to industrialization, modern health care, education, and other aspects of socio-economic development. It is widely agreed that families are better off with these changes than without them.

The positive effects of change on the modern family mirror negative changes discussed below. Modernization has commercialized many aspects of life that depended previously on much less commercialized exchanges within the traditional extended family and community. On the positive side, expanded communications networks create uniform global value standards in areas such as health care, nutrition, education, and basic human rights (as expressed, for example, in UNICEF's *The State of the World's Children, 1992*, which asserts that progress is ongoing). These value standards require technologies far exceeding those available to the traditional extended family.

15

Positive effects of changing child-rearing practices on child development

The ways in which parents train and stimulate their children also change systematically with the modernization of the family. These changes produce children who are more cognitively advanced by modern performance standards and are better nourished, and hence better prepared to participate in the modern workforce. Werner (1979) documented very similar differences in parenting styles between modernizing and traditional parents in the United States (Bronfenbrenner 1963; Becker and Krug 1964); Mexico (Holtzman, Diaz-Guerrero, and Swartz 1975); Lebanon (Prothro 1962); and Indonesia (Danzinger 1960a, 1960b; Thomas and Surachmad 1962); Nigeria (Lloyd 1966, 1970; LeVine, Klein, and Fries 1967); and Ghana (Grindal 1972). We found evidence of the same differences in the Nigerian and Indonesian data analysed in chapters 6 and 7; these differences were associated with better child growth and cognitive test performance (Zeitlin and Satoto 1990; Aina et al. 1992). We summarize these transformations as follows:

1. A change in parental discipline away from immediate physical punishment to tolerance of slower obedience, but expectation of greater understanding of the reasons for rules.
2. Acceptance of the child's physical dependency up to an older age.
3. More affection and intimacy, a more personal relationship with the father, and more recreation shared by parents and children.
4. Increased verbal responsiveness to the child and use of explanation rather than physical demonstration in teaching.

The first parents to alter their behaviours tend to be members of the élite and middle classes, who have the earliest contact with modernization. The same changes later occur as secular trends among less-privileged families. Our research demonstrated that the modernizing changes found in the élite families in Ibadan in the 1960s now also are seen among low-income families in Lagos State. The association of these factors with better child growth and cognitive scores tends to confirm the view that parents adopt these styles of interaction because they *are* adaptive, in that they *do* improve school achievement and the ability of children to compete in the modern world.

How various aspects of modernization and differences in social class produce changes in child-rearing, and how these changes alter cognitive and other outcomes, are ongoing topics of investigation

(Langman 1987). LeVine et al. (1991) documented that increased maternal schooling in Mexico is correlated with increased verbal responsiveness to infants and increased infant care by adults rather than siblings. They explain that

Formal education everywhere ... entails the presence of an adult whose role is entirely instructional, talking to children ... For girls in rural areas of countries where mass schooling is still a relatively recent innovation, this model of social interaction between an adult and children stands in contrast to their previous experience, and in time it reshapes their skills and preferences in social communication ... Identifying with the role of pupil, they continue to seek useful knowledge wherever they can find it; identifying with the role of teacher, they are verbally responsive to their children during infancy and after ... Their children grow up better prepared for school, equipped with verbal skills and with a new set of expectations concerning family life, fertility, parent–child relations, and health care. Thus, women's attendance at school initiates a cumulative process over the generations that contributes to the demographic transition. (LeVine et al. 1991, 492)

Parents need and welcome guidance and assistance in child development. Chapter 6 provides evidence for the effectiveness of early childhood education programmes that assist them in this task. Numerous evaluations of these programmes demonstrate that children's cognitive test scores and school success improve in response to their parent's verbal responsiveness and efforts to provide other forms of developmental stimulation.

Negative effects of development on the family and society

Sociologists, anthropologists, and women's study specialists also have documented negative effects of economic development on the family. Dizard and Gadlin, in their book *The Minimal Family* (1990), review extensive sociological literature in support of the premise, stated by Hirsch (1976), that the very success of capitalism entails the steady erosion of the "moral legacy" on which capitalism has rested, including the high levels of social responsibility found in the traditional family.

Dizard and Gadlin (1990, 41–42) present a negative view of the changes in family relationships away from cooperative endeavour towards modern goals of emotional fulfilment. They tend to view these changes as negative by-products of the forced expansion of industrial markets, which must grow at all costs because in the absence

17

of consumers industrial production would fall, unemployment would rise, and people would be unable to meet basic needs.

Commodification of family life

In this view, to remain profitable the economy must expand the sphere of needs that can be met through market-mediated exchanges. The expansion of markets is achieved by rendering more and more of the repertoire of human activity in commodity forms, thereby creating more opportunities for profit (Dizard and Gadlin 1990, 98). This process goes on at the expense of traditional production, economic exchange, entertainment, social support structures, personal relationships, and even biological functions such as breast-feeding.

Promotion of self-centred consumerism

According to this argument, the need to develop consumer markets to sustain the economy of capitalist systems leads not only to nuclear family formation but eventually to expressive, autonomous, and irresponsible individualism. In the upper class, such individualism translates into competitive upward mobility, while in the lower class it becomes "action seeking" – the constant quest for stimulation and excitement. Both types of individuals tend to have truncated human relationships, which are seen as instrumental rather than as ends in themselves (Dizard and Gadlin 1990, 188). Moreover, the emotional hothouse of the nuclear family tends to corrupt parental love (Dizard and Gadlin 1990, 79–81) by making it contingent on whether the child fulfils the parents' personal expectations.

Dizard and Gadlin (1990, 156) assert that "preparing children for autonomy tends to make them precocious, even unruly, yet there was reason to fear that imposing rules would inhibit or stultify a child's movement toward autonomy." Subjective aspirations for autonomy are reinforced and capitalized upon, literally and figuratively, by an economy whose existence is predicated upon the atrophy of traditional familism.

In the United States, immense advertising budgets for new consumer products have centred on two consuming social units – the nuclear family and the individual (Dizard and Gadlin 1990, 46) – and have not hesitated to awaken and appeal to such anti-family incitements as the desire for extramarital sex to sell products. The individualistic world view of the United States, however, may have created a particularly American experience of capitalism. Dizard and Gadlin (1990, 47) state that the advertising moguls of Madison Avenue were consciously actualizing a way of life that expressed the theories regarding human nature and social organization that were being formulated in esoteric journals and select conferences.

On the negative side, the most recent generation of young adults in America, born between 1965 and 1975, may appear to be the endpoint of this course of development. According to the description by Bradford and Raines (1992), the first priority of this group is themselves; they feel cheated by their parents' generation; they are materialistic; their adolescence is prolonged, with careers postponed in favour of travel and leisure; they are slow to commit themselves; they question authority and have a disregard for hierarchy. In the Nigerian context, Babatunde (1992) describes a sharp contrast in the essays of Nigerian schoolgirls about their ideal mates, between girls who seek men who can afford expensive consumer goods, versus girls who value a husband who is responsible and has a good character.

Reduction in altruism

In the field of cross-cultural child development, negative effects also have been noted. Whiting and Whiting (1975) studied children's behaviour in six cultures – in Kenya, Mexico, the Philippines, Japan, India, and the United States. They defined altruistic behaviour as actions to benefit another person and egoistic behaviour as actions to benefit the child himself. They found that the most altruistic children were from the most traditional society in rural Kenya and the most egoistic from the most complex modern society in the United States. The other children fell between these extremes according to their degree of modernization.

Focus groups with Lagos residents identified the issue of maintaining discipline and moral training in the presence of modern education and urban life as a major concern, particularly of grandparents who often were involved actively in bringing up their grandchildren (Aina et al. 1992).

Negative outcomes for poor families

The creation of new categories of industrial and post-industrial employment has had different effects on traditional family structures, depending on the numbers and types of jobs available and the employability of the applicants.

As noted above, the agrarian family could support its unskilled and psychologically marginal members by allotting them menial tasks. Such elasticity in African subsistence agriculture is captured in the Ghanaian proverb, "A guest is a guest for three days and then you give him a hoe" (to help on the farm). With departure from the farm, salaried families cannot support poor relatives who are unable to find stable employment. The majority of poor non-farm families often are left in the amorphous non-formal sector of petty trade and services. The non-formal process of living on "magic," as the Ghanaians termed it in the 1981 economic crisis, provides shifting sands for family formation.

Emergence of the modern two-parent nuclear family in developing countries has been primarily a middle-class phenomenon. The poorest classes tend to have high rates of relatively unstable consensual unions, low formal marriage rates, and high divorce rates. The direction taken by the urbanizing family towards an integrated, nuclear, upwardly mobile structure or an unstable female-headed structure may depend on the job success and attitudes of the father in the generation that migrates to the city, as described by Sennett (1970), for nineteenth century US urban migrants. Less successful urbanizing families devolve towards transient, male-headed or small, women-headed units, or extended family clusters in which women and their children are subunits (Buvinic 1992). Over time, women may bear children by different fathers in a manner that optimizes the probability that at least one of the men in their network will be able to provide remittances for child care, or social connections that help them to find a job (Gussler 1975; Guyer 1990). Often, as noted by Rao and Green (1991) in Brazil, women live in unstable consensual unions only because their partners will not agree to formal marriage or cannot afford it. By modern family standards, these irregular units are failed families; post-modern criteria may view them as normal variants (Doherty 1992).

The post-modern family, discussed in detail on pages 25–30, is sometimes termed the pluralistic (Doherty 1992) or permeable family (Elkind 1992). It consists of many small free-flowing groupings that include modern nuclear families; a few traditional families; single parents; blended, co-parent, adopted, test-tube, surrogate-mother, and gay and lesbian families, with or without formal marriage contracts.

Feminization of poverty

Women living alone or with their children are disproportionately represented among the poor. This trend, referred to as the feminization of poverty, may reflect changes in family structure (when nuclear families dissolve, the man usually retains his income and status, whereas the woman and her children enter the lower category of poor female-headed households). But others (Bane 1986) argue that often the underlying cause is poverty: resources for children living in poor female-headed households may be so inadequate that growth and development are adversely affected.

In general, women's economic power has become eroded with technological changes and with improvements in the market activities of poor rural households, which increase men's control over resources and simultaneously undercut women's control (Boserup 1970; Schultz 1989). By unbalancing traditional gender roles, modern agricultural technology may have negative effects on the caring capacity, cooperation between spouses, and emotional climate of families who adopt new cash crops and other technologies.

Female education has been shown to have a positive impact on the growth and development of children in many parts of the world (LeVine et al. 1991). Female education in sub-Saharan Africa, however, leads to the breakdown of the family values and codes of behaviour that govern the cooperative relations between co-wives (Bledsoe 1990), in which the first wife traditionally has seniority and supervisory duties over later wives, the second wife over the third, and so on. Education creates a different hierarchy: a young educated girl considers herself senior to an older, less-educated co-wife. As a mark of success, men now marry new wives who are more educated, socially presentable, and expensive to maintain than their earlier mate(s). With remarriage they cut off, or greatly reduce, support to children by the previous unions.

Negative effects of cultural distance

The greater the cultural distance between previous and new technologies, and between those who provide and those who receive assistance, the more negative the effects of change are likely to be on the family.

Extreme rates of alcoholism among Native Americans, and the hygiene and health problems of nomadic peoples moving into settled housing, are examples of numerous special problems that arise at the far reaches of cultural distance.

Changes in the late- and post-industrial era

The current ground swell of concern for the family in the United States reflects political and linguistic confusion for both conservatives and liberals. This resurgence of interest in the family coincides with an incipient shift away from a capitalistic system that depends for its survival on developing new consumer products that strip the family of its functions, and that are marketed at the expense of family cohesiveness.

New economic focus

The economic focus of the twenty-first century, according to Thurow (1992, 45), will be on new processes, not on new products. The seven key industries of the next few decades – micro-electronics, biotechnology, the materials industries, civilian aviation, telecommunications, robots plus machine tools, and computers plus software – will be brainpower industries that depend for their competitive advantage on new-process technologies and much less on new-product technologies.

These new industries can be located anywhere on the globe. The invention of new products, therefore, no longer leads to sustainable profits because these products can always be copied and reproduced less expensively elsewhere. "What used to be primary (inventing new products) becomes secondary, and what used to be secondary (inventing and perfecting new processes) becomes primary." (ibid.)

Profitability and high-wage employment depend increasingly on producing and marketing new versions of existing products. These existing products are transformed by information technology and biotechnology to be more powerful, efficient, and attractive. The competitive market advantages of the new information processes – e.g. facsimile machines built into notebook computers – may have as yet unforeseen transformational effects on lifestyles and values.

Viability in the competition for new processes does not depend on creative autonomy, but on high mathematical and technical skills from the top to bottom of a disciplined workforce. Much of the work involved requires high tolerance for detail and routine. According to Thurow (1992, 52),

If the route to success is inventing new products, the education of the smartest 25 percent of the labor force is critical ... If the route to success is being the cheapest and best producer of products, new or old, the education of the bottom 50 percent moves to center stage ... If the bottom 50 percent cannot learn what must be learned, new high-tech processes cannot be employed ... To learn what must be learned, every worker must have a level of basic mathematics that is far beyond that achieved by most American high school graduates.

Under these global conditions, it is hoped that the profitability of expanding markets for consumer goods at the expense of the family will yield to the profitability of recreating the family as a responsible unit for the production of disciplined children with strong technical skills.

If the highest profits lie in process competition rather than product competition, there also will be a need to develop the market for high-tech processes. This need should drive the education and training of consumers. Some high-tech processes, such as those in supermarket cash registers, reduce the need for thought on the part of the user, but the mastery of computers in the workplace and the home requires disciplined educational effort. This effort is best sustained by cohesive family life.

By constantly updating public awareness and lifestyle values, the new information technology also acts as a balancer between generations. When the older generation is no longer "out of touch," the younger generation loses its need to rebel, and cross-generational family ties may be strengthened. Amidst a glut of electronic images, the need to establish a unique personal identity separate from one's parents becomes less compelling.

Lessons from the East on the implications of the new conditions of production for family life

The fact that Japan has now surpassed the United States in many aspects of industrial and post-industrial development, without experiencing the same breakdown of family structures or the same growth in autonomy, indicates that highly disciplined, authoritarian, pre-industrial families may make the transition to the post-industrial family more efficiently than families that have yielded to the worst excesses of consumer society. The economic miracle currently occurring in Guangdong Province in China and in the "little dragons" of the Pacific Rim (Vogel 1992) – hardly the heartland of individualism –

further points to the importance of the simple cause-and-effect relationship between the acquisition of high mathematical skills through the school system and the family, and technological success in process industries that underprice those in the West. Philosophies of early childhood education that prepare children for these process-orientated skills may be very different from the extreme value placed on autonomy, self-expression, and uninhibited inquisitiveness in the United States.

The continued negative commodification of family life and other spheres of human activity that should not be commodified is apparently neither inevitable nor permanent. In the United States, for example, infant formula successfully competes with breast-feeding for close to a 40 per cent share of the newborn market, whereas in Sweden it captures only about 5 per cent.

Japan appears to have achieved economic supremacy in part by incorporating traditional family values into the capitalist production system. In fact, Japan is the only major industrialized country in the world never to have experienced a mass uprising against its feudal aristocracy. The fact that the Japanese aristocracy made a conscious decision to industrialize, leaving in place the psychology of feudalism, hierarchical family and group structures, and the value of subordinating one's ego to the group, worked to Japan's industrial advantage. In Italy, family lifestyles (Pitkin 1986) and the socialization of infants (LeVine, Miller, and West 1988) have responded to changing economic conditions with apparently little disintegration of the traditional family experience.

At the threshold of profound change

By the turn of the twenty-first century, new fibre-optic and other data transmission technologies will increase by a factor of about 60,000 the amount of information that can be carried into homes and offices over computer networks (David Wray, Bolt Beranek and Newman Internet Company 1994, personal communication). This new capacity is bringing down the walls between data, voice, and video communications in a universal network that delivers information of any kind, anywhere – seamlessly. This paradigm is called Total Area ATM Networking. This increased power will reduce so much further the effects of physical distance that its impact on family life cannot yet be imagined. With such communications, a wall in Boston could be opened visually into a house in London, and the occupants could sit facing each other and talk over dinner. An adult could supervise the care of an elderly parent confined to a nursing home or monitor a babysitter in another town. Work colleagues in separate locations will be able to converse face to face on computer screens while editing the same document on their computers. Such developments could greatly increase the ease with which multinational corporations relocate activities to take advantage of the world's cheapest labour markets. They also could make physical togetherness much less necessary for family members, leading to greatly accelerated fragmentation of the post-modern type described in the next section. The impact of these changes is predicted to be as profound as was the shift from agrarian to industrial society (Dertouzos 1989).

The post-modern family

Over 30 years ago, C. Wright Mills (1959) described the post-modern period as one in which the economy would shift employment from heavy industry to non-unionized clerical, service, and new industrial sectors. He foresaw the rise of multinational corporations, trouble in the social welfare system, and decline in human freedom and choice. At that time he wondered how the human family would respond to and adjust to this new period in world history.

Post-modernism, by no means simple to define, is characterized by a "close reading" of small units rather than general theorizing about big ideas. The post-modern tends towards elaboration, eclecticism, ornamentation, and inclusiveness; it dismisses the existence of an absolute reality and is deeply suspicious of the concept of human progress (Doherty 1991). If we define the current ongoing effort to remake contemporary family life as the post-modern family, such a definition carries with it overtones from the definition of post-modern art and literature. In these fields the term post-modern signals the end of a familiar pattern of activity and emergence of new areas of endeavour whose activities are unclear and whose meanings and implications are not yet well understood. Thus, the post-modern is characterized by uncertainty, insecurity, and doubt (Stacey 1990).

Full consensus on the definition of the emerging post-modern family structure has not been reached, despite recognition of the need for better understanding of the variety of human families in the post-modern period and insight into how large-scale social patterns affect personal and domestic relationships (Hossfeld 1991).

The post-modern world is shaped by pluralism, democracy, religious freedom, consumerism, mobility, and increasing access to news and entertainment. Residents of this post-modern world are able to see that there are many beliefs, multiple realities, and an exhilarating but daunting profusion of world views – a society that has lost its faith in absolute truth and in which people have to choose what to believe (O'Hara and Anderson 1991).

In the 1970s, Shorter (1975) may have been the first to describe the emerging post-modern family. He noted three important characteristics: adolescent indifference to the family's identity; instability in the lives of couples, accompanied by rapidly increasing divorce rates; and destruction of the "nest" notion of nuclear family life with the liberation of women. At that time, Shorter noted little change in patterns of child socialization. The dramatic shift from mothers caring for young children in the home to the use of paid providers occurred soon after in the developed world, reflecting mothers' increasing workplace participation.

While single-parent, surrogate-mother, and gay and lesbian families, and other variants of the post-modern family may be viewed as the negative results of the trends described above, or as breakdown products, they also reflect the following:

1. Disillusionment with the optimistic assumptions of human progress and with the universality and the regularity of the laws of science; hence, lack of faith in the previously established order.
2. The uncoupling of economic forces underlying social conformity, such as the need for women to marry advantageously to survive financially and to transmit their class status to the next generation, or the need to bear children in wedlock for them to inherit family land or other property that would be their source of livelihood.
3. The influence of the electronic media, which both reflect and legitimize family diversity.

In addition to reducing the separations that can be imposed between people by physical distance, physical barriers, and social barriers, electronic communications and other media also foster anonymous intimacy through radio talk shows, advice columns, electronic mail, computer bulletin boards, and commercially provided advisory/ counselling and other personal services available in the United States through area code 900. This relatively anonymous and instant intimacy in turn becomes a new basis for anonymous face-to-face social support, in which no names are mentioned, through 12-step programmes and similar self-help movements.

On-site day care, personal computers, electronic communications that permit work at home, and the lack of a defined working day for the higher occupational classes progressively blur the boundaries between the workplace and the home. This interpenetration of home, work, and global media coverage creates the permeability of the post-modern family. The media gather the post-modern family around the campfire of the global village, bringing the outside world into the living room and the bedroom.

Gergen (1991) has described the emerging family form as "the saturated family," whose members feel their lives scattering in intensified busyness. In addition to absorbing exposure to myriad values, attitudes, opinions, lifestyles, and personalities, family members have become embedded in a multiplicity of relationships. The technologies of social saturation (e.g. the car, telephone, television, and jet plane) have created family turmoil and a sense of fragmentation, chaos, and discontinuity.

The home, no longer a refuge of harmony, serenity, and understanding, may become the site of confrontation between people of different ages and genders, who have personal ideologies and social affiliations that are as diversely suspended as exotic species in a tropical rain forest. Human potential organizations, such as Landmark Education, ease this jangling overload by holding workshops in which participants learn to perceive their personal past history to be as mechanical and meaningless as television images. The human potential movements redefine personal identity in terms of the individual's choice of commitment to future goals.

The post-modern child

Children growing up in the post-modern family have been called post-modern children. Parents in the post-modern family may relinquish their roles as educators (Shorter 1975). For many post-modern children there is dual socialization by family and day-care provider. For example, in the Nordic welfare states, the family has been described as an intimacy sanctuary and a zone of stability while day-care centres develop the child's capacity to exercise self-control with respect to affective behaviour. The post-modern child is required to make continuous flexible adjustments between these spheres (Denick 1989).

With child care shared between family and day care, new problems have arisen. While some children thrive on dual socialization, others languish, unable to adjust to either environment or to the demands of daily transition from one environment to the other. The young child may be unable to form the necessary communication link between the two environments. Responsibilities may not be divided clearly between home and day-care centre; as a result, neither may provide some crucial aspects of child-rearing. For example, in the United States, neither the day-care centre nor working parents may perceive themselves in charge of helping the child to develop the capacity to exercise self-control nor of teaching the child basic social comportment, such as table manners, greeting rituals, narration of daily events, and interview skills required for social orientation and reconnaissance.

In the United States, concerns have been expressed about children raised in impoverished single-parent households by young mothers who are still children themselves. According to Elkind (1981), there also are problems with post-modern children of middle-class families as permeable families "hurry" their children to take on the physical, social, and psychological trappings of adulthood before they are prepared to deal with them. Permeable families tend to thrust children and teenagers forward to deal with realities of the outside world at ever-earlier ages, perceiving them as competent to deal with the steady diet of overt violence, sexuality, substance abuse, and environmental degradation that they view on television. Such abuses in the United States and Europe often translate into worse abuses in poor neighbourhoods of large third world cities, where unsupervised children of all ages are lured, together with adults, into watching sexually explicit "adult videos" for the equivalent of a few pennies (Dr. Tade Akin Aina 1992, personal communication). Countries such as the United States, as well as places in the developing world that have departed most widely from institutional family values, appear to be particularly vulnerable to such abuses in the post-modern era. Both Elkind (1981) and Spock and Rothenberg (1992) deplore the tendency of parents to rush children into adult roles.

Although parents remain very concerned about their children in the post-modern world, perceptions of parenting have changed. In the modern era, parenting was intuitive and child-health professionals guided parents by teaching them the general norms of development. The focus of parent education was development of the whole child. In contrast, parenting in the post-modern world is perceived as a learned technique with specific strategies for dealing with particular issues. The target has shifted from the whole child to developing the child's positive sense of self-esteem. In the modern era, parents made the effort to fit advice to the particular needs of the child; Elkind (1992) points out that the directive post-modern techniques may be easier for parents but the child may be deprived of customized treatment. Moreover, he strongly believes that the focus on the whole child should not be lost.

Certainly, the nuclear family was not perfect. In its attempts to explain the turbulence of the 1960s, the recent PBS documentary "Making Sense of the Sixties" powerfully indicted the stifling, conventional, and rigid nature of the nuclear family of the 1950s. The revolution that led to post-modern life corrected old imbalances in society through de-differentiation of parental and gender roles. Yet these radical social changes may have created new imbalances by increasing demands on children and adolescents.

Post-modern de-differentiation

Post-modern life appears to reverse, or de-differentiate, many characteristics of the modern family back to pre-modern lifestyles and values, as shown in table 2.1, re-creating at the level of electronic images and on a global scale certain aspects of the undifferentiated

Table 2.1   **Similarities between post-modern and pre-modern families**

Modern	Pre- and post-modern
Sharp distinction between home and workplace	Workplace and home are often the same
Romantic love	Contractual/consensual love
Idealization of mother as only legitimate caretaker	Shared parenting, working mother
Protected late-maturing child	Early social maturation in full view of adult activities
Child-centred parent focused on the needs of the child	Parent-centred parent looks to child lifestyle goals, social gratification
Individual identity uniquely defined by personal narrative and value judgments	Identity fluidly defined by social context
Stormy adolescence to establish autonomy and separate identity from parents	More peaceful adolescence with less need to establish separate residence

Table 2.2 **Differences between post-modern and pre-modern families**

Pre-modern	Post-modern
Largest and most dependent on kinship ties	Smallest, least dependent on kin
Most of life enacted on the immediate physical plane	Most of life enacted on the electronically removed, or symbolic plane
As illustrated by:	
Manual labour	Brain work
Direct social encounters	Electronically mediated or symbolic encounters
Physical conflicts	Symbolic conflicts
Small number of stable physical and social contexts	Very large number of shifting physical, symbolic and social contexts
Low requirements for information storage processing skills	Very high requirements for abstract information storage and abstract processing
Compulsory participation in all aspects of communal life, lack of privacy and personal choice	Optional participation in most aspects of communal life, high levels of privacy and choice
Functional identity limited to small number of predetermined social roles	Identity shifts with many discontinuous obligatory and optional social roles
Authority figures and set rules determining what is right and wrong; literal, fundamental beliefs	Pluralistic, relativistic values, non-literal symbolic interpretations of most claims to truth

life of the pre-modern village. Nevertheless, there remain quantum differences between pre- and post-modern lifestyles (table 2.2).

Reach of post-modern influences into the developing world

In this global village, developing country villages, such as in the North-West Frontier Province of Pakistan, are now dotted with satellite dishes bringing in the latest news and lifestyles of the West (Dr. Hank Shumacher 1992, USAID/Peshawar, personal communication). This permeability creates great uniformity in the standards, values, and lifestyles of the middle class throughout the world. Middle-class families in Boston, Lagos, Peshawar, Bangkok, Tokyo, and Tashkent feel obliged to buy Nintendo for their children. With the Super Mario

Brothers' Nintendo game, these children are instantly at home with each other. This permeability also makes it impossible to hide from the poor the extent of their disentitlement.

Lessons from the social change literature for family social health

Ability to adapt is a major characteristic of well-functioning families during rapid social change. While flexibility may be an inborn trait, families can be assisted to adapt through social policies and programmes that facilitate change through the provision of resources and education. Equally important is an authoritative reinterpretation of traditional values to meet the needs of emerging lifestyles.

In all industrialized countries the predominant family orientation has changed over the past hundred years from the extended institutional family to the small self-contained modern or post-modern family. Positive socio-economic development, limitation of the world's population, and protection of the environment depend on this transition in family type. Emotionally close families that invest heavily in the care and education of their few children are needed to provide skilled labour for industrial and post-industrial technologies and for sustainable agriculture.

The literature describes a single global megatrend in family life tied to the changing child-rearing strategies of the demographic transition (Zeitlin et al. 1982, ch. 2). This trend occurs in response to industrialization and the expansion both of markets for consumer goods and of electronic communications. The majority of developing countries now are engaged, to greater or lesser degrees, in this transition from the agrarian institutional extended family to the small modern or post-modern family.

Negative aspects of the global megatrend sometimes are overwhelming. Major social dysfunction occurs when the supports needed for small families are not yet in place. Urban families in cramped quarters default on their traditional obligations to take in and house many kin. They dissolve from lack of family mediation in times of stress. The need to rely on their own children for old-age care may inhibit these families from limiting births. Overdependency on kin networks for employment leads to "amoral familism" (Banfield 1958). The practice of diverting resources that belong to public and private sector enterprises to serve one's family, lineage, or ethnic faction is a major source of corruption and mismanagement (Babatunde 1992, 222–240). Deep disillusionment with the failure of family and state values and support systems is at the root of the "each-for-himself" mentality that corrodes public life and leadership in many developing countries. Chapter 10 recommends cultural renewal and social adjustments to overcome these problems.

For developing countries, the shortest line between the pre-modern and the socially healthy post-modern family may not run through the modern family. Child-rearing advice that repeats the earlier ideological positions of the modern US family, with its high emphasis on autonomy, personal gratification, and self-expression, is called into question. From infancy onward, certain post-modern child-care routines that influence individuation and altruism may draw upon pre-modern adaptations directly, just as the post-modern pattern of sustained breast-feeding reverts to early pre-modern practices. Some "hurrying" of children also may be needed – not in social roles but in cognitive skills that contribute to life-long learning, using methods appropriate to newly discovered infant learning processes and capacities. The literature points to the need for consumer values inherent in the "good life" of the modern family to shift radically for the protection of the family itself. It calls for new definitions of progress that reverse the negative aspects of the global megatrend.

A post-modern approach to progress

This book is based on faith that a post-modern concept or process of human progress is worth working for, and that a new awareness of the importance of families lies at the heart of new world views that reverse the negative aspects of the global megatrend. For deeply rooted shifts in world views and lifestyles to occur in a sustainable fashion, they must evolve within socially healthy reproductive units, i.e. within families.

Post-modern thinkers reject modern concepts of progress based on rational projections of current economic growth, food production, and technology transfer. This rejection appears to be well founded. According to *The State of the World, 1994* (Brown et al. 1994), the future rate of technological advances in global agricultural production will not keep pace with global population growth over the next 40 years. According to King (1992), many developing countries, including Nigeria, already are "trapped" by population growth that will lead to mass starvation or international welfare dependency, caused by insufficiency and environmental destruction of agricultural lands. In the view of Kaplan (1994), the combined effects of population expansion and a shrinking resource base will destabilize and reshape political and social structures at many levels.

Environmental advocates (Durning 1992) make a well-documented case that the rate at which consumer lifestyles use global resources is unsustainable for industrialized countries and untransferable to underdeveloped countries. Recent scientific discoveries reveal, for example, that routine use of the chemical fertilizers, pesticides, herbicides, plastics, and detergents that are the technological foundation for middle-class family lifestyles may significantly impair the reproductive ability of both wildlife and humans and may impair neurological integrity through a wide variety of chemicals that replace or amplify pathologically the normal effects of the female hormone, oestrogen (Wiles and Campbell 1993; Ginsberg et al. 1994; Raloff 1994). These writers agree that a major and as yet unclear shift in values – as expressed in titles such as *The Great U-Turn* (Goldsmith 1988) – may be needed if current destructive trends are to be reversed. Deep pessimism grows from the perception that the changes needed run counter to the rules of economics and human nature as modernist theories understand them (Brown et al. 1994).

Post-modern deconstruction clears the slate for the fundamental regrouping or reconstruction of reality into new underlying constructs and new paradigms. We may apply the word "progress" to reconstruction that is directed towards, and successful in, achieving improvement in various aspects of quality of life, viewed in a global perspective. Such a process of reconstruction produces new lenses through which we view the world, rather than new conclusions based on old premises. We step outside language when we deconstruct it (Anderson 1990). According to contemporary philosopher Richard Rorty (1989),

a talent for speaking differently, rather than for arguing well, is the chief instrument of cultural change ... it is the vocabulary itself which must be addressed ... The method is to redescribe ... things in new ways, until you have created a pattern of linguistic behavior which will tempt the rising generation to adopt it, thereby causing them to look for appropriate new forms of nonlinguistic behavior, for example, the adoption of new scientific equipment or new social institutions. (Rorty 1989)

Post-modern progress requires a continuing, ongoing "stepping out" of old reality constructs to engage in the social construction of reality (Anderson 1990). In chapter 10, we use the term "cultural renewal" to refer to the social construction of reality that is needed in both industrialized and developing countries.

The type of fine-grained and eclectic attention provided in this book to the internal and external dynamics of families is, we hope, an example of the post-modern process through which progress is constructed.

References

Aina, T.A., M.F. Zeitlin, K. Setiloane, and H. Armstrong. 1992. "Phase I Survey Results: Positive Deviance in Nutrition Research Project, Lagos State, Nigeria." Draft Report to UNICEF.

Anderson, W.T. 1990. *Reality Isn't What it Used to Be*. San Francisco: Harper and Row.

Babatunde, E.D. 1992. *A Critical Study of Bini and Yoruba Value Systems in Change: Culture, Religion and the Self*. Lewiston, NY: The Edwin Mellen Press.

Bane, M.J. 1986. "Household Composition and Poverty." In: S.H. Danzinger and D.H. Weinberg, eds. *Fighting Poverty*. Mass.: Harvard University Press, pp. 209–231.

Banfield, E. 1958. *The Moral Basis of a Backward Society*. Glencoe, Ill.: Free Press.

Becker, W.C., and R.S. Krug, 1964. "A Circumplex Model for Social Behavior in Children." *Child Development* 35: 391–396.

Bledsoe, C. 1990. "Transformations in Sub-Saharan African Marriage and Fertility." *Annals, AAPSS* 510: 115–125.

Boserup, E. 1970. "Women in the Urban Hierarchy." In: *Women's Role in Economic Development*. New York: St. Martin's Press, pp. 139–156.

Bradford, L.J., and C. Raines. 1992. *Twentysomething: Managing and Motivating Today's New Workforce*. New York: Master Media.

Bronfenbrenner, U. 1963. "The Changing American Child: A Speculative Analysis." In: Smelser, N.J. and W.T. Smelser, eds. *Personality and Social System*. New York: Wiley.

Brown, L., A. Durning, C. Flavin, H. French, N. Lenssen, M. Lowe, A. Misch, S. Postel, M. Renner, L. Starke, P. Weber, and J. Young. 1994. *State of the World 1994; a Worldwatch Institute Report on Progress Toward a Sustainable Society*. New York: Norton.

Burgess, E.W., and H.J. Locke. 1953. *The Family: From Institution to Companionship*. New York: American Book Co.

Buvinic, M. 1992. "Social Variables in Poverty Research: Example from a Case Study on the Intergenerational Transmission of Poverty in Santiago, Chile." Paper prepared for presentation at IFPRI–World Bank Conference on Intrahousehold Resource Allocation: Policies and Research Methods, 12–14 February 1992, IFPRI, Washington, DC.

Caldwell, J.C., and P. Caldwell. 1977. "The Economic Rationale of High Fertility: An Investigation Illustrated with Nigerian Survey Data." *Population Study* 31: 5–27.

———, and ———. 1990. "High Fertility in Sub-Saharan Africa." *Scientific American* (May): 118–125.

Danzinger, K. 1960a. "Independence Training and Social Class in Java, Indonesia." *Journal of Social Psychology* 51: 65–74.

———. 1960b. "Parental Demands and Social Class in Java, Indonesia." *Journal of Social Psychology* 51: 75–86.

Deng, F.M. 1972. *The Dinka of the Sudan*. New York: Holt, Rinehart, and Winston.

Denick, L. 1989. "Growing Up in the Post-Modern Age: On the Child's Situation in the Modern Family, and on the Position of the Family in the Modern Welfare State." *Acta Sociologica* 32: 155–180.

Dertouzos, M.L. 1989. *Made in America: Regaining the Productive Edge*. Cambridge, Mass.: MIT Press.

DHSL/Institute of Population Studies. 1992. *Demographic and Health Surveys of Pakistan, 1990–91*, Columbia, Md.: IRD/Macro Systems.

Dizard, J.E., and H. Gadlin, 1990. *The Minimal Family*. Amherst, Mass.: University of Amherst Press.

Doherty, W.J. 1991. "Family Therapy Goes Postmodern." *Networker*, September/October.

———. 1992. "Private Lives, Public Values." *Psychology Today*, May/June 32–37.

Durning, A.T. 1992. *How Much is Enough? The Consumer Society and the Future of the Earth*. World Watch Environmental Alert Series. New York: Norton.

Elkind, D. 1981. *The Hurried Child*. Reading, Mass.: Addison-Wesley.

———. 1992. *The Post-modern Family, A New Imbalance*. New York: Knopf.

Gergen, K.J. 1991. "The Saturated Family." *Networker*, September/October.

Ginsberg, J. and others. 1994. "Letter to the Editor, Residence in the London Area and Sperm Density," *Lancet* 343(1191): 230.

Goldsmith, E. 1988. *The Great U-Turn; Deindustrializing Society*. New York: Bootstrap Press.

Grindal, B. 1972. *Growing Up in Two Worlds: Education and Transition Among the Sisala of Northern Ghana*. New York: Holt, Rinehart, and Winston.

Gussler, J.D. 1975. "Adaptive Strategies and Social Networks of Women in St. Kitts." In: B. Bourguigno, ed. *A World of Women*. New York: Praeger, pp. 185–209.

Guyer, J.I. 1990. *Changing Nuptuality in a Nigerian Community: Observations from the Field, Working Papers in African Studies, No. 146*. Boston, Mass.: African Studies Center.

Hareven, T.K. 1987. "Historical Analysis of the Family." In: M.B. Sussman and S.K. Steinmetz, eds. *Handbook of Marriage and the Family*. New York: Plenum Press, pp. 37–55.

Hirsch, F. 1976. *Social Limits to Growth*. Cambridge, Mass.: Harvard University Press.

Holtzman, W.H., R. Diaz-Guerrerro, and J.D. Swartz. 1975. *Personality Development in Two Cultures: A Cross-cultural Longitudinal Study of School Children in Mexico and the United States*. Austin, Tex.: University of Texas Press.

Hossfeld, K.J. 1991. "Pondering the Post-modern Family." *Socialist Review* 3–4: 187–194.

Kaplan, R.D. 1994. "The Coming Anarchy." *Atlantic Monthly* (Feb. 1994), 44–76.

King, M. 1992. "Human Entrapment in India." *National Medical Journal of India* 4: 196–201.

Langman, L. 1987. "Social Stratification." In: M.G. Sussman and S.K. Steinmetz, eds. *Handbook of Marriage and the Family*. New York: Plenum Press, pp. 211–246.

Lasch, C. 1977. *Haven in a Heartless World*. New York: Basic Books.

LeVine, R.A. 1974. "Parental Goals: A Crosscultural View." *Teachers College Records* 76: 2.

———, N.H. Klein, and C.H. Fries. 1967. "Father–Child Relationships and Changing Lifestyles in Ibadan." In: H. Miner, ed. *The City in Modern Africa*. New York: Praeger, pp. 215–255.

———, P.M. Miller, and M.M. West, eds. 1988. *Parental Behavior in Diverse Societies. New Directions for Child Development, Number 40*. San Francisco: Jossey-Bass.

———, S.E. LeVine, R. Richman, F.M. Tapia Uribe, C. Sunderland Correa, and P.M. Miller. 1991. "Women's Schooling and Child Care in the Demographic Transition: A Mexican Case Study." *Population and Development Review* 17: 459–496.

Lloyd, B.B. 1966. "Education in Family Life in the Development of Class Identification Among the Yoruba." In: P.C. Lloyd, ed. *New Elites of Tropical Africa*. London: Oxford University Press, pp. 163–183.

———. 1970. "Yoruba Mothers' Reports of Child-rearing, Some Theoretical and Methodological Considerations." In: P. Mayer, ed. *Socialization, the Approach from Social Anthropology*. New York: Tavistock, pp. 75–108.

Maccoby, E.E. 1966. *The Development of Sex Differences*. Stanford, Calif.: Stanford University Press.

Mills, C.W. 1959. *The Sociological Imagination*. New York: Grove Press.

O'Hara, M., and W.T. Anderson. 1991. "Welcome to the Postmodern World." *Networker*, September/October.

Pitkin, D.S. 1986. *The House that Giacomo Built*. New York: Cambridge University Press.

Prothro, E.T. 1962. *Child Rearing in Lebanon*. Cambridge, Mass.: Harvard University Press.

Quale, G.R. 1988. *A History of Marriage Systems. Contributions in Family Studies, Number 13*. New York: Greenwood.

Raloff, J. 1994. "The Gender Benders: Are Environmental 'Hormones' Emasculating Wildlife?" *Science News* 8 January, 148: 24–27.

Rao, V., and M.E. Green. 1991. "Marital Instability, Inter-spouse Bargaining and their Implication for Fertility in Brazil." Paper presented at the Annual Meeting of the Population Association of America, 1991, Washington, DC.

Rorty, R. 1989. *Contingency, Irony, and Solidarity*. New York: Cambridge University Press.

Schneider, D.M., and K. Gough, eds. 1961. *Matrilineal Kinship*. Berkeley: University of California Press.

Schultz, T.P. 1989. *Women and Development: Objectives, Frameworks, and Policy Interventions. World Bank PPR/WID Working Papers WPS #200*. Washington, DC: World Bank.

Sennett, R. 1970. *Families Against the City*. Cambridge, Mass.: Harvard University Press.

Shorter, E. 1975. *The Making of the Modern Family*. New York: Basic Books.

Spock, B., and M.B. Rothenberg. 1992. *Dr. Spock's Baby and Child Care*, 6th revised edn. New York: Dutton.

Stacey, J. 1990. *Brave New Families*. New York: Basic Books.

Stone, L. 1977. *The Family, Sex and Marriage in England, 1500–1800*. New York: Harper and Row.

Sweet, L.E., ed. 1970. *Peoples and Cultures of the Middle East: Vol 1, Depth and Diversity; Vol 2, Life in the Cities, Towns and Countryside*. Garden City, NY: Natural History Press.

Thomas, M., and W. Surachmad. 1962. "Social Class Differences in Mothers' Expectations for Children in Indonesia." *Journal of Social Psychology* 57: 303–307.

Thurow, L.C. 1992. *Head to Head: The Coming Economic Battle among Japan, Europe, and America*. New York: William Morrow.

UNICEF. 1992. *The State of the World's Children, 1992*. Oxford: Oxford University Press.

Vogel, E.F. 1992. *The Four Little Dragons: The Spread of Industrialization in East Asia*. Cambridge, Mass.: Harvard University Press.

Wenke, R.J. 1984. *Patterns in Prehistory: Humankind's First Three Million Years*. Oxford: Oxford University Press.

Werner, E.E. 1979. *Cross-Cultural Child Development: A View from the Planet Earth*. Monterey, Calif.: Brooks Cole.

Whiting, B.B., and J.W.M. Whiting. 1975. *Children of Six Cultures: A Psycho-cultural Analysis*. Cambridge, Mass.: Harvard University Press.

Wiles, R., and C. Campbell. 1993. "U.S. Congress. Testimony Before the Subcommittee on Health and the Environment House Committee on Energy and Commerce." Environmental Working Group, 21 October 1993.

Zeitlin, M.F. 1977. "Report of Nutrition Survey Conducted in Abyei District S. Kordofan Province, Sudan, by the Nutrition Division of the Ministry of Health, Government of the Sudan and by Harvard Institute for International Development, November and December."

———, and Satoto. 1990. "Indonesian Positive Deviance in Nutrition Research Project, Phase I and Phase II Reports." Submitted by Tufts University School of Nutrition to UNICEF and the Italian Government.

———, J.D. Wray, J.B. Stanbury, N.P. Schlossman, J.J. Meurer, and P.J. Weinthal. 1982. *Nutrition and Population Growth: The Delicate Balance*. Cambridge, Mass.: Oelgeschlager, Gunn, and Hain.

3

Economic perspectives on the family

Introduction

The behaviour of families was neglected by economists until the 1950s (Becker 1981). Now, their growing awareness of family behaviour is hastening the incorporation of family life into the mainstream of economics. In turning their attention to the household or family, economists and economic demographers are analysing the underlying ways in which the rules of the market govern the consumption, production, and welfare of family members and the structure of the family itself. Family economics is now a respectable and growing field (Becker 1965).

Definitions of the family and household

Economists focus on the household – a residential unit – whose members pool their resources (at least to some degree) to provide for the welfare of all. Households usually consist of family members linked by blood or marriage, occasionally augmented by unrelated members. Households are defined on the basis of residence, while families are defined primarily by kinship.

The household is not an undifferentiated unit, but "an economy in microcosm, a system of exchanges, entitlements, and responsibilities allocated among members in a group whose boundaries are far from clear" (Rogers 1990). According to Guyer (1980), it is "a particularly dense center in a network of exchange relationships." Within the group residing together, there may be further distinctions between those who do and do not carry out domestic functions together, such as cooking, eating, child care, and farm labour (Webb 1989; Heywood 1990). Therefore different analyses of the same household may identify different subgroups of individuals.

The new home economics

The branch of economics concerned with intra-household or family dynamics is known as the "new household economics" (NHE). Prior to NHE, the household was treated as a "black box" (Pollak 1985) – no attempt was made to model the dynamics of intra-household decision-making. The tendency to treat the household as a black box tells us nothing about how its decision-making process is structured by the complex interests and different capacities of family members. The NHE brings economic theory into the microcosm of the household, building on the observation by Becker (1965), "A household is truly a 'small factory': it combines capital goods, raw materials and labour to clean, feed, procreate and otherwise produce useful commodities." NHE redefines household satisfaction in terms of intangible products or utilities. Households are viewed as "consuming" the things that satisfy them, such as the health of their members, bright and successful children, or relaxation (Berman, Kendall, and Bhattacharyya 1994). These ultimate consumption goods are considered to be "commodities."

Sen (1990), refines the terms that he believes should be applied to the measures of individual well-being in these analyses. He suggests that the intangible outcomes should be considered as capabilities of persons, or positive freedoms that the different members of the family can enjoy. He points out that such a capabilities perspective is particularly useful for evaluating social conditions and programmes in relation to children, in terms of freedom from undernourishment and nutrition-related diseases and of developmental capabilities. Such research should address both the immediate benefit aspects and the investment aspects of personal consumption – e.g. in looking after children, short-term considerations must be balanced against long-term concerns for the well-being of the next generation and the support of the parents in old age.

Concepts in the analysis of household/family behaviour

As explained by Kennedy and Rogers (1992), there are three common approaches to analysing intra-household behaviour, which contribute different useful perspectives to understanding family dynamics. These concepts are equally applicable to non-residential kinship or family structures, to the extent that these groups also share resources and responsibilities.

NHE research on the family began by questioning and rejecting the first of these approaches, which is the neoclassical "unified household preference function," or black box (Becker 1981; Folbre 1986). Theorists using this model tend to make an assumption of altruism in the family, in which all household resources are pooled and then reallocated according to some common rule that benefits all family members (Becker 1981). Neoclassical analysis uses relatively simple regression equations that calculate the "outcome" only as a function of inputs from outside the household, disregarding decision-making inside the household. These analyses assume that the household maximizes its unified household preferences (Rosenzweig and Schultz 1983), given its budget and production constraints. This assumption of altruism-unified preference within the household is in contrast to expectations of naked self-interest in the market (Berk 1980; Folbre 1989). Thus, the altruistic household was viewed as "the haven in the heartless world" of market competition (Lasch 1977).

Research within the past 15 years, however, has demonstrated the existence of separate, different, and often conflicting preference functions of individual members (Jones 1983). Given the different preferences, household behaviour can be described using a bargaining model (Manser and Brown 1980; McElroy and Horney 1981), according to which individual members pursue their own interests, given their relative bargaining positions inside the household. Simplistic assumptions that families are in harmonious agreement or consensus regarding the use of household resources (Samuelson 1956), or that each household has one altruistic member who works things out for the benefit of all (Becker 1974; 1981), have been shown to be inaccurate.

Some bargaining models apply mathematical game theory to

marriage and household decision-making (Manser and Brown 1980; McElroy and Horney 1981). They include models of cooperative conflict (Sen 1990), which address situations in which there are many cooperative outcomes that would be more beneficial to all the parties than non-cooperation, but where the different family members have conflicting interests in the choice among these cooperative arrangements.

Bargaining is supplemented by an "implicit contracts" model (Folbre 1989) that sees the family as governed by culturally determined expectations about the entitlements and obligations of individuals in different positions within a household unit. This model explains why people who lack bargaining power retain access to some household resources. Individuals pursuing their own self-interest also are bound by ties of affection as well as implicit contracts. These traditional norms can be viewed as the cultural "fall-back" position for men and women who are unwilling to invest time and energy in bargaining over alternative allocation (Pollak 1985), or as the upper and lower bounds on acceptable behaviour within which bargaining can be applied (Kennedy and Rogers 1992). These norms are often held in place by powerful legal and institutional factors that determine the disposition of household assets, such as family laws regarding property rights and social entitlements (Folbre 1992). Changes in these institutional factors may have greater effects on intra-household bargaining than changes in individual market earnings or assets.

Individual earning power increases bargaining power. An individual's bargaining power is determined in part by his or her "threat point" – the point at which the person believes he or she would be better off outside the household unit than in it. The greater a person's income-earning opportunities outside the household, the higher the threat point and thus the greater the bargaining power within the household. Another type of threat-point analysis defines the threat point not as divorce, but as a non-cooperative or asymmetric equilibrium within marriage, which may be reflected in different roles for men and women and different use of resources. Such analyses explain why child allowance schemes that pay the mother may have different effects from those that pay the father (Lundberg and Pollak 1992). To the extent that interventions alter the first type of threat point, they may create shifts in the family structure, while alterations in the second may influence intra-household tasks and benefits.

Pollak (1985) applies a less-developed "transaction cost" approach to intra-household transactions. The premise of transaction cost analysis is that organizations (including families and households) seek institutional modes for organizing transactions that minimize transaction costs. Pollak applies theories regarding the boundaries, structure, and internal organization of commercial firms to families, treating the family as a governance structure, with supplier–customer contract relationships. He views family governance in terms of incentives, monitoring, altruism, and loyalty.

Methods for predicting the impact of development inputs on families

The family's relationship to the use of development assistance is modelled in different ways for different purposes. Until now, the analysis of intra-household factors has been constrained by the expense of collecting detailed and highly accurate information.

Household unified preference function for aggregate policy

The unified preference function, according to which household members (e.g. parents) are assumed to allocate resources as if they have common preferences, remains useful for determining the effects of price changes on demand for basic commodities (i.e. foods or nutrients). This information is essential to permit governments to use such means as tariffs, support prices, or export prices to modify the price structure in ways that protect poor families. For macro or regional policy purposes, a price subsidy to increase food consumption of a population or a segment of the population can be implemented with the assumption that households will re-allocate this food to their members. This is the least expensive approach because household-level income and consumption data are sufficient.

Health reduced-form relation function

The household unified preference function, however, offers little information regarding to what extent changes in food prices affect individual family members (Rosenzweig 1990); for this purpose, individual food intake or other commodity consumption is needed. Collecting individual food intake data is difficult and costly (Behrman 1990). In place of food consumption data, Rosenzweig (1990) and Behrman (1990) suggest using individual biological outcomes (health or nutritional status) to analyse, for example, how changes in exogenous factors such as the prices of food or medical services result in changes in the health of individuals. This is called the "health reduced-form relation." If policy makers need to know the person-specific demand equations to analyse the consequences of government policy regarding the welfare of the individual, this framework can be used.

Household health production function: Household health/outcome technology

While the reduced-form relation permits policy makers to estimate the effects of aggregate policy on individuals, it does not reveal how programme interventions affect household allocations of inputs to family members. Decisions regarding which services are most productive with respect to health, or how food supplementation programmes can improve child nutrition, may require information obtained by using a framework that investigates household allocation *among* members. This framework, according to Behrman (1990), is an attempt to "peek into the black box" of the family.

This is a household production function whose outcomes are determined by various inputs. Unlike the "reduced-form" relation, in which outcomes are determined by exogenous factors (factors that cannot be controlled by the family), some inputs in this framework are under the control of household members. This framework is called the "technological/biological relationship between inputs and outcome indicators" (Rosenzweig and Schultz 1983; Behrman 1990; Rosenzweig 1990).

Estimations using this framework are very sensitive to factors that are known to family members but unknown to the researchers (Rosenzweig and Schultz 1983). Household allocation among family members is influenced by across-household and individual-specific endowments. Researchers should be aware of the existence of these factors to reach an accurate estimate: for example, a household with better sanitary conditions will inherently use less health services; if this factor is ignored, the estimated effect of the health services would be underestimated. In another example, if a child's perceived intelligence (endowment) influences the allocation of educational resources, unbiased anticipated resource effects on the child's schooling will be difficult to obtain.

A two-stage estimation procedure is commonly used in the attempt to overcome this problem. The first stage describes the household's "demand" for the inputs to welfare outcomes such as child health. The second stage estimates the production functions using predicted allocation based on the demand estimates. This procedure is very useful for better anticipating how the allocation of resources within the household will respond to outside changes induced by government programmes, and how foods and other inputs will directly affect health outcomes (Rosenzweig 1990). As an example of this two-stage procedure, Berman, Kendall, and Bhattacharyya (1994) cite the work of Popkin (1980), who applied this type of model to nutrition in the Philippines to demonstrate the effects of employment opportunities, for mothers outside the home, on child care and nutrition.

Such knowledge is important not only for a better understanding of the ways in which families allocate their resources but also for the design of family life education and home economics programmes to help families to allocate their resources better. It requires, however, large quantities of carefully collected data at both the family and the individual level. These data are expensive to gather, thereby hindering widespread use of the methods, especially in large surveys.

Findings relevant to the family

Much of the economic research bearing on the family is *gender role research*, arising from the fact that the main bargainers for family control are of opposite gender. Feminist issues also enter as, for example, in the concern of Folbre (1986) that the ways in which economic theory deals with altruism are sentimentalized by men who fail to see their discrimination against women or who perceive that women have a "taste" for altruism or voluntary sacrifice.

Major research findings applicable to the family are as follows:
1. Equity and adequacy of intra-household allocation of all types of resources increase as these resources become more adequate.
2. The household's sharing rules shift with any shift in the resources given to one member, whether child support to a mother, donated food to a child, or agricultural technology to a male household head (McElroy 1992). Unless counterbalanced by cultural or legal sanctions, programmes that enable one gender, either male or female, to earn comparatively more than before will raise their threat point both for leaving the family union and for demanding a larger share of services or other household resources from their partners. Therefore, reduced access to technology for women, who

already may be in subordinate overburdened positions, is a major issue for families in development.

3. From the cultural side, loosening social controls on the family that permit men to discontinue their support to wives and children increases the threat point for these men leaving the family by enabling them to keep more income for themselves if they leave than if they stay. According to the laws of the market, these forces will lead inevitably to the progressive detachment of men from women and children. Absolute insufficiency of wages for men and inability to live up to cultural ideals for family support contribute to this detachment.

   Where marital disruption rates are high, the risk of being a major or sole economic support of a household motivates women to enter the labour force and to take an active role in support of the family, even while co-resident with a spouse (Bruce and Lloyd 1992).

4. Actual earning power or economic profitability to the family of women in the current generation influences the allocation of food, health, and educational resources to female children (the next generation).

5. Income in the hands of women has effects on household expenditure that differ from those of income in the hands of men (Thomas 1990, 1992; Hoddinot and Haddad 1991; Engle 1993). Income in the hands of women is associated with a larger increase in the share of the household budget devoted to human capital. The inputs and outcomes measuring human capital in various studies have included household services, health and education, leisure and recreation, as well as more quantitative and biological measurements of child height, weight for height, immunizations, survival, and nutrient intake. In theory at least, this finding implies that increases in employment opportunities for women will have a greater positive effect on child welfare (Folbre 1992) than similar increases for men.

6. The work of poor women for pay both inside and outside the home has been associated with favourable child nutrition outcomes, if child care and pay rates are adequate (Engle 1993). This is more true for older than younger children. Favourable nutritional status of children with alternate child care while their mothers work may, however, not be matched by equally favourable cognitive development. Aina et al. (1992) found in Nigeria

that two-year-olds who went with their mothers to the worksite were more malnourished but had higher cognitive test scores than those left behind with a caregiver.

7. Poor women household heads with low incomes will make great personal sacrifices to achieve favourable child outcomes (Bruce and Lloyd 1992). These studies, however, have been done in societies where such women are highly dependent on their children for future support.

8. Intra-household dynamics differ regionally, with the predominant cultures of sub-Saharan Africa showing wider divergence from those of Europe, Asia, and Latin America than these regional cultures from each other (Bruce and Lloyd 1992; Desai 1992; Kabeer 1992).

Insights regarding family social wellness

Probably most important to social health of the family is the finding that poverty decreases the altruistic allocation of resources, or the ability and willingness of the family to satisfy the needs and preferences of its individual members.

According to Desai (1992), the important task for policy formation is "to identify the *conditions* influencing the degree of altruism or conflict within the family" (key components of social wellness). Very little research has investigated the explicit conditions under which households maximize the welfare of all of their members (Kabeer 1992). Desai (1992) calls for the examination of two sets of conditions, one rooted in the individual situation, and the second in institutional structures. As an example, Desai illustrates with data from Latin America that consensual rather than formal marriages are structures that significantly decrease the degree of family altruism as reflected by preschool nutritional status. She assumes that this negative outcome occurs because these less-committed households are less likely to pool their income.

A transaction cost approach to families

Also bearing on family social health, Pollak (1985) introduced an approach to viewing the family as a governance structure that applies the concept of "transaction cost" usually used by firms or institutions. The premise of transaction cost analysis is that organizations (including families and households) seek institutional modes for organizing transactions that minimize transaction costs. This approach expands the NHE recognition of the importance of internal structure and organization. Unlike the NHE approach, it treats the family as a governance structure rather than a preference ordering. This approach links the two debated spheres – the altruistic model and the bargaining model. This is done by recognizing the advantages of altruism to family governance in terms of incentives, loyalty, and monitoring; and the disadvantages to family governance of conflict, different family endowments, and nepotism.

Pollak's ideas on transaction costs provide a promising perspective, opening the door to new, broader economic analyses of families, not just in terms of economic production and consumption, but also in terms of their structures and the organizational characteristics that govern their activities. For family policy purposes this approach holds promise; however, it needs rigorous econometric investigations and has not been adequately modelled. The application of this approach still awaits further development of this model. In order to strengthen the management functions of the family as a responsible agent, the approach by Pollak (1985) to family governance should be further explored.

Acknowledgement

This chapter has benefited from discussions with Beatrice Rogers, Ph.D., at Tufts University School of Nutrition, Medford, Mass., USA.

References

Aina, T.A., M. Zeitlin, K. Setiolane, and H. Armstrong. 1992. "Phase I Survey Results: Positive Deviance in Nutrition Research Project, Lagos State, Nigeria." Draft Report to UNICEF.

Becker, G.S. 1965. "A Theory of the Allocation of Time." *Economic Journal* 299(75): 493–517.

———. 1974. "A Theory of Marriage: Part II." *Journal of Political Economy* March/April, 82(2): S11–S26.

———. 1981. *A Treatise on the Family*. Cambridge, Mass.: Harvard University Press.

Behrman, J.R. 1990. "The Action of Human Resources and Poverty on One Another: What We Have Yet to Learn." LSMS Working Paper No. 74, The World Bank.

Berk, R. 1980. "The New Home Economics: An Agenda for Sociological Research." In: S.F. Berk, ed. *Women and Household Labor*. Berkeley, Calif.: Sage Publications.

Berman, P., C. Kendall, and K. Bhattacharyya. 1994. "The Household Production of Health: Integrating Social Science Perspectives on Micro-level Health Determinants." *Social Science and Medicine* 38: 205–215.

Bruce, J., and C.B. Lloyd. 1992. "Beyond Female Headship: Family Research and Policy Issues for the 1990s." Paper prepared for presentation at IFPRI–World Bank Conference on Intrahousehold Resource Allocation: Policies and Research Methods, 12–14 February 1992, IFPRI, Washington, DC.

Desai, S. 1992. "Children at Risk: The Role of Family Structure in Latin America and West Africa." Paper prepared for presentation at IFPRI–World Bank Conference on Intrahousehold Resource Allocation: Policies and Research Methods, 12–14 February 1992, IFPRI, Washington, DC.

Engle, P.L. 1993. "Intrahousehold Food Distribution Among Guatemalan Families in a Supplementary Feed Program." *Social Science and Medicine* 36: 1605–1612.

Folbre, N. 1986. "Hearts and Spades: Paradigms of Household Economics." *World Development* 14: 245–255.

———. 1989. Presentation at the fourth seminar on Female-Headed Households, sponsored by the International Center for Research on Women and the Population Council, New York City, 28 November 1989.

———. 1992. "Rotten Kids, Bad Daddies, and Public Policy." Paper prepared for presentation at IFPRI–World Bank Conference on Intrahousehold Resource Allocation: Policies and Research Methods, 12–14 February 1992, IFPRI, Washington, DC.

Guyer, J. 1980. *Household Budgets and Women's Incomes. African Studies Center Working Paper No. 28*. Boston, Mass.: Boston University.

Heywood, P. 1990. "Multiple Groups Membership and Intrahousehold Resource Allocation." In: B.L. Rogers and N. Schlossman, eds. *Intrahousehold Resource Allocation: Issues and Methods for Development Planning. Food and Nutrition Bulletin, Supplement No. 15*. Tokyo: United Nations University Press.

Hoddinot, J., and L. Haddad. 1991. *Household Expenditures, Child Anthropometric Status and the Intrahousehold Division of Income: Evidence from the Côte d'Ivoire*. Washington, DC: IFPRI.

Jones, C. 1983. "The Mobilization of Women's Labor for Cash Crop Production: A Game Theoretic Approach." *American Journal of Agricultural Economcs* 65: 1049–1054.

Kabeer, N. 1992. "Beyond the Threshold: Intrahousehold Relations and Policy Perspectives." Paper prepared for presentation at IFPRI–World Bank Conference on Intrahousehold Resource Allocation: Policies and Research Methods, 12–14 February 1992, IFPRI, Washington, DC.

Kennedy, E., and B. Rogers. 1992. "The Implications of Income and Household Structure on the Intrahousehold Allocation of Resources: Evidence from Kenya." Paper prepared for presentation at IFPRI–World Bank Conference on Intrahousehold Resource Allocation: Policies and Research Methods, 12–14 February 1992, IFPRI, Washington, DC.

Lasch, C. 1977. *Haven in a Heartless World*. New York: Basic Books.

Lundberg, S., and R.A. Pollack. 1992. "Separate Spheres Bargaining and the Marriage Market." Paper prepared for presentation at IFPRI–World Bank Conference on Intrahousehold Resource Allocation: Policies and Research Methods, 12–14 February 1992, IFPRI, Washington, DC.

Manser, M., and M. Brown. 1980. "Marriage and Household Decision Making: A Bargaining Analysis." *International Economics Review* 21: 31–34.

McElroy, M.B. 1992. "The Policy Implications of Family Bargaining and Marriage Markets." Paper prepared for presentation at IFPRI–World Bank Conference on Intrahousehold Resource Allocation: Policies and Research Methods, 12–14 February 1992, IFPRI, Washington, DC.

———, and M.J. Horney. 1981. "Nash-bargained Household Decisions, a Theory of Demand." *International Economics Review* 22: 333–349.

Pollak, R.A. 1985. "A Transaction Cost Approach to Families and Households." *Journal of Economic Literature* 23: 581–608.

Popkin, B.M. 1980. "Time Allocation of the Mother and Child Nutrition." *Ecology of Food and Nutrition* 9: 1–14.

Rogers, B.L. 1990. "The Internal Dynamics of Households: A Critical Factor in Development Policy." In: B.L. Rogers and N.P. Schlossman, eds. *Intrahousehold Resource Allocation: Issues and Methods for Development Policy and Planning. Food and Nutrition Bulletin, Supplement No. 15*. Tokyo: United Nations University Press, pp. 1–19.

Rosenzweig, M. 1990. "Programme Interventions, Intrahousehold Allocation, and the Welfare of Individuals: Economic Model of the Household." In: B.L. Rogers and N.P. Schlossman, eds. *Intrahousehold Resource Allocation: Issues and Methods for Development Policy and Planning. Food and Nutrition Bulletin, Supplement No. 15*. Tokyo: United Nations University Press, pp. 233–243.

———, and T.P. Schultz. 1983. "Estimating a Household Production Function: Heterogeneity, the Demand for Health, Inputs, and Their Effects on Birth Weight." *Journal of Political Economy* 91: 723–746.

Samuelson, P. 1956. "Social Indifference Curve." *Quarterly Journal of Economics* 90: 1–22.

Sen, A. 1990. "Economics and the Family." *Asian Development Reviews* 15–26.

Thomas, D. 1990. "Intrahousehold Resource Allocation: An Inferential Approach." *Journal of Human Resources* 25: 635–664.

———. 1992. "The Distribution of Income and Expenditure within the Household." Paper prepared for presentation at IFPRI–World Bank Conference on Intrahousehold Resource Allocation: Policies and Research Methods, 12–14 February 1992, IFPRI, Washington, DC.

Webb, P. 1989. *Intrahousehold Decision Making and Resource Control: The Effects of Rice Commercialization in West Africa. Working Papers on Commercialization of Agriculture and Nutrition 3*. Washington, DC: IFPRI.

4

Psychological approaches to the family

The vastness of the field

Most of the more than 5,000 listings on the family in the Harvard libraries appear to be by professionals in social psychology and human development. Figure 4.1 illustrates the daunting quantity of this work in the subset of theories relating to family development over the life cycle (Mattessich and Hill 1987). Fortunately for our project, these fields produce periodic review volumes. While this body of work focuses on middle-class, largely White, North American families, it distinguishes and classifies various categories of findings that provide useful starting points for study and for comparison in other cultures and settings. Approaches can be broadly divided according to their focus:

1. On the family as an entity; its adjustment and preservation;
2. On child development, viewing the family in terms of its contributions to child welfare;
3. On the family as a system with internal dynamics that produce developmental and welfare outcomes of its members.

We reviewed selected aspects of this literature under these three headings.

The majority of family studies are not directly pertinent to inter-

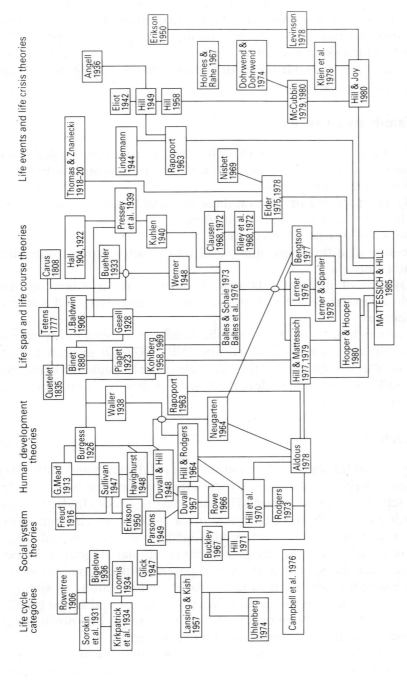

Fig. 4.1 **Genealogy of evolving family development frameworks from origins in family life-cycle categories, theories of human and life-span development, and theories of life events and life crises (source: Mattessich and Hill 1987)**

51

national development, yet they often suggest relevant research that might be conducted in the future. Many questions of relevance to international development remain to be investigated – for example, the extent to which skills and other traits made available through the social context are transmitted to the child through the agency of the family.

The family as an entity

Kreppner and Lerner (1989), in their introduction to the book *Family Systems and Lifetime Development*, note the following different perspectives on the family itself:
1. A system focusing on general dimensions of family interaction and taking into account all family members;
2. A series of dyadic interactions;
3. The sum of interactions among all family subgroupings – dyadic, triadic, tetradic;
4. A system of internal relations in reaction to broader contexts such as external social support, intergenerational, and historic influences.

Much research also has described the family as a social entity with a predictable life cycle (Mattessich and Hill 1987). Of interest for international development are the life-cycle models studies of work and stress and the systems models designed for family counselling and preservation activities.

Life-cycle models

Life-cycle and family development models (Mattessich and Hill 1987) commonly divide the family life cycle into seven stages: newly established (childless); child-bearing (infants and preschool children); with schoolchildren; with secondary-school or adolescent children; with young adults aged 18 or over; middle-aged (children launched); ageing in retirement. Within any given culture, similar stages can be defined and can be specified for single-parent, polygamous, or other family configurations, such as the number and functions of siblings. This approach dovetails with the concerns of Bruce and Lloyd (1992), noted in chapter 3 on economics, that more needs to be known about the effects of variation in household composition.

Figure 4.2 from Mattessich and Hill (1987, 460) illustrates the potential usefulness of life-cycle research for targeting development

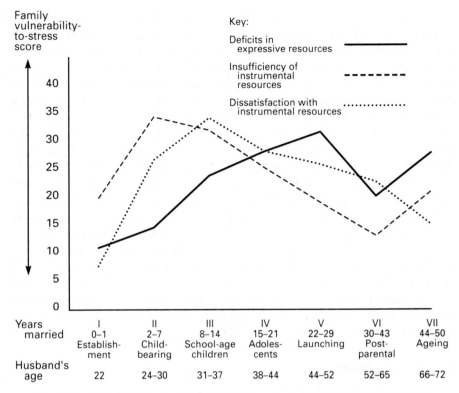

Fig. 4.2 **Stages of the family life cycle (source: Mattessich and Hill 1987)**

inputs by showing that families are most likely to have insufficient resources in the early child-bearing stage, but are most likely to be dissatisfied with their resources when their children reach school age. Stages at which the family is most susceptible to disintegration also might be identified by this method (with special reference to couples who separate not long after the birth of a child).

Families and work

Piotrkowski, Rapoport, and Rapoport (1987) review many industrialized country studies linking the work of spouses to family satisfaction, stability, and other welfare measures. The availability of alternate child care and the effects on the family of balancing domestic and income-generating tasks are major issues. This domestic literature provides hypotheses and discussion topics for international researchers in intra-household and women's economic studies. Some studies link male occupational status and earnings positively to marital satisfaction, but find the reverse for women, with high female job status and earnings correlated to low self-esteem and depression in males and greater probability of dissolution of the marriage. These findings are counterbalanced by other studies reporting positive family effects of women's work (Skinner 1980).

Poor family correlates of women's work appear linked to lower-middle-class beliefs that the wife's work is an indicator of the husband's failure as a breadwinner; favourable outcomes are linked to more egalitarian upper-middle-class beliefs. Job satisfaction is significantly linked to positive parent–child interactions, but very high job involvement requiring long work hours strains all aspects of family functioning, particularly when the female partner is job-involved.

Conventional gender roles that assign most domestic work to the female partner prove extremely resistant to change, even when both partners earn equally outside the home (Blumenstein and Schwartz 1985). Rather than evolving towards more egalitarian solutions over the course of a marriage, conventional roles become more rigid and restrictive (Mattessich and Hill 1987).

Stress and coping

Family stress theory can be applied to critical work events that negatively affect the family, such as job loss, and to chronic work stressors such as job dissatisfaction, instability, shift work, inadequate child care, and role overload (Piotrkowski and Kattz 1983). Other sources of family stress are death, divorce, separation, illness, and social dysfunction.

Stress theory (Boss 1987) studies the phenomenon of family coping, which is the management of a stressful event by the family as a group and by each individual in the family. "Coping refers to efforts to master conditions of harm, threat or challenge when a routine or automatic response is not readily available" (Monat and Lazarus 1977, 8).

Figure 4.3 shows a contextual model of family stress. The sequence A–B–C–X at the centre has been termed the ABC–X model, where A is the crisis event, B the resources available, C the perception of the event, and X the degree of manifested stress. On the basis of all the influences represented in the model, the family mobilizes its resources either into constructive coping or negatively into crisis. Thus,

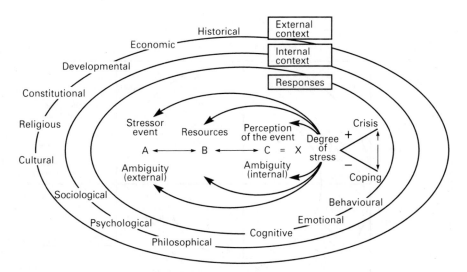

Fig. 4.3   **The contextual model of family stress (source: Boss 1987)**

coping is a process involving the cognitive, emotional, and behavioural responses of the family as a collective. Summarizing research in this field, Boss (1987) concludes that the main determinant of why some families cope while others fall into crisis is the *meaning* that the event holds for the family and the individuals within it. The extent to which constructive interpretations result in adequate coping depend on the degree of support provided by the internal and external contexts. We return to the theme of coping in our discussion of Schneewind's model of the family (Schneewind 1989) at the end of this chapter.

Counselling models

These family systems models provide conceptual frameworks that can be used in counselling by marital and family therapists. They draw their rationale from perceptions regarding the social changes in family structure discussed in chapter 2. Burgess (1926) theorized that the family had changed in function from an economic institution to a structure for providing companionship, and should henceforth be defined as a network of interpersonal relationships. These frameworks have tended to use circumplex models, with two-dimensional classification schemes (Becker and Krug 1964; Peterson and Rollins 1987).

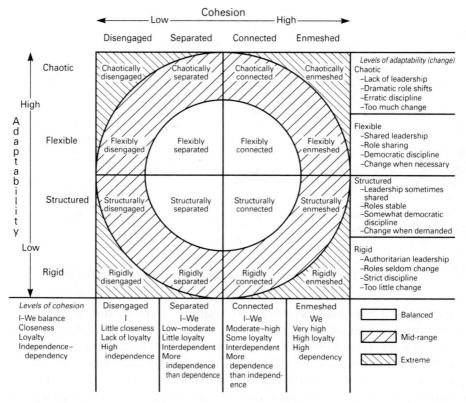

Fig. 4.4 **Circumplex model – couple and family map (source: Olson, Russell, and Sprengkle 1984)**

Olson (Olson, Sprengkle, and Russell 1979; Olson, Russell, and Sprengkle 1984; Olson and Lavee 1989) has been influential in designing a circumplex model of marital and family systems (fig. 4.4). The model depicts two dimensions – "cohesion" and "adaptability" – and makes use of a third dimension called "communication," which is not pictured (Olson and Lavee 1989). These three dimensions were drawn from the conceptual clustering of concepts from six social science fields, including family therapy (Kaslow 1987).

Family cohesion is defined as the "emotional bonding that family members have toward one another" (Olson, Russell, and Sprengkle 1984, 60). Specific indicators for measuring the family cohesion dimension are emotional bonding, boundaries, coalitions, time, space, friends, decision-making, and interests and recreation. The cohesion dimension ranges from "disengaged" (very low) to "separated" (low to moderate) to "connected" (moderate to high) to "enmeshed" (very high). The extremes (disengaged or enmeshed) are considered to be problematic. Families falling in the middle of the dimension (separated or connected) are healthy, because family members can be both independent of, and connected to, their families.

The second dimension, "adaptability," is defined as "the ability of the marital or family system to change in its power structure, role relationships, and relationship rules in response to situational and developmental stress" (Olson, Russell, and Sprengkle 1984, 60). This dimension ranges from "rigid" (very low) to "structured" (low to moderate), to "flexible" (moderate to high), to "chaotic" (very high). Again, a middle range of the dimension is considered to characterize a well-functioning family. A structured relationship is generally less rigid, less authoritarian, and more shared. A flexible relationship is even less rigid and the leadership is more equally shared. A rigid relationship (highly authoritarian) and a chaotic relationship (has erratic or limited leadership) are considered to be problematic for individual and relationship development in the long run.

Based on the two dimensions (cohesion and adaptability), the 16 types of marital and family systems shown in figure 4.4 have been used in clinical diagnosis and for specifying treatment goals with couples and families. The third dimension, family communication, is not pictured but is considered to be a facilitating dimension that enables families to move on the other two dimensions.

Olson and Lavee (1989) summarize similar work by 11 other theorists (table 4.1). In the variation represented by the Beavers system model (Beavers and Voeller 1963), cohesion is rephrased as a centripetal-to-centrifugal dimension: a centripetal family type finds the most relationship satisfaction within the family; a centrifugal family, in contrast, views most relationship satisfaction as coming from outside the family. Beavers' formulation brings in life-cycle considerations: for example, a family with small children is more centripetal; as the family matures and children grow up, such a family may move to a more centrifugal style. All such generalizations must be seen as culture specific, however: in certain societies, it may be mothers with young children who engage most frequently in neighbourhood activities (Fischer 1977), and grandparents who are most centripetally involved with their children and grandchildren.

Experience with these models may provide a useful starting point for designing similarly constructed culturally appropriate models in

Table 4.1 **Theoretical models using cohesion, adaptability, and communication**

Reference	Cohesion	Adaptability	Communication
Beavers and Voeller (1983)	Centripetal–centrifugal	Adaptability	Affect
Benjamin (1977)	Affiliation	Interdependence	
Epstein, Bishop, and Levin (1978)	Affective involvement	Behaviour control, problem-solving roles	Communication, affective responsiveness
French and Guidera (1974)		Capacity to change power	
Gottman (1979)	Validation	Contrasting	
Kantor and Lehr (1975)	Affect dimension	Power dimension	
L'Abate (1987)	Intimacy	Power	
Leary (1957); Constantine (1986)	Affection Hostility	Dominance Submission	
Leff and Vaughn (1985)	Distance	Problem solving	
Parsons and Bales (1955)	Expressive role	Instrumental role	
Reiss (1981)	Coordination	Closure	

Source: Olson and Lavee (1989).

other countries. The importance of the models may lie less in their accuracy of representation than in their ability to engage counsellors and families in a dialogue or bargaining process through which issues surface and are discussed, family communications improve, and problems such as anger or depression are resolved. Expressing the positions of different families and family members, along a continuum such as "cohesiveness" that is value free, relieves the negotiators from labelling them as good or bad. "Balance" may be viewed as a positive term for compromises that reduce family stress.

Every culture has its own polarizing issues, over which family members engage in bargaining. These issues could be determined through focus groups and other forms of research and then depicted experimentally along the axes of circumplex models. Acceptable degrees of cohesion are culture specific. The concept that enmeshment is undesirable is a value judgment that may be specific to US or Western culture of the twentieth century. As noted in chapter 2, the cultural ideal of the good family has changed in the West from one of greater to less "closeness." A leading American economist (Becker 1981, 244) endorsed this shift in values: "Nostalgia for the supposed closeness of traditional families overlooks the restrictions on privacy and free choice, the very imperfect protection against disasters, and the limited opportunities to transcend family background."

Many societies continue to value family togetherness above privacy, autonomy, or free choice, and yet the family seems to function well at the enmeshed extreme of Olson's model. (Olson, Russell, and Sprengkle [1984] did acknowledge that as long as all the members are willing to accept the expectation of family togetherness, the family can function well.)

While an adaptability dimension may prove universal, the degree to which adaptability implies shared decision-making is likely to vary. The Olson model assumes that certain structures, such as egalitarianism or democracy, are better than others. Some argue that in societies with highly differentiated gender roles, as in some African and Asian countries, a male-dominated leadership pattern within the family is perceived to be fair by the family members. Meanwhile, feminists within these cultures contend that such consensus is itself highly contested and a matter of struggle and power relations.

For purposes of modelling the effects of good versus poor management on developmental outcomes, these models are conceptually flawed by false sets of opposites. On the dimension of cohesion, for example, some of the worst-managed families are both disengaged from each other emotionally and overly enmeshed in each others' lives – where uncommunicative adult children continue to live intrusively in their parents' homes, for example. The "false opposites" problem also could explain why family members rarely rate themselves in the same quadrants as do the therapists working with them (Olson and Lavee 1989): Friedman, Utada, and Morissey (1987) found that family members tended to rate their families as disengaged, whereas therapists tended to rate these same families as enmeshed.

Marital and family therapy

Counselling on the basis of the above models is embedded in the broader field of marriage counselling and family therapy (Kaslow

1987). Marriage counselling in an informal context is as old as the family: family problems are a common reason for consulting elders and religious practitioners and for seeking dispute resolution. In Yoruba traditional society (chapter 7), it is not uncommon for domestic disputes to be brought before a third party, known for his or her wisdom. Like traditional midwives, such family counsellors may potentially serve as a resource for development.

In the United States, marriage counselling entered the formal practice of therapy in the 1920s (Kaslow 1987). Family therapy evolved, following World War II, out of frustration over the slow improvement of individuals in therapy under conditions in which their family contributed to their pathology. It continues to be primarily an adjunct to the treatment of troubled individuals who often are viewed as acting out the pathology of the family as a whole. Kaslow reviews the nine "schools" of marriage and family therapy, depicted on the horizontal axis of figure 4.5. Most recently, avantgarde or post-modern family therapists are interested in language and stories that families relate about themselves. The therapist and family together generate a new narrative, transforming the pathological tale that first created the family problem. Healing occurs during the process of searching for meaning (Doherty 1991).

The formal approaches of these and similar schools draw heavily on Western intellectual tradition. They could possibly contribute to the design of family preservation programmes in countries that have well-established therapeutic practitioners drawing on the same traditions; such countries might include Mexico and the Philippines. Knowledge of the techniques taught by these schools provides no substitute for personal ability: personal style and talent appear to determine the success of these approaches, which often are almost synonymous with the names of their founders (Kaslow 1987).

Counselling for family management

The circumplex models do not deal with the home economics issues of providing physical resources such as money, food, or health care. These aspects can affect family functioning; as noted by the National Academy of Sciences (1976), inadequate resources are the central villain in undermining the families' adequacy for child development.

The McMaster model of family functioning (MMFF), described by Epstein, Bishop, and Baldwin (1984), has been a workhorse model

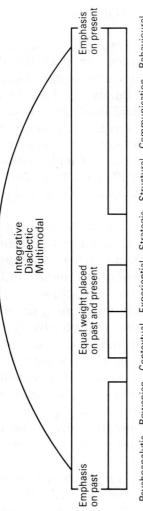

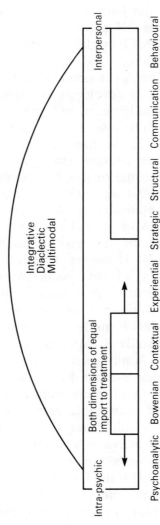

Fig. 4.5 **The nine schools of marriage and family theory (source: Kaslow 1987)**

for family management counselling for 25 years. This model's stated assumption is that the primary function of the family unit is to provide a setting for the development and maintenance of family members on the biological, social, and psychological levels (Epstein, Bishop, and Baldwin 1984, 78). Hence, family issues are grouped into three areas – the basic task area, the developmental task area, and the hazardous task area.

The MMFF model puts the basic task area (providing food, money, transportation, and shelter) as the most fundamental of the three areas. The developmental task area includes family issues related to the stages of developmental sequence of the family. At the individual level, these issues include crises in infancy, childhood, or adolescence; at the family level, these could be such issues as the beginning of the marriage or the first pregnancy. The hazardous tasks area encompasses how families handle crises resulting from accidents, illness, or loss of income or job, for example. The MMFF model suggests that families who are unable to handle these task areas are most likely to develop clinically significant problems.

The MMFF model has six dimensions of family functioning that designate the structure, organization, and transactional patterns of the family. These six dimensions are problem solving, communication, roles, affective responsiveness, affective involvement, and behaviour control. A summary outline is presented in table 4.2.

The definition of healthy or effective family functioning according to the MMFF model is summarized as follows. An effectively functioning family is expected to deal with each dimension successfully. Effective families solve their problems easily, whereas ineffectively functioning families do not deal with at least some of their problems. Effective families communicate in a clear and direct manner, have clear and reasonable roles and accountability, are capable of expressing a full range of emotions, have empathic involvement in particular activities and interests of individual family members, and have flexible behaviour control.

The MMFF model lays strong foundations for the transmission of coping skills and for conflict resolution. We believe that this model also provides a useful starting framework for developing other similar culture-specific tools. The use of the MMFF cross-culturally would require empirical testing of the skills dimensions appropriate to the setting: for example, in Javanese society it is socially unacceptable to express anger freely, even within the family; anger is usually shown very subtly or through refusal to speak.

Table 4.2   **Summary of dimension concepts of McMaster model of family functioning**

Problem solving
Two types of problems:
– Instrumental and affective
Seven stages to the process:
1. Identification of the problem
2. Communication of the problem to the appropriate person(s)
3. Development of action alternatives
4. Decision on one alternative
5. Action
6. Monitoring the action
7. Evaluation of success
Postulated:
– Most effective when all seven stages are carried out
– Least effective when families cannot identify problem (stop before step 1)

Communication
Instrumental and affective areas
Two independent dimensions:
1. Clear and direct
2. Clear and indirect
3. Masked and direct
4. Masked and indirect
Postulated:
– Most effective: clear and direct
– Least effective: masked and indirect

Roles: two family function types
Necessary and other

Two areas of family functions
Instrumental and affective

Necessary family function groupings
A. Instrumental
  1. Provision of resources
B. Affective
  1. Nurturance and support
  2. Adult sexual gratification
C. Mixed
  1. Life skills development
  2. Systems maintenance and management

Other family functions
Adaptive and maladaptive
– Role functioning is assessed by considering how the family allocates
  responsibilities and handles accountability for them

(*continued*)

Table 4.2 **(cont.)**

Postulated:
- Most effective when all necessary family functions have clear allocation to reasonable individual(s) and accountability is built in
- Least effective when necessary family functions are not addressed and/or allocation and accountability are not maintained.

Affective responsiveness
Two groupings:
1. Welfare emotions
2. Emergency emotions
Postulated:
- Most effective when a full range of responses is appropriate in amount and quality to stimulus
- Least effective when range is very narrow (one or two affects only) and/or amount and quality is distorted, given the context

Affective involvement
A range of involvement with six styles identified:
1. Absence of involvement
2. Involvement devoid of feelings
3. Narcissistic involvement
4. Empathic involvement
5. Overinvolvement
6. Symbiotic involvement
Postulated:
- Most effective: empathic involvement
- Least effective: symbiotic involvement and absence of involvement

Behaviour control
Applies to three situations:
1. Dangerous situations
2. Meeting and expressing psychobiological needs and drives (eating, drinking, sleeping, eliminating, sex, and aggression)
3. Interpersonal socializing behaviour inside and outside the family
Standard and latitude of acceptable behaviour determined by four styles:
1. Rigid
2. Flexible
3. *Laissez-faire*
4. Chaotic
To maintain the style, various techniques are used and implemented under "role" functions (systems maintenance and management)
Postulated:
- Most effective: flexible behaviour control
- Least effective: chaotic behaviour control

Source: Epstein, Bishop, and Baldwin (1984).

The family from a child development perspective

Theories of child development, which approach the family from the child perspective, include concerns with nature versus nurture, the flexibility or plasticity of the child at different ages to being moulded by the family, and the relative permanence of family influences (Kreppner and Lerner 1989). The development of the child is viewed as following a probabilistic epigenetic course – according to which, biology remains a prime mover but the developmental results depend on reciprocal interaction between biology and the social context, and hence on the probability that biological sensitive points in the child and the social and environmental resources of the family will come together to produce certain outcomes (Lerner 1989).

This approach to the family elaborates theories regarding family factors as determinants of child outcome that have been useful in the design of such social interventions as the Head Start Program, later championed by Lerner. It includes the investigation of psychological resilience, or why some children thrive in adverse circumstances. Exploration of family effects often is reduced to the examination of dyadic parent–child interactions, usually focusing on the mother–child dyad, with little attention to family dynamics.

The Bronfenbrenner model

Bronfenbrenner (1979) placed child development in an ecological perspective. His ground-breaking work combined aspects of sociology and developmental psychology and laid an enduring foundation for future approaches. The relationships between individuals and their environments are viewed as "mutually shaping." Brofenbrenner saw the individual's experience "as a set of nested structures, each inside the next, like a set of Russian dolls" (Bronfenbrenner 1979, 22). In studying human development, one has to see within, beyond, and "across" how the several systems interact (family, workplace, and economy). The study of the ability of families to access and manage resources across these systems would appear to be a logical extension of his investigations. His four interlocking systems that shape individual development are as follows:

1. *The micro-system*. At this level the family enters Bronfenbrenner's framework, but only in terms of its interpersonal interactions with the child. It is the level within which a child experiences immediate interactions with other people. At the beginning, the micro-system

65

is the home, involving interactions with only one or two people in the family ("dyadic" or "triadic" interaction). As the child ages, the micro-system is more complex, involving more people – such as in a child-care centre or preschool. Bronfenbrenner noted that as long as increased numbers in a child's micro-system mean more enduring reciprocal relationships, increasing the size of the system will enhance child development.

2. *The meso-system.* Meso-systems are the interrelationships among settings (i.e. the home, a day-care centre, and the schools). The stronger and more diverse the links among settings, the more powerful an influence the resulting systems will be on the child's development. In these interrelationships, the initiatives of the child, and the parents' involvement in linking the home and the school, play roles in determining the quality of the child's meso-system.

3. *The exo-system.* The quality of interrelationships among settings is influenced by forces in which the child does not participate, but which have a direct bearing on parents and other adults who interact with the child. These may include the parental workplace, school boards, social service agencies, and planning commissions.

4. *The macro-system.* Macro-systems are "blueprints" for interlocking social forces at the macro-level and their interrelationships in shaping human development. They provide the broad ideological and organizational patterns within which the meso- and exo-systems reflect the ecology of human development. Macro-systems are not static, but might change through evolution and revolution. For example, economic recession, war, and technological changes may produce such changes.

Bronfenbrenner's conceptual framework proved a useful starting point for multivariate systems research in which family considerations became secondary to the design of institution-based social programmes focusing on children.

The Belsky process model

Belsky (1984) pioneered theories of the processes of competent parental functioning. His model focused on factors affecting parental behaviour and how such factors affect child-rearing, which in turn influences child development. At the family level, Belsky's interest, like Bronfenbrenner's, is primarily on interpersonal interactions between parent and child. Developed to explain the causes of child abuse and neglect,

The model presumes that parenting is directly influenced by forces emanating from within the individual parent (personality), within the individual child (child characteristics of individuality), and from the broader social context in which the parent–child relationship is embedded. Specifically, marital relations, social networks, and jobs influence individual personality and general psychological well-being of parents and, thereby, parental functioning and, in turn, child development. (Belsky 1984, 84)

Through an intensive literature search, Belsky drew the following conclusions regarding the determinants of parenting (Belsky 1984, 84):

(1) parenting is multiply determined by characteristics of the parent, of the child, and of contextual subsystems of social support; (2) these three determinants are not equally influential in supporting or undermining parenting; and (3) developmental history and personality shape parenting indirectly, by first influencing the broader context in which parent–child relations exist (i.e., marital relations, social networks, occupational experience).

Belsky found that parental personality and psychological well-being were the most influential of the determinants in supporting parental functioning. When two of three determinants are in the stressful situation, he stated that parental functioning is most protected when parental personality and psychological well-being still function to promote sensitive caring. In other words, optimal parenting still occurs even when the personal psychological resources of parents are the only determinant remaining in positive mode.

The influence of contextual subsystems of social support is greater than the influence of child characteristics on parental functioning. On the basis of his review of the literature, Belsky determined that risk characteristics in the child are relatively easy to overcome, given that either one of the other two determinants is not at risk.

The Belsky process model does not specifically define the child's developmental outcome (Belsky defined it as competent offspring, without any further explanation). No special attention is given to the importance of the family's material resources, while the family's social resources are conceptualized impersonally as the contextual subsystem of support. Belsky's work is most useful in exonerating the child of blame for poor outcomes. Blame, however, might seem to shift to the parent, as parental personality is viewed as a relatively transcendent or intrinsic and immutable characteristic.

Table 4.3 **Characteristics of developmentally stimulating environments**

1. The optimal development of a young child requires an environment ensuring gratification of all basic physical needs and careful provisions for health and safety.

2. The development of a young child is fostered by the following:
   (a) a relatively high frequency of adult contact involving a relatively small number of adults;
   (b) a positive emotional climate in which the child learns to trust others and himself;
   (c) an optimal level of need gratification;
   (d) the provision of varied and patterned sensory input in an intensity range that does not overload the child's capacity to receive, classify, and respond;
   (e) people who respond physically, verbally, and emotionally with sufficient consistency and clarity to provide uses as to appropriate and valued behaviours and to reinforce such behaviours when they occur;
   (f) an environment containing a minimum of social restrictions on exploratory and motor behaviour;
   (g) careful organization of the physical and temporal environment that permits expectancies of objects and events to be confirmed or revised;
   (h) the provision of rich and varied cultural experiences rendered interpretable by consistent persons with whom the experiences are shared;
   (i) the availability of play materials that facilitate the coordination of sensori-motor processes and a play environment permitting their utilization;
   (j) contact with adults who value achievement and who attempt to generate in the child secondary motivational systems related to achievement;
   (k) the cumulative programming of experiences that provide an appropriate match for the child's current level of cognitive, social, and emotional organization.

Source: Caldwell and Bradley (1984).

The Caldwell HOME inventory

Caldwell and Bradley (1984) take an operational approach to defining the list of home, environmental, parental, and family characteristics needed to foster the development of the child (table 4.3). While consistent with Belsky's concept of the importance of parental personality, this approach operationalizes a set of propensities to interact behaviourally with the child in ways that are, or are not, conducive to the child's development. It then focuses on assessing and intervening on these behaviours and on the contextual support subsystem rather than on the personalities that produce them. Studies linking the HOME to cognitive development have been conducted (Caldwell and Bradley 1984). The two HOME assessment check-lists for children, aged 0–3 years, and 3–6 years, provide the behavioural variables used in our models. These check-list items, on the 0–3-year scale, are combined into subscales, derived from factor analysis of data from the US reference population, measuring emotional and verbal responsivity, acceptance of the child's behaviour, organization of the environment, provision of play materials, parental involvement with the child, and opportunities for variety.

The Caldwell HOME inventory has proven a very useful research tool, but should be viewed as a starting point for more culturally appropriate measures in each developing country setting. A modification of the Caldwell HOME inventory, along with other culturally appropriate items determined by rapid appraisal and preliminary qualitative research, could be used with factor analysis to identify the relevant factors. As an example, in analysing Caldwell HOME inventory data from Indonesia and Nigeria, we discovered that neither the Indonesian nor the Nigerian HOME data yielded an "acceptance" factor similar to the American data during factor analysis. Moreover, in these cultures the variables in the acceptance subscale seemed more indicative of parental neglect than of positive parenting (Satoto and Zeitlin 1990; Aina et al. 1992). By contrast, factor analysis on the Indonesian 0–3-year-old check-list identified a "community socialization" factor that was apparently not present in the US sample. These analyses sensitized us to the value placed by American culture on "acceptance" of what was viewed to be the child's emerging autonomy, and the fact that our two other cultures did not value autonomy similarly.

Resilience and positive deviance research

Belsky's conclusions regarding the central importance of parental personality/caregiving behaviours for children are supported by research on psychological resilience and positive deviance. Zeitlin, Ghassemi, and Mansour (1990), reviewing and conducting cross-cultural studies in developing countries on good physical growth and (in fewer studies) good cognitive test performance in the presence of poverty, concluded that children with the most favourable outcomes tend to live in cohesive, supportive, well-spaced, two-parent families, without major pathologies.

These findings contrast with studies from the United States that controlled for socio-economic status (Cashion 1982), showing that children in female-headed households have good emotional adjustment, if they are protected from stigma, and good intellectual development comparable to that of other children in studies. In fact, child outcomes were better in a low-conflict, single-parent household than in a high-conflict, nuclear family (Clingempeel and Reppucci 1982). Parents of children who are positive deviants typically have superior mental health, life satisfaction related to the child, greater upward mobility and initiative, and more efficient use of health, family planning, and educational services. They display favourable behaviours towards their children, such as rewarding achievement; giving clear instructions; frequent affectionate physical contact; and consistent, sensitive, and patiently sustained responsiveness to the children's needs (Zeitlin, Ghassemi, and Mansour 1990).

This research provides further empirical evidence for Belsky's conclusion that the psychological resources of the parents are particularly important in impoverished settings, where the support context and the child's own condition may be fragile or in a negative state.

The family both as an entity in itself and as the producer of developmental and welfare outcomes of its members

Perspectives on the family both as an entity and as a producer of developmental outcomes of its members (Kreppner and Lerner 1989) depict it as a social context or "climate" facilitating the individual's entry into other social contexts and as an environmental factor containing both genetically shared and non-shared components for the developing individual. Research in this area investigates the interplay between sensitive periods in individual development and family development – e.g. the birth of a child leading to changes in family relationships and structure that in turn affect the child (Kreppner and Lerner 1989). The family is seen as a dynamic context in which the child is both transformer and transformed.

The Schneewind model

Schneewind (1989) provides a psychological model of the family and its effects on children that is supported by empirical work, using an extensive field study of 570 West German families with children aged 9–14 years. The model, which Schneewind called "an integrative research model for studying the family system," is the only one we found that deals quantitatively with the family itself as a system as well as with measurable child outcomes that depend on the family system, and that clearly specifies causal relationships between factors. Using this model, Schneewind tried to understand how and to what extent the "extrafamilial world" is associated with the "intrafamilial world" in the processes of socialization within the family.

A general conceptual framework of the model can be seen in figure 4.6. Socio-economic and demographic variables are used as contextual variables reflecting the spatial and social organization, and social inequality. These variables represent the family's eco-context for further use. This eco-context is a potential source of stimulating agents that can be used by parents in performing their parental functioning. This potential source is transformed into the actual experience field of both parents and children. The process of transforming the potential into the actual is called the "inner-family socialization activity."

The inner-family socialization activity is divided into three parts:
1. The family system level, or the family climate that measures the overall quality of interpersonal relationships within the family;
2. The spouse subsystem level, or the marital relationship;
3. The parent–child subsystem level, or the educational style indicated by parental behaviours and attitudes or authoritarianism.

The family system/climate variables were based on factor analysis of the variables shown in table 4.4, which loaded on three factors referred to as positive emotional family climate, stimulating family climate, and normative–authoritarian family climate. We present these variables in detail because their measurement illustrates one approach that could be pursued to identify the component parts contributing to the family decision-making/management capabilities and to the contextual and resource variables contributing to family coping that we ultimately seek to define.

Schneewind's applied structural causal modelling used latent variables for hypothesis testing and formulation. His model, which served as a guide for our own, and its variables are shown in figure 4.7 and table 4.5. This type of modelling, sometimes known by the name LISREL (Jöreskog and Sörbom 1989), constructs abstract underlying (latent) variables using factor analysis and relates these to measured outcomes. The data supporting the causal model linked extrafamilial (measured by socio-economic status [SES], urban or rural location, and job experience) and intrafamilial variables (measured by family climate, and personal traits of the father and the son). The expressive family climate factor (measured by high degree of mutual control,

71

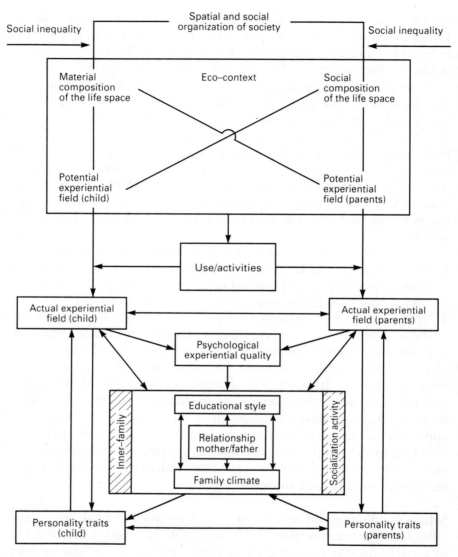

Fig. 4.6 **An integrative research model for studying family systems in context (source: Schneewind 1989)**

intellectual/cultural orientation, active-recreational orientation, and independence) appeared to be an important mediating factor in the child outcome variable, which was the social adjustment of the son (termed "extraverted temperament"). In another model in the same paper, he demonstrated that low socio-economic eco-context and

Table 4.4　**Subscales of the family environment scale**

Type of dimension	Dimension	Description
Relationship	1. Cohesion	The degree of commitment, help, and support family members provide for one another
	2. Expressiveness	The extent to which family members are encouraged to act openly and to express their feelings directly
	3. Conflict	The amount of openly expressed anger, aggression, and conflict among family members
Personal growth	4. Independence	The extent to which family members are assertive, are self-sufficient, and make their own decisions
	5. Achievement orientation	The extent to which activities (such as school and work) are cast into an achievement-orientated or competitive framework
	6. Intellectual–cultural orientation	The degree of interest in political, social, intellectual, and cultural activities
	7. Active-recreational orientation	The extent of participation in social and recreational activities
	8. Moral–religious emphasis	The degree of emphasis on ethical and religious issues and values
System maintenance	9. Organization	The degree of importance of clear organization and structure in planning family activities and responsibilities
	10. Control	The extent to which set rules and procedures are used to run family life

Source: Schneewind (1989), after Moos and Moos (1981).

rigid unstimulating job conditions of the father were associated with an authoritarian parenting style that produced sons with inferiority feelings and weakly internalized locus of control.

Schneewind found that at the same level of family eco-context are critical differences in the inner-family socialization activity. He concluded that "the psychological makeup of family life ... has an important influence on how a family's potential eco-context is actually utilized." This is similar to Belsky's conclusion that personality and

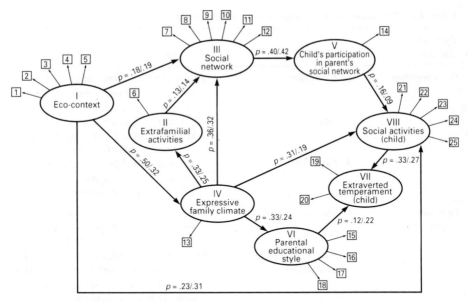

Fig. 4.7 **Antecedents and consequences of the family's social network (source: Schneewind 1989)**

the psychological well-being of the parents have the greatest influence on parental functioning.

Family social wellness

Measures for the evaluation of family functioning provide our major entry point into the study of family social health. Table 4.6 gives a sample of the variety of concepts measured in the subscales of seven instruments used to evaluate family functioning (Walker and Crocker 1988). Another set of instruments can be found in the coping literature (Krauss 1988). Many of the items in table 4.6 are designed to capture positive aspects of social wellness, such as mood and tone, marital satisfaction, happiness, and relationship quality. Only the first of the instruments, however – the Beavers–Timberlawn family evaluation scale – is based on observed measures, rather than self-report, and is claimed to be objective, quantifiable, multifactoral, focused on the entire family, and relatively simple to administer and score.

Walker and Crocker (1988) conclude that "a global measure of family functioning that is well standardized and relatively simple to administer does not now exist and may never be developed." We

Table 4.5   Latent and indicator variables of a causal model on the antecedents and consequences of the family's social network

			Factor structure coefficients	
			Mother–child	Father–child
Latent variables	No.	Description	($n = 570$)	
I. Eco-context	1.	Socio-economic status	.85	.85
	2.	Urban location	.62	.58
	3.	Action space density	.51	.48
	4.	Location of residence	.34	.41
	5.	Period of living in same house/flat	.46	.45
II. Extrafamilial activities (parents)	6.	Membership in sports and other leisure groups	1.00	1.00
III. Social network (parents)	7.	Intensity of primary contacts	.72	.75
	8.	No. of telephone contacts	.63	.57
	9.	No. of visiting contacts	.51	.18
	10.	No. of good friends	.68	.53
	11.	No. of close families with children	.54	.55
	12.	Addressee for educational problems	.44	.57
IV. Expressive family climate	13.	Stimulating family climate (second-order factor)	1.00	1.00
V. Child's participation in parents' social network	14.	Child's participation in parents' social contacts (composite score)	1.00	1.00
VI. Educational style	15.	Enhancing child's initiative	.49	.83
	16.	Enhancing child's autonomy	.37	.66
	17.	Loving support	.62	.48
	18.	Limited verbal reward	−.60	−.23
VII. Extraverted temperament (child)	19.	Will-power	.93	.90
	20.	Extraversion	.73	.77
VIII. Social activities (child)	21.	No. of telephone contacts	.62	.60
	22.	No. of activities in sports groups	.64	.68
	23.	No. of hours spent in group activities	.41	.48
	24.	No. of extracurricular activities	.73	.74
	25.	Social active field of experience (SAFE)	.60	.43

Source: Schneewind (1989).

Table 4.6 **Family measure subscales categorized by Fischer's schema** [a, b]

Measure	Subscale	SD	C and S	E and N	CA	DA
BTFES	Overt power		×			
	Parental coalitions	×				
	Closeness			×		
	Mythology	×				
	Goal-directed negotiation	×				
	Clarity of expression	×				
	Responsibility		×			
	Invasiveness	×				
	Permeability	×				
	Range of feelings			×		
	Mood and tone			×		
	Unresolvable conflict	×				
	Empathy			×		
FACES II	Family cohesion					
	Emotional bonding			×		
	Family boundaries	×				
	Coalitions	×				
	Time	×				
	Space	×				
	Friends			×		
	Decision-making	×				
	Interests and recreation			×		
	Family adaptability					
	Assertiveness		×			
	Leadership (control)		×			
	Discipline		×			
	Negotiation	×				
	Roles	×				
	Rules		×			
FCAM	Consideration versus conflict	×				
	Open communication	×				
	Togetherness versus separateness	×				
	Internal versus external locus of control		×			
	Family actualization versus inadequacy			×		
	Family loyalty			×		
	Closeness versus estrangement			×		
	Community sociability				×	
	Family ambition				×	

(*continued*)

Table 4.6 **(cont.)**

Measure	Subscale	SD	C and S	E and N	CA	DA
FES	Cohesion	×				
	Expressiveness			×		
	Conflict		×			
	Independence		×			
	Achievement orientation				×	
	Intellectual–cultural orientation				×	
	Active-recreational orientation				×	
	Moral–religious emphasis				×	
	Organization	×				
	Control		×			
FFL	Frequency of disagreement	×				
	Communication	×				
	Problem solving	×				
	Weekends together	×				
	Marital satisfaction			×		
	Happiness			×		
FIS	Clarity	×				
	Total continuity	×				
	Commitment			×		
	Agreement and disagreement	×				
	Affect intensity			×		
	Relationship quality			×		
FAD	Problem solving	×				
	Communication	×				
	Rules	×				
	Affective responsiveness			×		
	Affective involvement			×		
	Behaviour control		×			

a. Key to Fischer's schema: SD, structural descriptors; C and S, controls and sanctions; E and N, emotions and needs; CA, cultural aspects; DA, developmental aspects.

b. Source: Schneewind (1989) after Forman and Hagan.

view this perspective as overly pessimistic. Rather than looking to create any single measurement tool that serves as a "gold standard," we believe that sensitive use of qualitative research and rapid assessment methods in developing countries should be able to yield a variety of culture- and situation-specific measures that may be represented by relatively simple indicators for specific research purposes. Such research is actively needed, however, because the investigation of the dimensions of family functioning that are of greatest relevance to international development has yet to begin.

References

Aina, T.A., M. Zeitlin, K. Setiolane, and H. Amstrong. 1992. "Phase I Survey Results: Positive Deviance in Nutrition Research Project. Lagos State, Nigeria." Draft Report to UNICEF.

Beavers, W.R., and M.N. Voeller. 1983. "Family Models: Comparing and Contrasting the Olson Circumplex Model and the Beavers Systems Model." *Family Process* 22: 250–260.

Becker, G.S. 1981. *A Treatise on the Family*. Cambridge, Mass.: Harvard University Press.

Becker, W.C., and R.S. Krug. 1964. "A Circumplex Model for Social Behavior in Children." *Child Development* 35: 391–396.

Belsky, J. 1984. "The Determinants of Parenting: A Process Model." *Child Development* 55: 83–96.

Benjamin, L.S. 1977. "Structural Analysis of a Family in Therapy." *Journal of Counseling and Clinical Psychology* 45: 391–406.

Blumenstein, P., and P. Schwartz. 1985. *American Couples: Money, Work, Sex*. New York: Pocket Books.

Boss, P. 1987. "Family Stress." In: M.B. Sussman and S.K. Steinmetz, eds. *Handbook of Marriage and the Family*. New York: Plenum Press, pp. 835–859.

Bronfenbrenner, U. 1979. *The Ecology of Human Development: Experiments by Nature and Design*. Cambridge, Mass.: Harvard University Press.

Bruce, J., and C.B. Lloyd. 1992. "Beyond Female Headship: Family Research and Policy Issues for the 1990s." Paper presented at IFPRI–World Bank Conference on Intrahousehold Resource Allocation: Policies and Research Methods, 12–14 February 1992, IFPRI, Washington, DC.

Burgess, E.W. 1926. "The Family as a Unity of Interacting Personalities." *Family* 7: 3–9.

Caldwell, B.M., and R.H. Bradley. 1984. *Home Observation for Measurement of the Environment*. Little Rock, Ark.: University of Arkansas.

Cashion, B. 1982. "Female-headed Families' Effects on Children and Clinical Implications." *Journal of Marital and Family Therapy* 8: 77–85.

Clingempeel, W.G., and N.D. Reppucci. 1982. "Joint Custody after Divorce." *Psychological Bulletin* 91: 102–127.

Constantine, L. 1986. *Family Paradigms*. New York: Guilford Press.

Doherty, W.J. 1991. "Family Therapy Goes Post-modern." *Family Therapy Networker* 37–42.

Epstein, N.B., D.S. Bishop, and L.M. Baldwin. 1984. "McMaster Model of Family Functioning." In: D.H. Olson, and P.M. Miller, eds. *Family Studies Review Yearbook, Volume 2*. New Delhi: Sage Publications.

———, ———, and S. Levin. 1978. "The McMaster Model of Family Functioning." *Journal of Marriage and Family Counseling* 4: 19–31.

Fischer, C.S. 1977. *Networks and Places: Social Relations in the Urban Setting*. New York: Free Press.

French, A.P., and B.J. Guidera. 1974. "The Family as a System in Four Dimensions: A Theoretical Model." Paper presented at the American Academy of Child Psychology, San Francisco.

Friedman, A.S., A. Utada, and M.R. Morissey. 1987. "Families of Adolescent Drug Abusers are Rigid: Are These Families either Disengaged or Enmeshed or Both?" *Family Process* 26: 131–148.

Gottman, J.M. 1979. *Marital Interaction.* New York: Basic Books.

Jöreskog, K.G., and D. Sörbom, 1989. *LISREL7: G Guide to the Program and Applications.* Chicago, Ill.: SPSS.

Kantor, D., and W. Lehr. 1975. *Inside the Family.* San Francisco: Jossey-Bass.

Kaslow, F.W. 1987. "Marital and Family Therapy." In: M.B. Sussman and S.K. Steinmetz, eds. *Handbook of Marriage and the Family.* New York: Plenum Press, pp. 835–859.

Krauss, M.W. 1988. "Measures of Stress and Coping in Families." In: H.B. Weiss and F.H. Jacobs, eds. *Evaluating Family Programs.* New York: Aldine de Gruyter, pp. 177–194.

Kreppner, K., and R.M. Lerner, eds. 1989. *Family Systems and Life-Span Development.* Hillsdale, NJ: Lawrence Erlbaum Associates.

L'Abate, L. 1987. "The Emperor Has No Clothes! Long Live the Emperor! A Critique of Family Systems Thinking and a Reductionist Proposal." *American Journal of Family Therapy* 15: 19–33.

Leary, T. 1957. *Interpersonal Diagnosis of Personality.* New York: Ronald Press.

Leff, J., and C. Vaughn. 1985. *Expressed Emotion in Families.* New York: Guilford Press.

Lerner, R.M. 1989. "Individual Development and the Family System: A Life-Span Perspective." In: K. Kreppner and R.M. Lerner, eds. *Family Systems and Life-Span Development.* Hillsdale, NJ: Lawrence Erlbaum Associates, pp. 15–27.

Mattessich, P., and R. Hill. 1987. "Life Cycle and Family Development." In: M.B. Sussman and S.K. Steinmetz, eds. *Handbook of Marriage and the Family.* New York: Plenum Press, pp. 437–470.

Monat, A., and R. Lazarus, eds. 1977. *Stress and Coping.* New York: Columbia University Press.

Moos, R.H., and B.S. Moos. 1981. *Family Environment Scale* (Manual). Palo Alto, Calif.: Consulting Psychologists Press.

National Academy of Sciences. 1976. *Toward a National Policy for Child and Families.* Washington, DC: US Government Printing Office.

Olson, D.H., and Y. Lavee. 1989. "Family System and Family Stress: A Family Life Cycle Perspective." In: K. Kreppner and R.M. Lerner, eds. *Family Systems and Life-Span Development.* Hillsdale, NJ: Lawrence Erlbaum Associates, pp. 165–193.

————., C.S. Russell, and D.H. Sprengkle. 1984. "Circumplex Model of Marital and Family Systems: VI. Theoretical Update. In: D.H. Olson and P.M. Miller, eds. *Family Studies Review Yearbook. Volume 2.* New Delhi: Sage Publications.

————. D.H. Sprengkle, and C.S. Russell. 1979. "Circumplex Model of Marital and Family System: Cohesion and Adaptability Dimensions, Family Types, and Clinical Applications." *Family Process* 18: 3–28.

Parsons, T., and R.F. Bales. 1955. *Family Socialization and Interaction Process.* Glencoe, Ill.: Free Press.

Peterson, G.W., and B.C. Rollins. 1987. "Parent–Child Socialization." In: M.B. Sussman and S.K. Steinmetz, eds. *Handbook of Marriage and the Family*. New York: Plenum Press, pp. 471–507.

Piotrkowski, C.S., and M.H. Kattz. 1983. "Work Experience and Family Relations among Working Class and Lower Middle Class Families." In: H.Z. Lopata and J.H. Plecks, eds. *Research in the Interweave of Social Roles, Volume 3: Families and Jobs*. Greenwich, Conn.: JAI Press.

———, R.N. Rapoport, and R. Rapoport. 1987. "Families and Work." In: M.B. Sussman and S.K. Steinmetz, eds. *Handbook of Marriage and the Family*. New York: Plenum Press, pp. 251–284.

Reiss, D. 1981. *The Family's Construction of Reality*. Cambridge, Mass.: Harvard University Press.

Satoto, and M.F. Zeitlin. 1990. "Indonesian Positive Deviance in Nutrition Research Project. Phase I and Phase II Reports." Submitted by Tufts University School of Nutrition to UNICEF and the Italian Government.

Schneewind, K.A. 1989. "Contextual Approaches to Family Systems Research: The Macro–Micro Puzzle." In: K. Kreppner and R.M. Lerner, eds. *Family Systems and Lifespan Development*. Hillsdale, NJ: Lawrence Erlbaum Associates, pp. 197–221.

Skinner, D.A. 1980. "Dual Career Family Stress and Coping: A Literature Review." *Family Relations* 29: 473–480.

Walker, D.K., and R.W. Crocker. 1988. "Measuring Family Systems Outcomes." In: H.B. Weiss and F.H. Jacobs, eds. *Evaluating Family Programs*. New York: Aldine de Gruyter, pp. 153–176.

Zeitlin, M.F., H. Ghassemi, and M. Mansour. 1990. "Research Considerations." In: *Positive Deviance in Child Nutrition: With Emphasis on Psychosocial and Behavioural Aspects and Implications for Development*. Tokyo: United Nations University Press, pp. 80–149.

5

Perspectives from international development assistance and from family programmes

The flagship role of early childhood development programmes

A number of programmes of various types have worked for many years with families in poverty. Social workers and home economists work with families, family planning with couples, and farming systems projects with households. Micro-enterprise programmes increasingly recognize the role of families as managers of strategic resources (Foss 1992). Nevertheless, until now, almost all of the pioneering work and literature on family programmes *per se* has been in the area of early childhood development.

Early childhood intervention family programmes take a two-generational approach, averting future poverty in the child's generation while improving family conditions in the present generation. They enter more intimately into the psychological environment of the family than other programme types, and they are based on evidence that interventions with children before the age of five have long-term benefits on rates of school completion, employment, teen pregnancy, and other indicators of family social health and economic development (Berrueta-Clement et al. 1984). This evidence supports a continuing focus on child development in multipurpose family initiatives.

Across the world, as early childhood development interventions start up, they show a progression from minimal to extensive family involvement (Simeonsson and Bailey 1990). Programmes are typically child-centred when they begin: they offer services directly to children, with the parent as passive observer. In a next step some parental involvement is encouraged, with a parent taking on the role of "teacher" and providing stimulation for the child. As programmes evolve, they typically recognize that community services also must be offered to the family, as a unit, to enable it to care for its children.

The movement towards greater family involvement probably has occurred in the majority of programme types. According to Weiss and Jacobs (1988), US programmes with different service objectives, in child health, child development, prenatal care, teen pregnancy prevention, and treatment of children with special needs, increasingly use similar models for involving the family. Community-based programmes in Indonesia and programmes in other developing countries based on the primary health care (PHC) concept have moved in very similar directions. According to Weiss and Jacobs (1988), these programmes:

1. Demonstrate an ecological approach to promoting child and adult growth by
   (a) enhancing both the family's child-rearing capacity and the community context;
   (b) building on and strengthening the interdependent relationships between the family and the community.
2. Are community-based and hence
   (a) are sensitive to local needs and resources, even when government sponsored;
   (b) use horizontal multilateral rather than vertical approaches to service delivery through creative use of volunteers, paraprofessionals, peer support, and social networks, in addition to professional services.
3. Provide services in the domains typically classified under the heading of "social support," including
   (a) information;
   (b) emotional and appraisal support (empathy, feedback, and reinforcement to adults in parenting roles, and access to other parents);
   (c) instrumental support (referrals, transportation, etc.).
4. Emphasize prevention of mortality and of child and family dysfunctions.

These programmes, employing similar means to achieve overlapping ends, are likely to have a common set of outcomes that benefit families, such as enhanced parenting skills, reduced social isolation, and richer, more developmentally appropriate parent–child interactions.

In international child health and nutrition, such family-level outcomes are only beginning to become a part of the explicit goals of programmes in which they may have exerted beneficial effects for some time. During the 1980s, the international focus for children gradually shifted from child survival alone to child survival and development. The concept of vulnerable groups, which applied earlier to preschool children and to pregnant and lactating women, was extended to women and girl children. The family focus builds on development work in health, nutrition, population, agriculture, and rural development.

Myers (1992), writing for UNICEF in his book, *The Twelve Who Survive*, reviewed international development frameworks for child survival, health, nutrition, and development, with the child as the focus. These frameworks usually represent the family by the mother alone, although the word "parent" may be used instead. Some depict macro-systems of development inputs pointing through the mother to the child; others depict parent–child transactional relationships, and still others (Zeitlin, Ghassemi, and Mansour 1990) include the social system, the mother, and the child. Myers (1992) reported the following trends towards perspectives which increasingly engage with the micro-ecology of the family level in the fields of child survival, growth, and development:

1. From a definition of survival, growth, and development as states or conditions to considering them as processes.
2. From isolated emphasis on one or another dimension of child survival and development to a multidimensional and "integrated" view (Mosley and Chen 1984; L. Bennett, as cited in Myers 1992), to models including physical and psychosocial dimensions of development (Zeitlin, Ghassemi, and Mansour 1990).
3. From a one-way relationship between health or nutrition actions affecting early childhood development (Mosley and Chen 1984) to a two-way interactive relationship in which developmentally sensitive interactions affect health and nutritional status (Zeitlin, Ghassemi, and Mansour 1990).
4. From a view of the child as a passive recipient of "stimulation", or

of other interventions, to the child as an actor, influencing the development process (Bronfenbrenner 1979; Super and Harkness 1987; Zeitlin, Ghassemi, and Mansour 1990).

5. From a "universal" definition of the goals and outcome of child development to a more culturally relative and sensitive view (Bronfenbrenner 1979; Super and Harkness 1987).

The emphasis on the family can be viewed as one more step in this process of integration and contextualization. It also is a step in the direction of respect for the social structures and the cultural integrity of the participants in the development process. These programmes move away from deficit and didactic models to partnerships in which all participants, parents, and professionals have expertise and support to share (Weiss and Jacobs 1988).

Myers speaks for our current effort to combine the "piecemeal thinking" of the various disciplines:

... we are victims of the age of specialization in which we live. Academic and bureaucratic divisions of labour cut the child into small pieces. The "whole single child," so often present in the rhetoric of child development, is slowly dissected in a series of unconnected, narrowly conceived analyses. Doctors, psychologists, nutritionists, sociologists, educators, anthropologists, economists, and others, each approach the topic from a distinct point of view. (Myers 1992, 49)

Our return to dealing with the whole child in the whole family may be viewed as a part of the de-differentiation that is characteristic of the post-modern era (Lash 1990). A corresponding process of integrating research disciplines also has occurred among the epidemiologists, nutritionists, economists, child psychologists, anthropologists, and other researchers who specialize in the problems of children in poverty. These researchers have become social science generalists, drawing across many disciplines for research techniques to flesh out the increasingly detailed and complete pictures that can be generated using data processing technology (see ch. 9).

The UNICEF conceptual framework

The UNICEF conceptual framework shown in figure 5.1 (Jonsson 1992) provides a basis for assessment, analysis, and action to improve child nutrition and development and is an effective tool for mobilizing communities and designing programmes. This framework deliberately leaves vague the ecological levels to permit emergence of

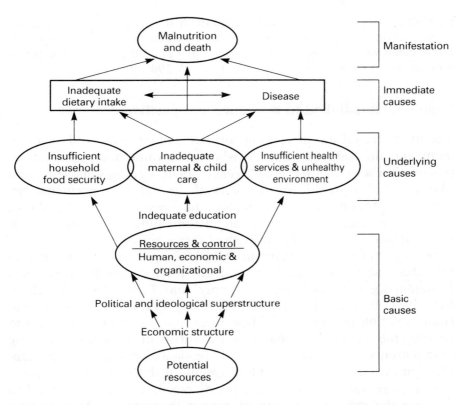

Fig. 5.1   **Causes of malnutrition: the UNICEF model (source: Jonsson 1992)**

different causal patterns in different context-specific circumstances. This flexibility permits specification of family-level variables, as one context of analysis. Accordingly, we drew on this framework in designing our latent variables for the analyses in chapter 9.

Family factors and programmes that protect high-risk children

This section first reviews naturally occurring, informal, or family circumstances that protect children, followed by the formal circumstances established in intervention programmes designed for children alone or children and their families. We present evidence for the view of Meisels (1985) that,

The family and its sociocultural and economic context is the crucible in which forces for good and ill are transformed into developmental patterns for high risk and handicapped children in the first years of life. The evidence from a whole generation of research demonstrates that the quality of parents' behavior as caregivers and teachers makes a difference in the development of infants and young children. (Meisels 1985, 9)

Family factors linked to resilience and positive deviance

The literature on the caretaking correlates of optimal child development and the data on children who are invulnerable, resilient, or positive deviants (Rutter 1987; Werner 1990; Zeitlin, Ghassemi, and Mansour 1990) provide descriptions of the naturally occurring circumstances that protect children from the worst effects of the illness, absence, or death of a parent; of an unstimulating environment; or of the limitations of highly impoverished surroundings.

Of key importance to resilient children is at least one person who provides stable care, affection, and attention during the first years (Furstenberg 1976; Kellam, Ensminger, and Turner 1977; Crockenberg 1981; Werner and Smith 1982; Sheey 1987). Such a warm and stable relationship allows children to develop trust in others and to develop the secure sense that they are worthy of being loved. Loving grandparents, sibling caregivers, or friends and neighbours can supplement the care of overextended, absent, or dysfunctional parents.

There are also ways of caring for or raising children that tend to increase the children's ability to cope with problems. Longitudinal studies have shown that resilience in boys and girls is promoted by different parental behaviours (Werner and Smith 1982; Block and Gjerde 1986). Boys appear to be most resilient when they are raised in families that have more rules, structure, parental supervision, and a male role model, and where the expression of feelings is encouraged. Girls appear to do best where they are not overprotected, where they are encouraged to be independent and to take risks, and when they receive consistent emotional support from their primary caregiver.

Positive experiences in school also support resilient children. Rutter (1987) points out that schools that support high-risk children have high academic standards, offer incentives for good work, encourage performance with feedback and praise, and offer children opportunities to experience trust and responsibility. Supportive schools have a more organized and predictable environment, with clear rules, and defined student responsibilities. Teachers also may serve as positive role models and protective influences for highly stressed or disadvantaged children.

In developing countries, descriptions of resilient children are largely based on field observations rather than on longitudinal data. The protective factors that appear to be most common in developing countries (Dash and Dash 1982; Swaminathan 1986; International Development Research Center 1988; Colletta and Satoto 1989; Landers 1989; Zeitlin, Ghassemi, and Mansour 1990) include the following:

1. A high value placed on children and female commitment to mothering;
2. Emotional security and close bonding with mother;
3. Intense caretaking, high in tactile and verbal stimulation;
4. Sense of belonging fostered by involvement in a family-based social network with multiple family caregivers;
5. A well-structured, organized, and clean home;
6. Learning by observing and interacting with adults;
7. Emphasis on self-reliance and self-help skills;
8. High manual dexterity and attentiveness to changes in the environment.

The effects of early intervention programmes

Programmes that provide services directly to children

There have been a number of reviews of the effects of early interventions on children (Simeonsson, Cooper, and Scheiner 1982; Halpern and Myers 1984; White and Casto 1985; Dunst 1986; Farran 1990; Myers 1992). Despite the considerable methodological flaws in the database, there are by now enough studies to allow us to draw conclusions for practice.

The majority of the studies reviewed focused on children at high risk for school problems, developmental delays, or problems in learning to read. The children studied also tended to be of low socioeconomic status and most were Black, though some studies included Hispanics and children in developing countries. While most studies were carried out in North America or Europe, two reviews (Halpern and Myers 1984; Myers 1992) considered the impact of programmes in developing countries.

From the data on children in developed countries, it may be concluded that when intervention services are provided directly to the child there is gain in school achievement and intelligence test performance. Intelligence test score gains are of the magnitude of up to one standard deviation (10–15 IQ points) in the short term. In developing countries (Myers and Hertenberg 1987) it may be concluded that most, if not all, early childhood intervention programmes have the effect of making children more alert, sociable, curious, and well prepared for primary school. Consistent with the findings from developed countries, children from the most deprived backgrounds (lower income, more socially distressed) tend to benefit the most from programme participation.

Data on the long-term impact of early intervention suggest that continued intervention is necessary for continued higher IQ scores but not for some improvements in school achievement. Data from the United States show that by five years of age, intervention children tend to score one-half standard deviation above control children; by the time they are seven years old and older there are no reported remaining intervention–control group differences in IQ scores, though a number of studies show decreased drop-out rates, fewer special education placements, and fewer grade retentions (Berrueta-Clement et al. 1984). Programmes in developing countries have not yet produced documentation of long-term effects beyond the third grade, but field experiences suggest that the readiness of the school to respond to more active and curious children is crucial in the process of maintaining the effects. While initial adjustment to school is better, the long-term impact seems to be overwhelmed by the limitations of the schools that the children enter.

While there are few data to suggest that preschool intervention, which is not continued into elementary school, has a long-term impact on IQ scores (Farran 1990), when the intervention is continued into the early elementary grades the effects are long lasting. Effects include intervention children both performing on grade level and graduating from high school at a higher rate than the controls (Becker and Gersten 1982; Meyer, Gersten, and Gutkin 1983; Gersten and Carnine 1984; Meyer 1984). Effective interventions tended to consist of improving the quality of the school day, for instance monitoring the teachers to make sure that classes receive academic instruction for 60 per cent of the school day (Farran 1990).

Programmes that provide services to families

Interest in family-based interventions has been spurred by the evidence that early interventions, when focused on the child alone, have a time-limited impact (Simeonsson, Cooper, and Scheiner 1982) and that a multifaceted approach appears to be more effective in both developed and developing countries (Farran 1990; Myers 1992).

Interventions focusing on providing services to children through their parents generally foster a partnership between the parent and programme on behalf of the child. In reviewing interventions nearly two decades ago, Bronfenbrenner (1979, 595) concluded that,

The involvement of the child's family as an active participant is critical to the success of any intervention program. Without such family involvement, any effects of intervention, at least in the cognitive sphere, appear to erode fairly rapidly once the program ends.

One approach to parental involvement considers the parent to be the primary teacher of the child, with the intervention team showing the parent how to work with the child. Home intervention programmes typically have used this approach, in which a paraprofessional home visitor makes a home visit, showing the parent how the child's development can be furthered if the parent engages the child in specific cognitive or language-based activities. These programmes have the advantages of keeping responsibility for children centred in the family, increasing the likelihood of long-term improvements through changes in parental behaviours, and providing services to children at a relatively low cost. As Myers (1992) points out, field experience with home visiting programmes suggests that they have the greatest impact if:
1. The learning is reinforced with occasional group meetings;
2. All family members, not just mothers, are involved;
3. The home visits focus on concrete problems and activities;
4. Parents are active participants in working out the details of the activities, rather than having the home visitor use a "cookbook" approach.

Another approach to parental involvement is to educate the parent about children and their development. Such parent education programmes tend to be training programmes in which the main goals are to direct changes in parental knowledge, attitudes, and behaviours. Bailey and Simeonsson (1990) summarize the outcome of research on parent training:
1. Parents can be taught to use correct and consistent educational interventions, behaviour management techniques, or therapeutic techniques.
2. Parent training programmes often result in desired changes in child behaviour and development.

3. Effective training includes modelling, practice, and specific feedback as well as a way of monitoring parental performance.
4. Long-term maintenance of changes in parental behaviour has not been adequately documented.

Seitz and Provence (1990, 423) review caregiver-focused models of early intervention, concluding that the following outcomes "appear open to influence through caregiver-focused early intervention":
1. Raising children's development and intelligence quotients (DQs and IQs);
2. Improving children's school adjustment;
3. Increasing maternal education;
4. Increasing spacing of subsequent child-bearing;
5. Improving the quality of parent–child interaction;
6. Improving parental responsiveness to children;
7. Improving children's socialization.

The evidence on direct training interventions with families seems convincing, that parents can be taught skills, knowledge, and techniques that facilitate their children's development. This instruction also is applicable to other children in the family and seems to be related to greater feelings of parental satisfaction and control (Myers and Hertenberg 1987). We also know, however, that the more negative circumstances the family suffers, the less they are able to benefit from a highly focused intervention programme. For such families, a more comprehensive system of community support and crisis interventions also may be necessary.

Impacts on family functioning or social health

Child-centred programmes with goals for family functioning

Although most programmes have targeted child outcomes only, Weiss (1988) lists four US programmes that have set goals for family economic self-sufficiency and one for life events stress. Evaluations of these programmes have measured educational advancement, employment and training, different sources of income, rate of subsequent births, quality of life, recent stressful experience, and high-risk status.

Programmes for handicapped children with special needs have pioneered the process of creating individualized family plans for meeting needs for nurturance and emotional support (Walker and Crocker 1988). Family preservation programmes that intervene with crisis counselling and programmes providing social support to teenage parents are models that need further investigation for international application. Weiss (1988) also calls for more investigation of the beneficial impact that family programmes have on service delivery systems, by increasing family-level demand for, and use of, a wide range of services.

Community-based interventions

In reviewing community-based early childhood interventions in the United States, Halpern (1990) concludes that community-based parenting programmes can influence maternal emotional responsiveness, affection, praise, appropriate control, and encouragement of child verbalization. The programmes are most effective when there is a strong focus on improving parenting knowledge and skills. When the focus is a more diffuse attempt to improve the parents' personal adjustment, there tend to be fewer significant gains for either the parent or the child. Halpern concludes that because the influence of these programmes on the child is indirect (mediated through the parent) there tend to be modest short-term effects on child development. We believe that this conclusion underestimates the potential for positive gain.

As noted above, the trend is towards community-based interventions, which most typically are neighbourhood based, employ workers from the local area, and attempt to improve overall family conditions to remove or decrease those circumstances known to be damaging to child development. To meet these goals, model programmes such as Parent–Child Center programs (PCC), the Parent–Child Development Centers (PCDs), and the Child and Family Resource Programs (CFRPs) have been run in the United States.

Myers (1992) looks at community-based programmes in developing countries, pointing out that general improvements in child survival and development hinge on improvements in the community that protects, nourishes, and challenges the young child. Community development approaches in developing countries tend to focus on improving family achievements in the basic task areas of income, food, health, shelter, and sanitation. Community development programmes favour the continuity and sustainability of programmes that are run for the community by the community. Such programmes also have the potential for improving life for everyone in the community, not just the children (Myers 1992).

References

Becker, W.C., and R. Gersten. 1982. "A Follow-up of a Follow Through: The Latter Effects of the Direct Instruction Method on Children in 5th and 6th Grade." *American Educational Research Journal* 19: 75–92.

Berrueta-Clement, J.R., L.J. Schweinhart, W.S. Barnett, A.S. Epstein, and D.P. Weikart. 1984. *Changed Lives. The Effects of the Perry Preschool Program on Youths through Age 19.* Ypsilanti, Michigan: High Scope Press.

Block, J., and P.F. Gjerde. 1986. "Early Antecedents of Ego Resiliency in Late Adolescence." Paper presented at American Psychological Association meeting, Washington, DC.

Bronfenbrenner, U. 1979. *The Ecology of Human Development: Experiments by Nature and Design.* Cambridge, Mass.: Harvard University Press.

Colletta, N.D., and Satoto. 1989. "Messages from Invulnerable Children in Asian Villages: The Conditions that Protect Development." Paper presented at International Conference on Early Education and Development, sponsored by K.C. Wong Educational Foundation, UNICEF, Bernard van Leer Foundation, and High Scope Foundation, Hong Kong.

Crockenberg, S.B. 1981. "Infant Irritability, Mother Responsiveness, and Social Support Influences on the Security of Infant–Mother Attachment." *Child Development* 52: 857–865.

Dash, R., and A.S. Dash. 1982. A study of perceptual motor and intellectual abilities of tribal and non-tribal children. In: R. Rath, H.S. Asthana, D. Sinha, and J.H. Sinha, eds. *Diversity and Unity in Cross-Cultural Psychology.* Lisse, Netherlands: Swets-Zeilinger.

Dunst, C.J. 1986. "Overview of the Efficacy of Early Intervention Programs: Methodological and Conceptual Considerations." In: L. Bickman and D. Wheatherford, eds. *Evaluating Early Intervention Programs for Severely Handicapped Children and Their Family.* Austin, Tex.: PRO-ED, pp. 79–147.

Farran, D.C. 1990. "Effects of Interventions with Disadvantaged and Disabled Children: A Decade Review." In: S.J. Meisels and J.P. Shonkoff, eds. *Handbook of Early Childhood Intervention.* Cambridge: Cambridge University Press, pp. 428–444.

Foss, S. 1992. "Looking at Families as Managers of Strategic Resources." Family and Development Initiative Seminar. Brief No. 1, Washington, DC: USAID.

Furstenberg, F.F. 1976. *Unplanned Parenthood: The Social Consequences of Teenage Child-bearing.* New York: Free Press.

Gersten, R., and D. Carnine. 1984. "Direct Instruction Mathematics: A Longitudinal Evaluation of Low-income Elementary School Students." *Elementary School Journal* 84: 395–407.

Halpern, R. 1990. "Community-based Early Intervention". In: S.J. Meisels and J.P. Shonkoff, eds. *Handbook of Early Childhood Intervention.* Cambridge: Cambridge University Press, pp. 469–498.

———, and R. Myers. 1984. "Effects of Early Childhood Interventions on Primary School Progress and Performance in the Developing Countries." Paper prepared for USAID. Ypsilanti, Michigan: High Scope Press.

International Development Research Center, Ontario. 1988. *The Learning Environment of Early Childhood in Asia: Research Perspectives and Changing Programmes.* Bangkok: UNESCO.

Jonsson, U. 1992. "Nutrition and Ethics." Paper presented at meeting on Nutrition, Ethics, and Human Rights, Norwegian Institute of Human Rights, Oslo, 9–11 July 1992.

Kellam, S.G., M.T. Ensminger, and R.J. Turner. 1977. "Family Structure and the Mental Health of Children." *Archives of General Psychiatry* 34: 1012–1022.

Landers, C. 1989. "A Psychobiological Study of Infant Development in South India." In: J.K. Nugent, B.M. Lester, and T.B. Brazelton, eds. *The Cultural Context of Infancy*. New York: Ablex, pp. 169–208.

Lash, S. 1990. *Sociology of Postmodernism*. London: Routledge.

Meisels, S.J. 1985. "The Efficacy of Early Intervention: Why Are We Still Asking This Question?" *Topics in Early Childhood Special Education* 5: 1–11.

Meyer, L. 1984. "Long-term Academic Effects of the Direct Instruction Follow-through." *Elementary School Journal* 834: 380–394.

———, R. Gersten, and J. Gutkin. 1983. "Direct Instruction: A Project Follow-through Success Story in an Inner-city School." *Elementary School Journal* 81: 241–252.

Mosley, W.H., and L. Chen. 1984. "An Analytical Framework for the Study of Child Survival in Developing Countries." *Population and Development Review* 10 (supplement): 25–45.

Myers, R. 1992. *The Twelve Who Survive, Strengthening Programmes of Early Childhood Development in the Third World*. London: Routledge.

———, and R. Hertenberg. 1987. "The Eleven Who Survive: Toward a Re-examination of Early Childhood Development Program Options and Costs." Discussion paper produced for the World Bank, Education and Training Department, Washington, DC.

Rutter, M. 1987. "Psychosocial Resilience and Protective Mechanisms." *American Journal of Orthopsychiatry* 57: 316–331.

Seitz, V., and S. Provence. 1990. "Caregiver-focused Models of Early Intervention." In: S.J. Meisels and J.P. Shonkoff, eds. *Handbook of Early Childhood Intervention*. Cambridge (UK): Cambridge University Press, pp. 400–427.

Sheey, G. 1987. *Spirit of Survival*. New York: Bantam Books.

Simeonsson, R.J., and D.B. Bailey. 1990. "Family Dimensions in Early Intervention." In: S.J. Meisels and J.P. Shonkoff, eds. *Handbook of Early Childhood Intervention*. Cambridge (UK): Cambridge University Press, pp. 428–444.

———, D.H. Cooper, and A.P. Scheiner. 1982. "A Review and Analysis of the Effectiveness of Early Intervention Programs." *Pediatrics* 69: 635–641.

Super, C., and S. Harkness. 1987. "The Development Niche: A Conceptual Look at the Interface of Child and Culture." *International Journal of Behavioral Development* 9: 1–25.

Swaminathan, I. 1986. *The Coordinators' Notebooks*. April, p. 16. New York: The Consultative Group on Early Childhood Care and Development.

Walker, D.K., and W.R. Crocker. 1988. Measuring Family Systems Outcomes. In: H.B. Weiss and F.H. Jacobs, eds. *Evaluating Family Programs*. New York: Aldine de Gruyter, pp. 153–176.

Weiss, H.B. 1988. "Family Support and Education Programs: Working through Ecological Theories of Human Development." In: H.B. Weiss and F.H. Jacobs, eds. *Evaluating Family Programs*. New York: Aldine de Gruyter, pp. 3–36.

Weiss, H.B., and F.H. Jacobs, eds. 1988. "Introduction." In: *Evaluating Family Programs*. New York: Aldine de Gruyter pp. xix–xxix.

Werner, E.E. 1990. "Protective Factors and Individual Resilience." In: S.J. Meisels and J.P. Shonkoff, eds. *Handbook of Early Childhood Intervention*. Cambridge (UK): Cambridge University Press, pp. 97–116.

————, and R.S. Smith. 1982. *Vulnerable but Invincible: A Longitudinal Study of Resilient Children and Youth*. New York: McGraw-Hill.

White, K., and G. Casto. 1985. "An Integrative Review of Early Intervention Efficacy Studies with At-risk Children: Implications for the Handicapped. *Analysis and Intervention in Developmental Disabilities* 5: 7–31.

Zeitlin, M.F., H. Ghassemi, and M. Mansour. 1990. *Positive Deviance in Child Nutrition*. Tokyo: United Nations University Press.

6

The Javanese family

Introduction to the Javanese model

To test the effects of family-level variables on child welfare, one needs to develop a culturally appropriate conceptual model that reveals both family dynamics as well as the relationships between the child and other variables. Before developing such a model for the Javanese family, we review the concepts of family, kinship, and socialization in Java, and present an overview of socio-economic development in East Asian countries, focusing on family transitions caused by modernization. Where applicable, we have included data collected during the evaluation phase of a two-year intervention project (PANDAI) designed to change caretaking behaviours and home/environmental stimulation to improve child cognitive development (Satoto and Colletta 1987). The data were not originally collected to identify family structure and dynamics and thus the results reported are limited in their scope.

The survey data

Dietary, anthropometric, demographic, and social/behavioural data on 235 Javanese children, aged 24–79 months, are included in the analysis presented here. Details of the methodology are reported elsewhere (Chomitz 1992). The households included were non-randomly selected from eight villages in Central Java where *kaders* (volunteer workers from the growth monitoring and under-five clinics) were available to conduct the intervention and participate in the research. Each participating *kader* chose five children, aged one to five years, from her growth-monitoring case-load. The *kader* was likely to have selected children and households she believed would benefit from the child stimulation programme and reflect well on her own participation. The *kader* may have disproportionately included more middle- to upper-income families or families with positive care-taking behaviours that lead to regular participation in health care.

Data analysed from the evaluation survey of the PANDAI project included:
1. Food frequencies and 24-hour recalls for the children. Mothers were surrogate respondents for their child's food intake. Food level data, as well as the percentage of recommended dietary intake (%RDI) for energy, protein, vitamin A, and iron were evaluated.
2. A sociodemographic questionnaire and the Caldwell HOME inventory for preschool-aged children (Caldwell and Bradley 1984).
3. Anthropometric measurements, including weights, heights, mid-arm and head circumference of the children, and heights and weights of the mothers.

The Caldwell HOME inventory was modified to describe factors related to attained size and nutrient intake. We used age-controlled partial correlation analysis to identify relevant individual items in the HOME, and principal components analysis to cluster the variables into independent factors. Least-squares and logistic regression analysis was used to explain variation in the adequacy of nutrient intake and attained height.

East Asian relationship to socio-economic development

Some countries in East Asia have experienced rapid economic growth and improved quality of life. Although in the West economic prosperity coexists with increased crime and divorce, in the East the family remains stable and the crime rate remains low despite economic development (Rozman 1991).

According to East Asian experts, such as Colcutt (1991), Ebrey (1991), Haboush (1991), and Rozman (1991), Confucian tradition continues to influence culture and lifestyle in East Asian countries, particularly Japan. Confucian values revolve around the family and tradition, using the harmonious family as a building block for constructing a harmonious society. Therefore, East Asians continue to value group orientation, acceptance of authority, dependence, conflict avoidance, interest in harmony, seniority consciousness, and dutifulness (Rozman 1991). These characteristics may have helped to maintain social stability during the recent period of rapid economic growth.

Observers around the globe now marvel at the dynamism of this region. Some have tallied the statistics on economic performance, exclaiming about the quadrupling or quintupling of GNP over barely two decades since the 1950s or 1960s. Many have reported on the avalanche of high-quality and competitively priced exports that draw foreign customers by the throngs, provoking anguish as well as envy among leaders in other countries concerned with their balance of payments. Appreciation for the achievements of this region can be found in commentaries on superior educational performance, low crime rates, high life expectancies, and an unusual degree of family stability. (Rozman 1991, 5)

Despite the positive aspects of the region's development, some have raised concern regarding the lack of personal choice and individuality. In reviewing the East Asian literature, Ketcham (1987) found that so-called "negative" Eastern traits, such as the dependent relationship between a senior and a junior, and paternalistic management practices, have been credited by some East Asian authors for the remarkable social, human resources, and economic progress in East Asia.

With regard to dependency, Takeo Doi, a Japanese psychiatrist, explained in his book, *The Anatomy of Dependence* (Doi 1981), that the concept of dependence is the cultural foundation of Japanese social relationships, creating feelings of pleasure, comfort, and acceptance in hierarchical relationships. Such relationships involve intense emotional attachments, which further promote a sense of obligation or duty and establish interdependence. The family most nearly embodies these kinds of relationships, although similar relationships exist at work, school, and in the community.

The mother–child bond is perhaps the most important in shaping the attitude of dependence in Japanese society. This bond is formed through close physical proximity in the first years of life. The child usually lives in the parent's house until at least the time of marriage (Rozman 1991). In a cross-cultural study on parenting, Bornstein and co-workers (Bornstein, Tal, and Tamis-LeMonda 1991) stated that parents in collectivist cultures (such as Japan) encourage children to follow rules and to conform to norms (obedient and proper behaviour, with respect for the elder), whereas parents in individualist cultures (such as the United States) allow children a good deal of autonomy and encourage independent exploration of the environment (self-reliant and creative behaviour). The Eastern type of parenting combined with the inculcation of feelings of dependence and emotional obligation, which is distinct from that of the Western countries, may have influenced socio-economic development.

Indonesian culture (i.e. Javanese) shares much with its neighbouring countries and their Confucian values in terms of familial values, child-raising practices, and the idea of social conformity. Yet, in terms of socio-economic development, Indonesia, although growing rapidly, still lags behind other Eastern countries. Mulder (1978) hypothesized that one reason why economic development in Indonesia has not progressed as rapidly as it has in Japan and South Korea is because the Javanese view of the material world is less positive. According to Mulder, the Javanese see modernity as

material accomplishment, or *pembangunan* (development) ... Modern times also mean individual mobility, the upsetting of the harmonious social whole, frustrated feelings, and lack of a sense of social well-being. (Mulder 1978, 103)

Mulder's hypothesis, that the negative view of the material world held by the Javanese has impeded Indonesian development, may not be true according to new theories of modernization. As noted by So (1990),

The new modernization studies avoid treating tradition and modernity as a set of mutually exclusive concepts. In the new modernization research, tradition and modernity not only can co-exist but can penetrate and intermingle with each other. In addition, instead of arguing that tradition is an obstacle to development, the new modernization studies attempt to show the beneficial role of tradition (such as familism and folk religion). (So 1990, 61)

Therefore, the Javanese negative view of the material world does not necessarily lead to national backwardness. Indonesia's rapid income growth is confirmed by a World Bank report (1992) stating that the economy continues to grow strongly, and that it is possible for Indonesia to move towards solid middle-income status by the year 2000. Mulder's (1978) research, however, was conducted in 1969–1970, during which time the growth of manufacturing sectors was not as rapid as it was in the 1980s.

Economic development and modernization produce changes in family roles that may erode family ties and traditional values that bind relatives together. As in the United States since the 1940s (Dizard and Gadlin 1990), "extreme individualism" has increased in many large cities in Korea, where the small nuclear family is becoming the norm (Ketcham 1987). The degree to which the development process transforms family roles in East Asian countries, especially Indonesia, however, is not yet well documented, nor is the extent to which traditional family values can promote resilience and flexibility in adapting to new circumstances. More research in this area is needed.

An overview of Java

Java is the most heavily populated island in Indonesia, with 60 per cent of the population occupying only 7 per cent of the total land area (CBS 1987). As the centre of colonial activity, by 1930 Java already had experienced a long period of agricultural intensification, construction of irrigation facilities, and development of the infrastructure for colonial economic activities, making it the dominant region in Indonesia (Hugo et al. 1987).

The Javanese are the largest of Indonesia's 36 major ethnic groups. Their homelands are in the central and eastern parts of the island. The second-largest ethnic and linguistic group, the Sundanese, occupy the western part of Java. Because the post-Independence Indonesian government has not allowed the inclusion of an ethnicity question in the census,[1] the total population by ethnic groups is not available. Hugo et al. (1987) estimated Javanese dominance in Indonesia by using the language spoken in the homes in the 1980 census data, which showed that 40 per cent of the Indonesians speak Javanese at home, and 58 per cent living in Java speak this language.

Population growth, leading to conversion of agricultural land to residences, reduced both the total area of land under cultivation on Java and the size of the average farm (Booth and Sundrum 1976). At the same time, overinvestment in manufacturing drew people to seek non-agricultural, urban jobs. According to the World Bank (1988), the urban population is growing five times as fast as the rural population.

As a part of South-East Asia, Javanese culture shares several aspects with neighbouring countries, including the heritage of Hinduism, Buddhism, and Confucianism. But although Islam was introduced after the arrival of Shunni Muslim merchants from Gujarat, India, in the thirteenth century, in Indonesia (notably Java), Muslims blend their religion with the Hindu and Buddhist heritage. Most Javanese Muslims adhere to Islam by confession, but do not closely practise Islamic rituals and regulations. This group is called the *abangan*. A smaller percentage of Javanese Muslims adhere to a rather purist form of Islam, which is called the *santri* (people who follow Islamic principles seriously).

The distinction between *abangan* and *santri* is made when people are classified with reference to religious behavior. A *santri* person is more religious than an *abangan* person. The term *priyayi*, on the other hand, cannot be regarded as a category of the same classification, since there are definitely *priyayi* people who are religious, and thus *santri*, and those who have no interest in religious affairs and, accordingly, are considered to be *abangan*. The term *priyayi* refers to social class, to the traditional legitimate elite; it refers to those who by right are considered to be different from the commoners, called ... *wong cilik* (little men). (Bachtiar 1973)

Cultural practices surrounding weddings, funerals, and the birth of children are influenced by the Hindu heritage. Therefore, even though the country is one of the two largest Islamic nations in the world, local traditions have made Javanese Islamic culture distinct from that of Middle Eastern Moslems.

After extensive research, Mulder (1978) concluded that mysticism is the essence of Javanese culture. In fact, mystical practices have recently gained popularity (Koentjaraningrat 1985). The rise of Javanese mysticism, as explained by Mulder (1978), is not merely a reaction against modernization, as some have implied, but is primarily an effort to search for, and to preserve, the cultural identity that dominates the Javanese quest to deal with the present.

Like the Yoruba of Nigeria, Javanese society had pre-modern characteristics commonly associated with urban development. The Yoruba lived for many centuries in towns while remaining predominantly farmers; the Javanese also developed typically urban governmental and cultural institutions while remaining rice farmers living in rural villages. Despite an agrarian economy, there are almost no isolated peasant villages in Java (Koentjaraningrat 1985).

In terms of social stratification, the Javanese distinguish between two broad social levels – the *wong cilik* (or common people), consisting of peasants and the urban lower classes, and the *priyayi* (or high-class society), comprising civil servants, intellectuals, and the aristocracy (Koentjaraningrat 1957). Javanese society is, however, relatively open and socially mobile (Koentjaraningrat 1985). Peasants may move upward, by way of education, into white-collar governmental positions. But regardless of social rank, cultural values and attitudes toward children remain fairly constant (Koentjaraningrat 1985). In describing the Javanese family, therefore, we do not explicitly distinguish between *wong cilik* and *priyayi* families, although some distinctions between social classes are noted.

Regression analysis on our sample found that income and other economic measures were only marginally associated with dietary adequacy and nutritional status. These associations disappeared when social and behavioural variables entered the equations. Certain behaviours, however, appeared to be associated with middle-class and others with lower-class lifestyles and values. We characterized middle-class households as having a home built of relatively modern or expensive materials, better-educated parents who belonged to social or community organizations, and a non-working mother/housewife. These characteristics of middle-class families are consistent with the literature on Javanese household structure (Hull 1982; Koentjaraningrat 1985).

Features in the children's socio-economic environment that were found to have a positive association with the adequacy of their dietary intake were the sanitation and safety of the home, and television ownership. Morbidity was not evaluated in this model, and a relationship between sanitation and reduced morbidity may have influenced the adequacy of the nutrient intake (World Health Organization 1985). Owning a television implied that the family had electricity and a "window on the world" through communication networking and exposure to outside influences. The Indonesian government frequently uses television for health and nutrition promotion; thus the relationship between television ownership and the adequacy of intake may be an education effect and/or a reflection of wealth and income.

Concepts of individual, family, and community

To be Javanese means to be a person who is civilized and who knows his manners and his place (Geertz 1961; Mulder 1978; Koentjaraningrat 1985). The individual serves as a harmonious part of the family or group. Life in society should be characterized by *rukun* (harmonious unity), which Mulder (1978) has described:

Rukun is soothing over of differences, cooperation, mutual acceptance, quietness of heart, and harmonious existence. The whole of society should be characterized by the spirit of *rukun*, but whereas its behavioral expression in relation to the supernatural and to superiors is respectful, polite, obedient, and distant, its expression in the community and among one's peers should be *akrab* (intimate) as in a family, cozy, and *kangen* (full of the feeling of belonging). (Mulder 1978, 39)

To achieve *rukun*, persons should be primarily group members; their individuality should be expressed through the group. All overt expressions of conflict should be avoided. Unlike Western culture, which regards individualism and group belonging as mutually exclusive, most Javanese consider the two intimately related (Mulder 1978). Mutual assistance and sharing of burdens (*gotong royong*), within both the family and the community, should reflect the concept of *rukun* (Mulder 1978; Koentjaraningrat 1985).

Harmony and unity are complemented by social hierarchy. Everyone should know his or her place and duty, honouring and respecting those in higher positions, while remaining benevolent towards, and responsible for, those in lower positions. This hierarchy is captured in the Javanese language, which has three pronoun and verb forms for addressing the second person (the "you" who is above, equal, or inferior in rank) that express the respect to which the other person is entitled. Such respect is counterbalanced by a reciprocal claim of patronage and protection (Mulder 1978). Husken (1991) has described the relationship between relatives as generosity of the rich or senior relatives and reciprocal loyalties of the less well-to-do relatives or juniors. For example, some wealthy farmers support poor relatives by permitting them to become sharecroppers on their land.

The family arrangements

Ideally, marriage is meant by the Javanese to establish a new, nuclear, and autonomous household. Since it is not easy to acquire a new house in Java, young couples usually live in the home of the wife's parents for three to five years until they become economically and residentially independent (Koentjaraningrat 1985). There is a marked tendency towards matrilocal establishment of the new home close to that of the wife's parents, who may actually give the new house to them (Geertz 1961; Williams 1990). The wife will remain in close contact with her parents, assisting them as they age. If the married children live separately from their parents, the husband and wife maintain close contact with their own parents (Jay 1969).

Peasant households have been categorized into four family types (Jay 1969): the simple nuclear family consists of husband and wife and their unmarried children, or one parent and his/her children; the augmented nuclear family is the same as the nuclear family but also includes elderly retired parents; the extended family consists of husband and wife and their married children, whereas the joint family consists of siblings and their respective spouses. According to Jay's data from Mancanegari village, the simple nuclear family dominates (74.4 per cent), followed by the augmented nuclear family (15.0 per cent), the extended family (5.3 per cent), and the joint family (0.7 per cent). Geertz's data from Modjokuto (Central Java) shows comparable findings, with simple nuclear families comprising 75 per cent of households in the village and 58 per cent in the town (Geertz 1961). However, Koentjaraningrat (1985) found in his study village in Central Java that many simple nuclear families lived in the same compound of the parental house; when the parental gardens became crowded, a new house frequently was built attached to the wife's parents' house but with a separate kitchen so that the new couple could cook their own food and manage their own household affairs. The apparent lack of female-headed households in Jay's definition is consistent with statistics from a national survey in East Java and Nasatenggara Timur Barat (NTB) (Megawangi 1991) showing only 5.6 per cent of female-headed households. In general, divorced mothers and their children live in households headed by the mother's father.

The architecture of most village houses is standardized, with rooms usually divided by woven bamboo or wood plank partitions. The husband, wife, and baby sleep in one sleeping chamber, and older children sleep in other rooms. Figure 6.1 shows floor plans of typical Javanese houses (Jay 1969).

In our sample, about one-half of the families (46 per cent) lived in traditional homes with dirt floors and bamboo thatch siding; 17 per cent of the homes were more modern with brick and cement or tile floors; the rest of the families lived in transitional homes, with thatch siding and cement floors, or dirt floors with partial or full brick siding. The children's stature and nutrient intake (%RDI of energy, protein, vitamin A, and iron) were associated with the modernization of the

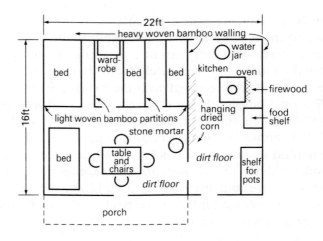

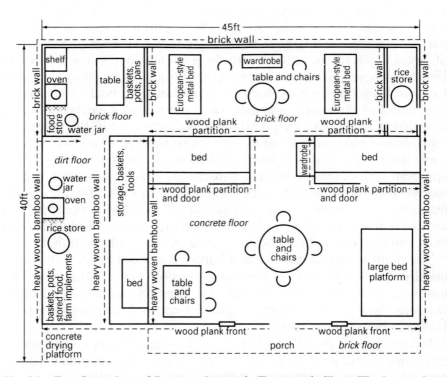

Fig. 6.1 **Two floor plans of Javanese houses in Tamansari village. The house above is relatively modest; the house below accommodates family members of two generations and guests (source: Jay 1969)**

home. A more modern/expensively constructed home also was associated with the measures of better cleanliness/sanitation in the home, more educated and older parents, and television ownership – indicative of middle-class ranking (Hull 1982; Koentjaraningrat 1985).

A more recent study in Sukaharjo, Central Java, conducted by Williams (1990), shows that among couples who relocated or moved away from their parents after marriage (62 per cent of the males and 72 per cent of the females experienced the post-wedding move by the time of her survey), roughly one-half moved within the village, while the remainder moved elsewhere. Even though they established their own households, they continued to maintain close contact with their parents. The average number of visits to parents on both sides (n = 274 couples) was between 5.0 and 6.7 per month.

It has been suggested that a woman's decision-making process is influenced by the intensity of parental contact and whether the family is nuclear or extended. Williams (1990) found that women had less overall decision-making power (measured by contraceptive and child-bearing decisions) when the couple did not move than when they relocated within the first four years. Also, the wife's intrafamilial status suffered when regular contact with parents from both sides was maintained. Williams' findings agree with those of Whyte (1978) and Warner, Lee, and Lee (1986) from other countries, who found that women in nuclear households are likely to have more power than those from extended families. When women move away from the extended family, their power in making major household decisions increases. Although moving away from family ties gives the new couple increasing autonomy and power to control their lives, it also may erode the kin network as the major source of child care and social and emotional support for the family. There are few data, however, regarding the effect of residential mobility on child welfare.

The status of women in the Javanese family

Much literature documents the favourable position of Javanese women. Hull (1982) noted that the status of women in Java appears to be ahead of that in other Asian countries. A recent study conducted by Wolfe (1988), comparing female autonomy in Java and in Taiwan,[2] confirms Hull's notion. The situation of Javanese women impressed Crawfurd (1820, in Winzeler 1982) during the European presence in the region, at which time Crawfurd remarked:

... women are not treated with contempt or disdain. They eat with the men, and associate with them in all respects on terms of equality, as surprised us in such a condition of society ... women appear in public without any scandal; they take an active concern in all the business of life; they are consulted by men on all public affairs, and are frequently raised to the throne, and that too when the monarchy is elective ... At public festivals, women appear among the men; and those invested with authority sit in their councils when affairs of state are discussed, possessing, it is often alleged, even more than their due share in the deliberations ... The Javanese women are industrious and laborious beyond all those of the archipelago, but their labor, instead of being imposed upon them by the men, becomes through its utility to the latter, a source of distinction. (Winzeler 1982, 178)

This pattern has remained relatively constant over time, as others have documented (see Geertz 1961; Mangkuprawira 1981; Hull 1982; Williams 1990). In general, Javanese women contribute to the household economy by earning income from wages, trading, and agricultural activities. Some jobs, however, women cannot perform, including ploughing; carrying extremely heavy loads; and performing heavy manual labour, such as road work, carpentry, or bricklaying (Geertz 1961). Since many Javanese women are economically independent, the typical woman has no difficulty in supporting herself and her children, should she wish to (Geertz 1961). Javanese women also have the right to own and control land, since it is transferred bilineally. This is in contrast to the Yoruba society, where until recently land was owned by the clan and its usage rights were inherited mainly through the male line (Afonja 1990). Social class, however, affects women's contributions to the household economy. According to Hull (1982), upper-class women are more financially dependent on their husbands because there is no economic necessity for them to work and the husband's status increases if he is able to support the family alone.

In our sample, children of mothers who purchased, prepared, and served the food to their child themselves consumed a higher proportion of their recommended dietary intake than did children for whom someone else performed food-related tasks. Mothers who completed the household food tasks themselves were less likely to work outside the home, and had a television and modern home. Although mothers who were less intimately involved in food preparation and feeding may have underreported their children's intake, it is likely that the children had better diets when the mother herself handled the tasks. Traditionally, it was principally the lower-class women who worked outside the home. Being a housewife is considered a privilege in Java, and women who work are thought not to be able to care properly for their children (Hull 1982). In our sample, 34 per cent of the mothers worked outside the home.

In the domestic domain, female autonomy also has been widely recognized. The Javanese believe that husband and wife should work together as a team. Hull (1982) found that, in each income category and social class, 80 per cent of married women (n = 950) claim that it is they who keep the household income. In a town in central Java, Geertz (1961) observed that wives make most household decisions. They usually consult with their husbands only on major matters. "Strong-willed men may have a relationship of equal partnership with their wives, but families actually dominated by the man are exceedingly rare" (Geertz 1961, 45). In a study in Maguwohardjo (central Java) conducted by Hull (1982), about 75 per cent of married couples (n = 950) agreed with the statement, "In general, females are more clever than males." The strong position of the Javanese woman in the domestic domain influences her role as mother. The woman is the main and direct authority figure over the children (Koentjaraningrat 1985), dominating in the management of the household and family decision making (Geertz 1961).

Kinship organization in Java is bilateral (Geertz 1961), with descent reckoned equally through father and mother. A strong network of ties between related Javanese women produces a "matrifocal" kinship system. The Javanese try to avoid conflict by minimizing interaction between potentially opposing relatives. Usually, the wife's kinswomen, who interact intensively with the family through exchange of mutual aid and child care, dominate. As Geertz described:

The woman has more authority, influence, and responsibility than her husband, and at the same time receives more affection and loyalty. The concentration of both of these features in the female role leaves the male relatively functionless in regard to the internal affairs of the nuclear family. (Geertz 1961, 79)

Blumberg (1984) also found that the Javanese bilateral and matrifocal system ranked high on the scale of female power.

The relatively high status and independence of women can be linked to the farming system in Java. Winzeler (1982) hypothesized that when men and women are both involved equally, as in other South-East Asian countries, the status of women tends to be favourable. In contrast to the sub-Saharan African women, who usually are the primary agricultural producers, Javanese women are seen to be equal participants in the household economy. The extent to which this pattern influences the practice of polygamy can be related to Boserup's hypothesis (Boserup 1970) that, since women do not commonly form the primary labour force in South-East Asian agriculture, polygyny is not as economically attractive a marriage pattern for men as it is in areas where women are the major agricultural producers. Even though polygyny is permitted in Javanese culture, it is not generally practised among the peasant society and is officially discouraged in the *priyayi* class. Geertz (1961) reported in her study in Modjokuto that only 2 per cent of marriages were polygynous (n = 1,939 marriages), and Koentjaraningrat (1985) observed that in two subdistricts in South Central Java, only a little over 3 per cent of the households were polygynous. In contrast to the peasants in rural areas, polygamy seems to be more common in urban classes and among wealthy men. If polygyny is practised, the living arrangement is still nucleatic, in which wives usually live in socially and economically separate households (Geertz 1961). Although there are no data estimating the prevalence of polygyny among the wealthy, Geertz noted that the practice of polygyny is still rare, owing to the strong resistance of wives who do not want to share their husbands. The law (Marriage Law no. 1 of 1974) requires the first wife to consent to her husband's marriage to another wife. Government employees also must obtain official consent of their supervisors before taking another wife. If a man were caught taking another wife without obtaining appropriate permission, his career would usually be in jeopardy.

Although the status of women in the family is clear, their position in society is less well defined. Williams (1990) reviewed the literature regarding the role of Indonesian women within the society. According to government reports,

The history and literature of Indonesia show how high the position and how great the role were of women during the periods of kingdoms in Indonesia. (Indonesia, Department of Information 1986, 7; from Williams 1990)

Under customary law of the various regions of the country, the position of women within society was viewed as no different from that of men, and women were frequently found in positions of military and political leadership. (Williams 1990, 35)

Some evidence, however, suggests that the situation of women has deteriorated, especially for women from lower social classes. Koentjaraningrat (1985, 139) found that

In public, social and political affairs ... the village women do not play an overt leading role, and although female landholders do have the same voting rights as men, they are usually not interested in such matters, and prefer to send their sons to represent them at village meetings.

According to Hull (1982), lower class women are not only poorly educated and busy with daily activities, but they are also socially isolated from organizations that are dominated primarily by women of higher social class. In contrast, however, other findings showed that wealth did not affect the participation of poor women in some development activities in East Java and Bali (e.g. Community Systems Foundation 1988). It may be that while upper-class village women had power, lower-class women were still very much involved.

Estimates of women's literacy in Java are still lower than for men, with the 1980 census figures showing that 90 per cent of men and 75 per cent of women are literate. The large number of illiterate females aged 50 or older contributed to the high illiteracy rate. At the turn of the century, few schools were available to the villagers, and daughters of poor villagers did not attend. Even daughters of wealthy villagers received no schooling, as they married between the ages of 12 and 15 (Williams 1990). The Marriage Law, enacted in 1974, sets the minimum age for marriage at 16 for girls and 19 for boys. With primary enrolment rates now approaching 100 per cent for both boys and girls, the number of new illiterates entering the adult population is becoming smaller. Enrolment rates for higher education are still greater for males than for females (Supas 1987), a trend that can be linked to tuition fees for secondary school. Because poor parents cannot afford to pay the tuition for all their children's education, they pay only for the males (Mangkuprawira 1981). The reason may be that it is socially acceptable for females to depend on their husband financially once married, but not vice versa.

In our Central Java sample, about one-half of the fathers (51 per cent) and mothers (48 per cent) had completed primary school; 10 per cent of the fathers and 8 per cent of the mothers had 12 years of school. The large majority of the fathers (74 per cent) and the mothers (84 per cent) belonged to at least one community organization.

The Javanese value of children

In Java, large families traditionally have been desirable. Some studies argue that the high value placed on fertility is mainly due to expected economic returns (White 1975; Nag, White, and Peet 1980; Williams 1990) that parents receive in the form of additional labour power and security in old age.

In Javanese peasant families in economically poor villages, very young children are actively involved in housework, care of younger siblings, and some agricultural chores (White 1975). Children's direct contribution to income is limited until about the age of 10 (White 1975). It is very common, especially in poor households, to see children from the age of five or six involved in looking after younger siblings, both before and after school. According to Jay (1969), children are not forced to work. He observed that it is through appreciation and praise of their activity that children's labour is encouraged. Jay explained further:

I observed children to be industrious, even at an early age, in picking up small piecework jobs such as hulling peanuts or sorting and bundling onions for sale ... there was a general notion that whatever a child might earn at such work belonged to the household purse. At lower levels, though, there was a feeling that most children would spend the proceeds on snacks for themselves and their age mates, and overt praise was given children who had turned their earnings over to their mothers. (Jay 1969, 69)

Yet higher-class Javanese families, who do not need their children's economic contribution, have more children than peasant families. Koentjaraningrat (1985) noted that having many children is perceived as prestigious; a man can have as many children as he can afford. The number of children a man has also increases his status at work. Javanese in white-collar occupations consider persons with many children higher in status than those with only a few. Also, in social etiquette, those with more children should be addressed in formal terms, even if their age, education, and experience are the same. Consequently, attempts in the early 1970s to introduce family planning were less successful among urban families than among peasants.

Since the introduction of rigorous family planning campaigns, however, the Javanese attitude towards the ideal number of children has begun to change (Koentjaraningrat 1985). Recent findings based on a study of 400 families in East Java (Megawangi, Sumarwan, and Hartoyo 1994), show that almost 90 per cent of couples, in both the urban and the rural areas, no longer agree with the statement, "Having many children can bring luck"; about 55 per cent of both rural and urban couples state that the ideal number of children is one or two. Among the Javanese peasant community, parents are now more future orientated and limit the number of children for the benefit of the children, foregoing the value of additional labour for the family (Koentjaraningrat 1985). A finding based on the Indonesian National Survey in East Java (Megawangi 1991) shows that the total parity of women from the lowest income category did not differ at all from the total parity of those from the highest income category. This attitude change seems to contradict the idea of high economic returns of the children mentioned earlier.

Koentjaraningrat (1957; 1985) and Geertz (1961) describe children as a source of family warmth, joy, and happiness. The Javanese believe that children bring luck and happiness and that if there is warmth in the family there will be calm and peace in the heart. Geertz (1961) wrote, "A woman with many children is envied; a barren woman is pitied." Infertility may become a source of family problems that end in divorce. A childless couple usually adopts a child, usually from relatives either on the husband's or the wife's side.

Many Javanese have children to provide security in old age. There is an expression for this in Javanese (Geertz 1961): "When you are old, your children will care for you. Even if you are very rich, the kind of care your children give you cannot be bought." Children are obligated to care for elderly parents. However, a shift in value of this kind of obligation may have occurred, as the most recent finding shows that only 53 per cent of Javanese parents agree with the statement, "Children can provide security in old age" (Megawangi, Sumarwan, and Hartoyo 1994). Parents traditionally endow their houses in their wills to the youngest child, especially the youngest daughter, who usually remains in the parents' home even after her marriage and is later charged with the obligation to care for elderly parents, living with them until the parents die.

In Javanese society, children of both sexes are equally wanted. Preferential treatment based on gender has never been noted in Indonesia, except for willingness to pay for tuition for higher education for boys, as noted above. A study conducted by Megawangi (1991) in East Java, Nusa Tenggara Timur, and Nusa Tenggara Barat (n = 6,796), showed that female children have better nutritional status, as measured by weight for age, than male children. The male infant mortality rate was also 30 per cent higher than for females (CBS 1985). Since preferential treatment does not explain this trend, biol-

111

ogy may be implicated. Stini (1983) and Stinson (1985) noted that female children might have a higher survival rate than male children. In addition, the long-term effects of prenatal undernutrition of the mother are more pronounced in males than females.

In our data, parental investment in the child's future, as measured by a modified HOME subscale describing learning and academic stimulation in the home, was significantly associated with taller child stature and the adequacy of nutrient intake. The subscale measured the provision of toys and books, and encouragement to learn the alphabet and numbers, and to read words. The type of behavioural interactions involved in teaching, and providing toys and books, may have been conducive to an investment in the child's nutrient intake and subsequent growth. This relationship of stature to child investment strategies was also seen in a study with slightly younger children living in the same geographical area (Sockalingam et al. 1990) and in the positive deviance literature (Zeitlin, Ghassemi, and Mansour 1990). Super, Herrera, and Mora (1990) also found that a group of Columbian children whose mothers had been tutored in cognitive and social stimulation had increased adequacy of protein and energy intake, as well as a distinct growth advantage over those children whose mothers did not receive tutoring. The learning and academic stimulation factor in our study was associated with characteristics typical of the middle-class Javanese family, and may reflect a more privileged lifestyle where the mother is more educated and is a non-working housewife intimately involved in child-rearing (Hull 1982; Koentjaraningrat 1985).

The Javanese child is the centre of social attention from the time of conception (Koentjaraningrat 1957; 1985). Before the birth, at least one ceremony in the seventh month of pregnancy is held to secure a successful delivery; this is usually a big party of relatives and neighbours. After the child is born, the father and other adult members stay awake every night until the umbilical cord has fallen off. They usually invite relatives, friends, or neighbours to spend the time chatting the whole night. There is an additional ceremony in the night when the umbilical cord has fallen off. This custom, however, has disappeared in urban families (Koentjaraningrat 1985), although other ceremonies are still held, including a naming ceremony usually held on the seventh day after birth; *kekah*, an offering after the thirty-fifth day that is especially common among Moslems; and *selapan*, a ceremony marking the thirty-fifth day after birth (Koentjaraningrat 1957).

Marital relationships

It is a Javanese ideal that husbands and wives should show affection and love to each other, although they cannot demonstrate their affection publicly (Koentjaraningrat 1957; 1985). The wife must show respect to the husband, as the husband is assumed to be older than the wife. The husband is supposed to be the leader of the household, but is concerned primarily with external matters. The wife's sphere of interest is internal household matters. Husbands and wives cooperate on significant financial decisions, but usually husbands take little interest in the day-to-day household management, including daily expenses, which are handled by the wife. Internal affairs of the household are not usually a source of conflict between husband and wife. Conflicts usually relate to compatibility of individual character traits, to sexual infidelity, and to larger affinal conflicts (Geertz 1961; Koentjaraningrat 1985). Communication between husbands and wives varies, depending on their education (Hull 1982; Williams 1990). For example, over one-half of lower-class married women surveyed in Maguwoharjo, Central Java (Hull 1982), said they never discussed either the number of children they wanted or the use of contraception with their husbands. In contrast, most educated women claimed to have discussed both issues.

Besides education, husband–wife communication appears to be related to whether the marriage was arranged or not (Hull 1982). Marriages arranged by parents, although declining, are still common among lower-class families (Geertz 1961). Among younger-generation women in Hull's study, marriages were arranged for 53 per cent of lower-income women, compared with 35 per cent of upper-income women.

Arranged first marriages account for high divorce rates in lower-class families (Geertz 1961; Hull 1982). The divorce rate in Modjo-kuto in 1953 was 47.2 per cent, mostly among arranged first marriages. Parents of low social class usually are aware that the first arranged marriage of their daughter can easily end in divorce, with little social stigma attached to such a divorce. Geertz (1961) compared the attitude towards divorce among the lower- and upper-class women in Java, stating that in the lower class divorce is neither right nor wrong, but often is the easiest solution to an unsatisfactory marriage. This is because the courtship period is extremely limited and sometimes completely omitted. According to Geertz, Javanese couples may have the wedding first and then, in the months following, find out whether or not they are compatible. In contrast, upper-class women perceive divorce as showing a lack of self-control and refinement, making divorce shameful. In Hull's study, 47 per cent of women aged 45 and over in the lower income group had their first marriage end in divorce, compared with only 24 per cent of upper-income women in that age group. A more recent survey reported by UNICEF and the Government of Indonesia (1988) shows that female-headed households tend to fall into a low or lower-middle income category.

The economic self-reliance of Javanese women in the lower income group is also considered a "facilitating factor" to divorce (Geertz 1961). This differs from the middle-class women who depend on their husbands for support (Hull 1982). Hull found that divorced lower-class women were completely self-supporting, except at very young ages. The few upper-class women who were divorced or widowed were more likely to depend on other family members until they could remarry.

Few factors discourage divorce. Although a mother may feel that she needs to maintain her marriage to support her children or to prevent them from living with a stepmother, this is a weak opposing factor, "... children of a divorced couple are always easily added to the families of their siblings and the divorced girl always has a place in her parents' family" (Geertz 1961, 144). Children of divorced parents usually live with the mother or the grandparents. Often siblings take care of their siblings' children. The custom of taking nephews and nieces into the household, or the so-called *ngenger* custom, according to Koentjaraningrat (1985) is very common among middle-class households. Impoverished relatives who come to live with a prosperous uncle or aunt are usually given proper care, education, and even a wedding. In return, they help with household chores.

According to Geertz (1961), quarrels between husband and wife generally are not explosive. Couples try to avoid anger; the neighbours, and even the children, must not know about the quarrel. When tempers flared, nearly every couple interviewed by Geertz used a form of silent expression, called *satru*, during which they did not speak to each other for a week or so. Direct contact is rarely used to settle differences. Couples use a mediator, usually the parents of both sides, to help solve the problem. Geertz further explained that "the go-between pattern appears in other contexts in Javanese life, particularly in delicate matters such as arranging a loan or a marriage, and is part of a more pervasive pattern of general avoidance of direct contacts that are potentially explosive" (Geertz 1961, 136).

The presence of children can strengthen the tie between husband and wife. After the birth of a child, a husband will address his wife as "mother of Slamet" (*Mbokne Slamet*) and the wife addresses her husband as "father of Slamet" (*Pakne Slamet*) (Geertz 1961). A husband is required to try to satisfy his wife's wishes, no matter how difficult, during her pregnancy. He also should share the pregnancy taboos, and supervise his wife's eating behaviour to avoid endangering the baby. He cannot hunt or kill animals. If he happens to kill an animal he should forestall the evil by shouting out "A thousand pardons, infant child!" The husband's positive attitude towards his wife during pregnancy still continues. A study conducted in East Java (n = 400) reveals that 95 per cent of Javanese husbands agree with the statement, "The husband should please his wife during her pregnancy"; 88 per cent with the statement that "his pregnant wife should rest more"; and 80 per cent that "a pregnant woman should eat more" (Megawangi, Sumarwan, and Hartoyo 1994). The husband's involvement in his wife's pregnancy can be seen in his active role in delivery: during the delivery, the husband should support his wife as she leans back while pushing her baby out; it is the task of the husband, and his alone, to wash away the blood from the birth. A Javanese friend of the authors told us of watching her brother wash his wife's dirty clothes every morning for several days following his wife's delivery; this washing, according to the husband, could not be done by a substitute.

Relationships in the family

The principles of social harmony and respect guide Javanese social behaviour outside the family. Parents begin to teach their children very early about the concepts of *isin* (shyness), *wedi* (fear), and *sungkan* (respectful politeness) to encourage social harmony and respect in their outside relationships. These three concepts are considered appropriate to situations demanding respectful behaviour (Geertz 1961). According to Magnis-Suseno (1988), the Javanese strive to control their natural impulses in order to maintain social harmony. Therefore, within the family is the only place where the Javanese are relatively free from such tensions, and Javanese relationships among family members should be based on unconditional love, or *tresna* (Magnis-Suseno 1988). Feelings of *isin* and *sungkan* should not be felt among members of the family; rather, family members can express their emotions freely, without fearing the loss of family support, especially that of the parents (Magnis-Suseno 1988). It should be noted that other authors cited in this report indicate that a certain degree of behaviour restriction exists towards the father and older siblings.

Parent-and-child relationships

According to the Javanese, the love given by biological parents to their children is incomparable and there is no substitute for it (Jay 1969). Before the age of five or six, children are provided by their parents, especially the mother, with nurturance, unconditional emotional support, and love, (Geertz 1961; Magnis-Suseno 1988). As the child ages, this kind of relationship with the father gradually disappears because the father should receive "respect" from his children.

Young children always sleep with their mother and usually also with their father, a practice that involves a good deal of physical intimacy (Geertz 1961). Bedtime for Javanese children was described by Geertz as a pleasant time, when "his mother lies down with him on his mat and puts her arms about him, cuddling him till he is asleep." When Geertz did her study in the 1950s, every child in her village was sent to sleep in this way.

Mother–child relationship and infant care

During the first one or two years, until the child is weaned or begins to walk, the mother is the most important person in the child's life. She is with the baby whenever she can be. If she works outside the home, she leaves the baby with someone she trusts, usually her sister or mother (Geertz 1961). Every early transition is managed with extreme care. Magnis-Suseno (1988) described the weaning period as very difficult for the mother, since she was constantly aware of the possible frustrations the child might undergo. This may explain why prolonged breast-feeding in East Java (Megawangi 1991) is quite common. In the villages studied, about 35 per cent of the children between the ages of 49 and 60 months were still partially breast-fed. Piwoz (1986) found that 58 per cent of children in East Java and West Nusatenggara still breast-fed at the age of two to three years, and in some cases, until well over four years of age. In our sample, 6 per cent of the total, and 16.4 per cent of the children aged two to four years, consumed some breast milk.

Geertz observed that a crying baby is rarely heard because no Javanese can bear to hear the sound without trying to calm the baby, no matter whose baby it is. A baby is handled with great care and in a completely supportive manner.

For if the baby were suddenly or severely disturbed by a loud noise, rough handling, or physical discomfort, he would be "shocked," "startled," or "upset," his weak psychic defenses would fall and the evil spirits, which hover constantly around the mother and child, could enter the infant and cause him to be ill. (Geertz 1961, 92)

This pattern is in marked contrast to earlier Western practices of leaving infants alone to cry, out of fear that picking them up would spoil their moral character (Zeitlin, Ghassemi, and Mansour 1990). Richman, Miller, and Solomon (1988) also found that US mothers in Boston value the child's independence and separateness. The use of infant seats and playpens that do not need human physical contact reflects this attitude.

Maternal behaviour that emphasizes soothing, holding, and over-protection of infants is typical, according to LeVine (1988), in an agricultural society. This represents a historical adaptation of culturally constituted maternal behaviour to high infant mortality rates. This also may be a way to keep the baby quiet and easily managed. Richman, Miller, and Solomon (1988) reported from a study of the Gusii society in Kenya that an infant care pattern similar to that of the Javanese was considered to be a means not only of keeping the infant safe and healthy but also of reducing the mother's energy output from her heavy workload.

Javanese babies spend most of their time carried in front of the mother's body in a shawl where they can nurse on demand. Geertz observed that most infants under the age of three seem to prefer to be carried rather than to be left to run around. She also found that because infants were constantly carried, they had no opportunity to crawl. Out of fear of damage to the baby's muscles and bones, which may result in a localized "fever," infants are held in a horizontal position at least until they lift up their own heads and often until they pull themselves upright. Before the baby is seven months old, he is not supposed to set foot on the ground. The child is permitted to walk by himself only when the mother is certain his muscles are developed enough to support him. In contrast, Yoruba mothers prop their infants upright and promote crawling and walking as early as possible (Zeitlin, Ghassemi, and Mansour 1990). The strong emphasis on rapid motor development might once have been related to "survival skills requiring physical dexterity, and activities such as hunting" (Aina et al. 1992). Bary, Child, and Bacon (1959) also stated that children in hunting societies tend to be pressured to be self-reliant and achievement-oriented. The overprotection of the Javanese mothers may be related to Whiting and Whiting's hypothesis that when a mother's workload is not demanding, or she has little involvement in the production of foods, it is not essential to encourage children to be self-reliant (Whiting and Whiting 1975). In addition, some Javanese mothers start to feed large amounts of starchy food, such as rice or banana, to their infants from the fifth day of life, and this diet may not promote early physical strength and motor development.

The general pattern of infant care in the Javanese society seems to have positive outcomes. Mothers who are concerned about reducing their children's discomforts are more likely to give them more love when they grow older than are mothers who fail to attend to infantile needs as nurturantly (Rohner 1975).

According to Geertz, "strong" and "secure" mother-and-child relationships will last a lifetime. It is usually the mother with whom both boys and girls discuss private matters and from whom they seek emotional support. The mother also teaches social manners, makes important decisions for her children, and administers most punishment (Geertz 1961; Magnis-Suseno 1988). Although children respect their mothers, they never address them in the formal *kromo* style of speech used in the Javanese language when speaking to an older or higher-status person, as they do their fathers. Some argue that this style of speech is disappearing as the result of modern education (Satoto 1990, personal communication).

Father-and-child relationships

A Javanese child does not have an intense relationship with the father until the child begins to walk. During the first year of life, the father may carry the child when the mother is busy, but he is not an important part of the child's life. During the period when the child is being weaned and is learning to walk, the father begins to show a more active interest in the child. Geertz observed that, during this period, fathers play with their children, feed and bathe them, and cuddle them to sleep; she described this relationship as a bond of warmth and affection. In their cross-cultural study, Whiting and Whiting (1975) observed that, in societies where a father shares a bed with his wife and children (with a monogamous marriage and a nuclear household), he tends to be more involved in child care than are fathers with polygynous marriages, who sleep in a different room from their wives and young children. Coltrane (1988) found that fathers participate more in child care in cultures in which women have high status. The relationships within Javanese families correspond to these findings.

Young children remain close to their fathers only until they are about five years old. After that they are taught to approach him more formally and to stay respectfully away from him. Although a Javanese child is seldom punished by his father, the father is accorded much respect. This trend was confirmed by Koentjaraningrat (1985) and Magnis-Suseno (1988). The ideal Javanese father should be "patient and dignified with his wife and children: he should lead them with a gentle though firm hand, not interfering with their petty quarrels, but being always available to give solemn sanction to his wife's punishment of disobedient children" (Geertz 1961, 107). Jay (1969) argued that because of these high expectations the father cannot be as free as his wife in expressing his emotions. According to Koentjaraningrat (1985), however, more educated fathers are less aloof and try to maintain closeness with their children.

Relationships among siblings

In Java, the relationship between the elder and the younger sister is close and warm (Magnis-Suseno 1988), as is the relationship between the elder sister and the younger brother (Geertz 1961; Magnis-Suseno 1988). Older siblings who already show a degree of responsibility are expected to take care of the small children, and they, according to Geertz's observations, seem happily unaware of jealousies. Jay (1969) described the relationship between the older child and the younger ones:

The tenderness an older child regularly shows toward a baby sibling leads him to feel strongly affectionate and protective toward the infant. The parents and older kin encourage this behavior and also gently encourage the baby to respond to the older child's attention and direction. The patient, loving, and solicitous manner of older children to the very young is indeed touching. Yet in this they are simply following the adult's lead. (Jay 1969, 118)

Because parents want to protect small children from dangerous accidents and frustrations, older siblings are instructed to fulfil the wishes of the younger one. The older sibling is usually blamed for a quarrel with a younger sibling. A personal communication with a Javanese friend confirms Geertz's observation (W. Rachmat Adi 1991, personal communication). He told us that being the eldest brother during childhood was not easy: he always had to maintain minimal conflict with the younger siblings or he would be blamed, no matter how right he was. As younger siblings get older, they gradually learn that they are supposed to follow their elder siblings' suggestions and, to some extent, to obey them (Koentjaraningrat 1957).

The pattern of intersibling interactions within the family is the first step in learning the Javanese value of repressing one's own desire and avoiding conflict, an essential step in adopting socially acceptable behaviour outside the family. Since the process of instilling Javanese values begins very early with the continual process of intersibling interactions, it is usually the only child or the youngest one who is spoiled and does not have self-control, a phenomenon that is captured in Javanese folklore and stories (Geertz 1961).

Geertz (1961) documented the close relationship between elder sister and younger brother. A boy's elder sister is like a mother, showing *tresna* (unconditional love) to her younger siblings. The relationship between a female and her younger sisters, however, differs somewhat (Jay 1969). Since girls are expected to help with the household chores, a younger sister is usually under the supervision of her elder sister as well as of the mother. Although the elder sister's authority is only mildly exercised (Jay 1969), conflicts between sisters are common. After marriage, the relationships between sisters are very intense, warm, and cooperative (Jay 1969).

The relationship between elder brother and younger brother is usually restrained and formal (Magnis-Suseno 1988). As reported by Jay (1969, 121), "I have often seen a teenage boy leave the room when an older brother appears, and the patterns of avoidance reveal occasional flashes of hostility." Jay observed that this constrained relationship between brothers had nothing to do with the exercise of authority and seniority by the older brother. The avoidance between brothers starts when the younger brother understands that he must play with his own age mates.

Mutual assistance among siblings is obligatory, especially when there are problems (Koentjaraningrat 1957). The elder siblings should take care of their younger siblings if financial problems arise or if the younger siblings are orphaned before adulthood.

Social network and family support system

Javanese behaviour and etiquette, as previously indicated, focus on achieving social conformity. Because the Javanese rely on other persons, especially on relatives and close neighbours, for support in times of need, they maintain good relationships by following socially acceptable behaviour. These values are embedded in the structure of social relations among relatives and within the community.

Relationships with relatives

The nuclear family is the most important kin group. Attention and care, as well as mandatory obligations, are expected among family members, and neglecting obligation is a serious infraction (Koentjaraningrat 1957). Conflicts with parents are believed to remove the parents' blessing, and such a loss is believed to threaten the child's life. Children are obliged to care for and maintain their parents when they are old and no longer self-supporting (Geertz 1961; Koentjaraningrat 1985). Women maintain closer contacts with their kindred than do men (Geertz 1961). Elderly parents live with both daughters and sons, but especially with daughters. However, this trend may change in the future, as current couples in East Java (n = 400) may have changed their perceptions about living with children in old age: 34 per cent do not expect this, 27 per cent are uncertain, and only 38 per cent say they expect to live with their children in the future (Megawangi, Sumarwan, and Hartoyo 1994).

The relationship with affinal relatives is usually formal, requiring constant politeness and reserve (Geertz 1961). Relatives through the male line always address each other in the language of respect. One reason why Javanese tend to limit the household occupancy to nuclear family members is to avoid psychological tension between affinal relatives (Geertz 1961). For parents to live with a daughter-in-law is undesirable, because conflicts about household matters may erupt. Conflict between parents and a son-in-law is rare, however, since husbands are usually uninterested in internal household matters.

According to Koentjaraningrat, there are two defined kin groups – close relatives, extending collaterally up through first cousins, and distant relatives, consisting of second and third cousins. In practice, the intensity of these relationships is fluid. Close relatives separated by geographical distance may have little contact, whereas distant relatives may have intense relationships because of proximity and frequent contact (Geertz 1961). A pattern of frequent contact is confirmed by more recent findings, in which 92 per cent of couples in East Java claim that they visit their relatives regularly (Megawangi, Sumarwan, and Hartoyo 1994). While relationships between cousins are generally friendly, no special obligations exist regarding mutual assistance (Koentjaraningrat 1985, 157).

A family usually pays attention to its nephews and nieces, although no authority is exerted over them. The relationship between girls and their aunts can be very close: girls may discuss private problems with their aunts (Koentjaraningrat 1957). There is a moral obligation to help a destitute aunt or a nephew/niece if no one closer is available to care for them (Geertz 1961). More fortunate families often support their nephews or nieces, who sometimes live with them.

While there are few mandatory obligations towards relatives outside the nuclear family, respect towards older and senior relatives is required. In addition, participation in, and contribution to (money, supplies, or labour), some festivities, such as weddings, circumcisions, and births are required (Koentjaraningrat 1985).

Relationships in the community and community support system

The Javanese frequently use the following phrase to describe the relationship between close neighbours: "If there is only little, (each) will receive little, but if there is much, (each) will receive a big share" (Koentjaraningrat 1985, 458). One should maintain good relations and share with one's neighbours. Two terms denote ideals of community behaviour among all classes (Koentjaraningrat 1957): *gotong royong*, which means "mutual help," and *rukun tangga*, which means "the bond of households" (Koentjaraningrat 1957, 74). These ideals require mutual attention and assistance among neighbours, especially in times of sickness and death. Neighbours assist one another either morally or financially when there is a death in the community. Neighbours also participate in various ceremonies (e.g. wedding ceremonies, circumcisions). The study by Megawangi, Sumarwan, and Hartoyo (1994) in East Java showed that 79 per cent of couples claimed always, 19 per cent sometimes and 2 per cent never to participate in wedding ceremonies/circumcisions in the neighbourhood.

Also, the majority of respondents said that they always help when there has been a death in the neighbourhood and visit their neighbours in times of sickness.

With regard to *gotong royong*, or mutual help, there is an institution called *sambatan*, which formerly provided mutual help among neighbours in corporate functions, such as building or repairing someone's house, participating in celebrations, or cooperating in farming (Koentjaraningrat 1984). However, the role of this institution is declining since, according to Koentjaraningrat (1984; 1985), the number of professional workers such as carpenters, bricklayers, painters, and handymen in the village has increased. The increased dependency of villagers on commercial goods also contributes to the declining role of *sambatan* (Koentjaraningrat 1984). This can explain why only 27 per cent of couples in East Java (n = 200) said that they participate in building neighbourhood houses, and only 53 per cent claim to help neighbours in agricultural activities (Megawangi, Sumarwan, and Hartoyo 1994).

The daily interactions among village women are warm and friendly. Hull (1982) observed in Maguwohardjo that women develop bonds through interactions with both kin and non-kin. Lower-class women chat and joke together during shared activities, obtaining, according to Hull (1982, 114) "interpersonal gratification" as a substitute for the lack of close conjugal ties. In contrast, middle-class women are more home centred, with limited daily interaction outside the family, although to a certain extent they are part of a female network in the village. Hull questioned whether decreasing participation in the world outside the home among middle-class women represents "progress" or "regress."

Given their lineal value orientation, the Javanese respect and trust their seniors and superiors (Koentjaraningrat 1985). Older people in the community, village notables, and village administrators are respected. If someone disagrees with these people, it is done by not responding or by agreeing in a particular manner, which actually indicates subtle disagreement (Koentjaraningrat 1985).

According to Koentjaraningrat, this type of lineal system is less pronounced in rural areas. Although villagers still rely on, and respect, their superiors within the family and the kin group, their hierarchical orientation is diminished outside the circle of relatives. Their attitudes toward village notables are more critical. However, peasants rarely interact with superiors. Decreasing respect for village authority, according to Koentjaraningrat (1985), is due to the seasonal mobility of the peasants looking for a living in the towns, which reduces their reliance on village superiors. In contrast, among the *priyayi* class or administrative officials, the lineal value system is still maintained and is still characterized by reliance on, and respect for, the superiors.

The participation of women in organizations also influences their extrafamilial relationships. Hull (1982) observed in her village in central Java that lower-class women's involvement in formal organizations was not as great as that of the upper-middle-class women. This is consistent with the lineal value system, in which lower-class women feel *sungkan* or awkward associating with upper-class women. In addition, lower-class women are heavily involved in economic activities. Lower-class women, however, usually belong to some informal organization that meets regularly, such as a rotating credit association or Koran-reciting group. According to Hull, membership of formal organizations does not promise improved opportunities for women to develop. Most formal women's organizations are orientated towards skills relating to middle-class social status, such as cooking, flower arranging, and home decoration.

Health facilities in every village are available through the *puskesmas* (community health centre), and community-organized activities are at the *posyandu* (integrated service delivery and nutrition post). There is at least one *puskesmas* in every subdistrict (*kecamatan*). The *posyandu* serves as the first contact for basic health services at the village level. It is orientated primarily towards family planning services and preventive and promotional health and nutrition services for children and mothers. Data from 1987 indicate that the average *posyandu* in central Java serves around 120 children. The current objective is to provide one integrated service post for every 100 children in the country under the age of five (UNICEF and the Government of Indonesia 1988).

In terms of education, both religious schools and public schools are available in most villages. A policy of free and compulsory primary education, introduced in 1984, has increased school attendance by almost 100 per cent (Supas 1987).

Javanese concept of life

Javanese parents tend to teach their children a "pessimistic view about life" and describe life as a series of hardships and misfortunes (Koentjaraningrat 1985). Children are taught to be in a continuous state of *eling* and *prihatin*, or "forever feeling concern" (Koentjar-aningrat 1985, 121). They should develop an attitude to accept hard-ships and misfortunes of fate willingly. Koentjaraningrat also noted that they are taught that exertion is important to overcome hardships. Their willingness to work is reflected in their activities in agricultural production, economic life, and social matters, which require an active life through constant endeavour.

The Javanese religion is mainly Islam, strongly influenced by Is-lamic mysticism. The Javanese seek hardship and suffering deliber-ately for religious reasons (Koentjaraningrat 1985). This practice, called *tirakat*, usually involves fasting during the month of Ramadhan or every Monday and Thursday, or eating only rice with no side dishes, and eating only small amounts of food for one or two days. The Javanese believe that experiencing suffering builds perseverance, making a person mentally strong and resistant to discomfort, dissat-isfaction, and disappointment. In fact, one of the authors' family tra-ditions is influenced by this practice: her mother is half Javanese, and her grandfather was a devout Javanese ascetic; she was introduced to fasting every Monday and Thursday during adolescence.

The Javanese also perform *tirakat* fasting in any critical situation, such as facing a difficult task; experiencing a crisis in family life, in career, or in social relations; or when the entire community faces hard times (Koentjaraningrat 1985).

Teaching manners and values

Javanese culture values virtues that contribute to harmonious so-cial integration. Ideal human virtues include obedience to superiors (*manut*), generosity, avoidance of conflict, understanding of others, and empathy (Geertz 1961; Koentjaraningrat 1985; Magnis-Suseno 1988). The traditional Javanese view that all men are socially unequal is demonstrated in numerous aspects of social behaviour. Therefore, respectful behaviours are constantly instilled in Javanese children.

The permissiveness noted earlier towards children younger than five or six years is mainly to structure affairs so as to minimize the emergence of impulses disruptive of social life. The child is consid-ered *durung Jawa* (not yet Javanese) or *durung ngerti* (does not yet understand) (Geertz 1961), so the use of force or punishment for in-comprehensible mistakes is considered useless. Magnis-Suseno (1988) observed that parents rarely become angry with their small children.

Unacceptable behaviour is indirectly opposed by frightening the child with the bogey man, strangers, or dogs, which, according to Magnis-Suseno (1988), also turns the child to the parents for emotional security. However, Koentjaraningrat (1985) noted that some Javanese peasants threaten their children with punishment, and even with a fit of anger. He agrees, however, that children's behaviour is generally controlled without punishment.

In contrast to the importance of punishment among the Yoruba, only 5 per cent of the Javanese mothers slapped or spanked their child while the observer was present, and only 10 per cent punished the child more than once a week. Geertz (1961) notes that as the child grows older, training for adulthood may involve discipline – even physical punishment to instil "correct" behaviour. Older children in our data set were more likely to have been disciplined than the younger children.

Geertz (1961) illustrated the kind of permissiveness that the mother may display towards the child:

If a child wants to stay up late there is usually no objection from the parents, and at the shadow plays the children sit all night in front of the screen, watching and napping alternately. On ordinary evenings the mother will simply ask the child if he wants to go to sleep and will keep asking him until he says yes. There is rarely a battle of wills; there is no direct opposition ... If the child gets out of hand and the quiet methods do not work, the mother may frighten him with talk of the bogey man he will see if he does not shut his eyes. (Geertz 1961, 103)

Mothers are also generally very permissive or indulgent in treating children to snacks and other food on demand, and children are not usually expected to wait for food throughout the day (Geertz 1961; Tan et al. 1970). Only 26 per cent of the mothers in our sample replied that the child cannot snack any time he/she is hungry and must wait until meal time to be fed; 84 per cent of the children had consumed sweet and salty snacks – providing 15 per cent of the total energy consumed. These snack products, or "Javanese junk food" (sweet cassava and glutinous rice products, salty commercially produced fried puffs and drinks) are generally low in micronutrients. Anecdotal evidence has suggested that children may consume so much of these high-calorie, low nutrient density snack foods between meals that more "nutritious" foods in the diet may be short-changed.

Young children have little opportunity to develop their own initiative and to be independent, according to Geertz, since they are heavily protected from frustration and danger. According to Koentjaraningrat, this remains true only until the child reaches about five years of age, after which he is free to play with his peers in the neighbourhood. By contrast, however, Megawangi, Sumarwan, and Hartoyo (1994) found that 94 per cent of Javanese parents want to have independent children.

As the child gets older, he gradually becomes inculcated with the Javanese concepts of self-control and obedience. He realizes that people around him are not responding as they used to, and they punish him when he does not obey. This transition, according to Geertz, has a significant impact:

The shift in the father's role from one of affection and warmth to one of distance and reserve, although it is only one step in the whole series of events by which the child learns the specific Javanese concepts of self-control and respect, is probably the most significant both because of the crucial place of the father in the child's emotional life and because this transition period occurs during the period of the oedipal crisis. But it would not have the impact it has if it were not presaged and followed up by other events in the child's life, or perhaps more important, if it were not for the meaningful context of Javanese ideas and values in which the whole transition is set. (Geertz 1961, 110)

In psychodynamic terms, protection from shock or frustration may delay or reduce the intensity of the child's individuation by preventing any sense of break in feelings of belonging to the gratifying family environment created by his parents and siblings. This pattern is related to what Bary, Child, and Bacon (1959) have observed through cross-cultural observations. Under the Javanese concept of obedience, which is typical of agricultural or pastoral societies, children are trained to be more compliant, obedient, and responsible than are children from hunting or fishing societies.

There is a little difference between peasant parents and the higher rank *priyayi* or noble families in terms of punishment (Koentjaraningrat 1985). The *priyayi* philosophy regarding the education of the children is *Tut wuri andayani*, which means "following from behind, constantly giving encouragement" (Koentjaraningrat 1985, 241). Therefore, children in *priyayi* families are more free to explore their own world, which according to Koentjaraningrat reflects early European or Dutch influences. But the child is actively guided to conform to socially acceptable behaviour. Unlike the father in traditional families, the father in the *priyayi* family also plays an active role in guiding his children, applying punishment more frequently. Physical punishment, however, is rarely used because Javanese children, ac-

127

cording to Geertz, are markedly well behaved, obedient, quiet, and shy.

If a child does not behave according to the norm, attention from or contact with his brothers or sisters may be withdrawn, and he may not be spoken to (*disatru*). Playmates also *satru* or shun each other for several days. Regarding this matter, Geertz noted: "It is an excellent mechanism for the adjustment of hostility in a society that plays down violence and the expression of real feelings, since it allows for the avoidance of the outbreak of rage while still permitting significant expression of it" (Geertz 1961, 117–118). Physical fights between children are rare (Geertz 1961). Parents always maintain good relationships with their neighbours. They always punish their own children if they have a fight with other children in the neighbourhood, regardless of who is wrong. In this way, children prepare for later social interactions in which they must successfully conceal their anger.

Obedience is considered not only a useful quality in social interactions, but it is also considered more safe (Koentjaraningrat 1985). The act of giving in to other people with whom one is not familiar is considered safe, avoiding conflict. Obedience is widely praised in both peasant and *priyayi* values. A child is taught obedience by forcing a sense of apprehension of unpleasant consequences of an action, or *wedi* (afraid). The usual method used by parents, which according to Koentjaraningrat is unfortunate, is frightening children with threats of punishment at the hand of spirits or strangers. He further explains that this has stimulated the easy emergence of feelings of fear towards others. According to Geertz, the concept of *wedi* is taught before the concept of shaming is inculcated. Geertz also describes the way in which parents instill *wedi* by frightening the child. She once observed "the two-year-old, silent in fear that the strange visiting man will, as his mother had warned, bite him if he makes a noise ..." (Geertz 1961, 113). This feeling conveys Javanese adult norms in social interaction to feel *wedi* first when they deal with unfamiliar people. Not knowing whether they will harm, hurt, or shame him (Koentjaraningrat 1985), the Javanese waits and remains inactive until he is sure how the situation will develop.

In teaching self-control and respectful behaviour to Javanese children, parents emphasize the concept of *isin* or shaming. The parents always try to arouse feelings of shame towards bad behaviour that will be "noticed by people from the street" (Koentjaraningrat 1985, 242) The children should feel *isin* toward their superiors. Geertz found that as the result of the inculcation of *isin*, Javanese children can sit quietly and well behaved for hours on any public occasion. In the Javanese culture, to know when to feel *isin* is to know the "basic social properties of self-control and avoidance of disapproval" (Geertz 1961, 114).

As the child enters adolescence, the concept of *sungkan* (respectful politeness) (Geertz 1961), is gradually introduced. This feeling is addressed to a superior or an unfamiliar equal. Koentjaraningrat (1985) described it as "feeling awkward" towards a superior or someone whom he respects. They will act timidly in their social interactions, trying not to bother their superiors. According to Geertz, the concept of *sungkan* is basic for the Javanese "to be able to perform the social minuet with grace" (Geertz 1961, 114).

The teaching of *wedi*, *isin*, and *sungkan* is considered prerequisite for adopting the basic elements of human virtue. As mentioned earlier, obedience, generosity, avoidance of conflict, understanding others, and empathy are basic values for the Javanese in their relationships, reflected in their emphasis on the interconnection of fellow humans. This value obliges the Javanese to conform to the community in their social interactions.

In our data from Central Java, a breakdown in the teaching or enforcing of this self-control or respectful behaviour may be accompanied, among children, by significantly lower nutrient intake and, to a lesser extent, a shorter stature. A modified HOME subscale from our study apparently captured an acceptance, on the part of lower-class parents, of culturally inappropriate behaviours from their children. These behaviours – hitting parents or expressing negative feelings – are generally inappropriate for Javanese children. Koentjaraningrat (1985) also noted that, among the lower class and rural peasant families, there was permissiveness or delinquency in teaching this respect behaviour – possibly linked with poverty and the migration to the towns in search of work due to land pressures. These poorer children also were taught more self-reliance and greater responsibility; in fact, "one has the impression that the development of more self-reliance and self-responsibility is still neglected among families who can afford a prosperous and comfortable life" (Koentjaraningrat 1985). These observations were consistent with our correlation analysis – the "acceptance of inappropriate behaviours" factor was negatively correlated with the household's expenses, home sanitation, membership of community organizations, home safety, and learning stimulation subscale.

129

Social implications of the Javanese value system

The Javanese values of respect and the maintenance of social harmony (*rukun*) are basic principles of normative and moral guidance for social interaction within both the family and the community. The attitude of respect, described before by Geertz and Koentjaraningrat, is based on the lineal value orientation in social relationships. This respect also is reflected in Javanese social behaviour in other contexts, such as the workplace, schools, and political organizations. The strong emphasis on *rukun* (social harmony) has marked the typical Javanese as inexpressive, avoiding social and personal conflict. Geertz noted that to the Javanese " ... emotional equilibrium, emotional stasis, is of highest worth, and on the corresponding moral imperative to control one's impulses, to keep them out of awareness or at least unexpressed, so as not to set up reverberating emotional responses in others" (Geertz 1961, 147).

All of these values colour Javanese society. These ideals also are reflected in the national Indonesian state ideology, *Pancasila*, which stresses mutual help, mutual understanding, and tolerance as important principles in human relations and Indonesian society. The President of Indonesia, Suharto, who is Javanese, made a presidential decree to launch an intensive and pervasive educational programme on *Pancasila* ideology to introduce it to schoolchildren, university students, and various groups of employers and employees.

We have seen how the family, as the first place for children to learn models for social relationships, works in preparing children to act as full members of Javanese society. Socialization within the family has implications that permeate both individual personality and the entire social system. The moral components of familial institutions are internalized by the child during the earliest years and are significant forces motivating the child's behaviour later in adulthood (Geertz 1961).

Koentjaraningrat (1985), however, hypothesized that to the extent that the concept of respect and social harmony are achieved in day-to-day life, they entail a certain "cost." The great reliance on, and respect for, seniors and superiors in the civil servant class (*priyayi*) can diminish the sense of self-reliance. Obedience to superiors can prove detrimental to the mentality of civil servants, leading to an unwillingness to take risks because they do not feel safe in acting without the support of other people with whom they can share the responsibility (Koentjaraningrat 1985). Such weaknesses are sometimes regarded as unfortunate by-products of a strong culture, rather than as singular attitudes to be eliminated (Hull 1986).

The organizational structure of the government corresponds to these cultural values. In general, there is a strong centralistic tendency in some government programming. The local administrators' task is only to implement centrally designed packages that contain detailed activities and a budget. This presentation of the task leaves little opportunity for creativity, and can create an attitude of passive implementation among the local managers. Given the lineal value orientation, they feel comfortable with this kind of central structure. The impressive achievements of the immunization programme, for example, are partly due to adhering to norms for obedience and respect. President Suharto once was photographed while administering a polio vaccine to an infant. A poster of this was widely distributed to gain the support and involvement of provincial governors and local leaders. Because of this poster, the provincial governors have become involved, with good coordination between the governors and local heads being key features of the programme's success.

The strong passive tendency among Javanese civil servants relates to Geertz's description of the enculturation process within the family. Before children can comprehend the concept of "respect" and "the maintenance of social harmony," the psychological groundwork is laid. These values presuppose an ability to control any expressive behaviour, and to choose inaction rather than action. Constant protection from any unpleasant shock, and hence from exploration during infancy, may serve to build a passive attitude. Passivity also is encouraged through teaching polite behaviour. Children are actively supervised and repetitively advised to adopt proper behaviour or be frightened by threats of strangers and bogey men. Mothers also discourage children from any spontaneous behaviour and teach them to be sensitive to any subtle reactions of other people.

In contrast, Rohner (1975) described treatment of the *Papago* children (one of the American Indian tribes), who are treated with support, affection, warmth, and comfort by their elders. He found that these children made few "dependency bids" because their needs for affection had been met. When they were older, they became more self-reliant and independent and left their compounds for wages for extended periods of time. A similar style exists in the Javanese peasantry. As Jay (1969) observed, Javanese children exhibit industriousness by imitating adults' work, which is thus praised and rewarded by their parents. Although self-reliance has not been mentioned as a typical Javanese attitude by authors we reviewed, we can argue that Javanese children have a certain degree of independence. As available land in Java becomes more scarce, the Javanese youth frequently leave the village to work for wages or to engage in informal sector jobs, activities that require a certain degree of self-reliance and independence.

Geertz also noted some undesirable features of Javanese life resulting from their adherence to norms for respect and external social harmony. Since expressions of open hostility or direct opposition are not socially acceptable, the only way to deal with such situations is through evasion, covert disobedience, and mutual avoidance. This behaviour pattern is often difficult for other ethnic groups working with the Javanese. A personal communication conducted with an Indonesian anthropologist (anonymous 1991) who is not Javanese stated that one should be overly cautious when Javanese say "yes" because "yes" may mean yes, no, or maybe. "If you are not sensitive enough, a Javanese would avoid you."

Challenges for transition

As described earlier, values of respect and obedience still are preserved in the higher *priyayi* class of society, although they are diminishing in peasant society. Because lower-class persons are more likely to engage in informal sector employment, they do not necessarily rely on superiors; nevertheless, they maintain these values within the family and kin group (Koentjaraningrat 1985).

The changing attitudes towards obedience in peasant societies is in accord with theories proposed by LeVine (1974) that suggest that obedience is a particularly valued trait in a child in agricultural economies because it is necessary for economic survival as an adult. According to LeVine, obedience becomes more important in traditional agricultural societies when economic survival is in greatest jeopardy. Reduced land availability and increasing reliance on commercial activity require that the Javanese peasant moves towards less respectful behaviour and more autonomy.

However, these trends appear to be manifested unevenly in the different social strata in Java. While the *priyayi* class shows other characteristics considered typical of modern parenting, such as greater emotional closeness between father and child, high levels of obedience and hierarchical respect are, nevertheless, maintained. This pattern is inconsistent with the generalizations reported in chapter 4 on the effects of middle-class status and modernization on parenting practices. As discussed in chapter 4, Kohn (1969) and other researchers have found that obedience and following the rules were highly valued in parents with blue-collar or traditional occupations, whereas independence and initiative were believed to pay off by professional and managerial parents. Hoffman's findings (Hoffman 1988) in the United States, Turkey, and Singapore supported Kohn's hypothesis. However, he found that the percentage of fathers endorsing the child's obedience in the highest social stratum was 50 per cent in Indonesia and 63 per cent in the Philippines, while in the other countries the percentage was less than 20 per cent in the same social class.

Comparing social strata within each country figure in Hoffman's study (Hoffman 1988), the same trend was observed as in Kohn's (Kohn 1969) and LeVine's (LeVine 1963) findings (except for the Philippines): the higher the social stratum, the more likely were the fathers not to expect a child's obedience. Looking at the data for mothers in Indonesia, however, the opposite trend was observed, in which the expectation of a child's obedience in the highest class category was very high overall and marginally higher (79.3 per cent) than in the lowest social stratum (73.7 per cent). This suggests either the persistence of pre-modern values in the two social classes or that Javanese women, in the process of modernization, are more resistant than the men to changing their culturally embedded behaviour. Since our literature review shows that mothers are closer than men to their children, the modernization process may not affect the child-rearing strategy in high-class families, at least in the near future.

Hoffman (1988) has theorized that the endorsement of obedience relates to the subsistence level of a country. Using cross-national samples (Indonesia, Korea, the Philippines, Singapore, Taiwan, Thailand, Turkey, and the United States), he found that obedience is stressed most in agricultural countries where subsistence resources are scarce. He used per capita energy supply and per capita protein supply to measure subsistence level. Indonesia now has reached beyond the subsistence level in terms of rice production: socioeconomic figures indicate rapid improvements, and Indonesia has been ranked by the World Bank (1983) as a middle-income, oil-producing country. Indonesians (e.g. the Javanese) are, indeed, rapidly entering the mainstream of contemporary civilization, yet the traditional value orientation is still preserved by the higher-class society. Koentjaraningrat (1985) may be right in proposing a hypothesis: "... whenever a culture or subculture in a particular class of the society concerned has an established ancient tradition and therefore a vested interest in protecting the great tradition, it will show greater resistance towards change than cultures or subcultures with few such traditions" (Koentjaraningrat 1985, 462). This is, in fact, the same argument made by Barnlund (1989, 161–171) in explaining why Japanese culture succeeds in maintaining respectful behaviour while North American culture does not. This hypothesis, however, needs to be supported by more extensive research.

Another, simpler, hypothesis regarding the relationship between respect and physical punishment also should be examined. Modernization reduces the use of physical punishment in favour of verbal explanation. Where physical punishment has been used to maintain respect, formality, and distance between parents and children, its removal may lessen respectful behaviour. In a culture such as the Javanese, however, where physical punishment is non-existent and respectful behaviour historically has been taught verbally and modelled through concepts of shyness, fear, and shame, there may be less cause for the erosion of respect.

Javanese parents appear to be highly adaptive in terms of the survival, health, and economic capacities of children. Javanese parents tend to be very responsive to new ideas in child care, as demonstrated by the widespread use of growth monitoring and the popularity of a new tool for child-development assessment and parent teaching, introduced into the *posyandu* (Satoto and Colletta 1987). At the macro-level are increased primary school enrolment, decline in infant mortality, impressive immunization coverage, and a decline in the fertility rate (UNICEF and the Government of Indonesia 1988).

From a historical point of view, in Javanese society maternal attention during the child's vulnerable period agrees with LeVine's theory (LeVine 1988) that the optimal parental strategy for an agrarian society is high fertility with maximization of the number of surviving children. This is because the agrarian subsistence economy seems to rely on child labour. The goal of high fertility was historically difficult to achieve, given the high infant mortality rate. The period of exclusive maternal attention, which also includes breast-feeding and co-sleeping, is a way to provide confidence in the child's survival. The practice of high physical nurturance and protection before the child is weaned is still prevalent in Javanese culture, even if the infant mortality rate (IMR) has declined. (The official IMR reported by the Indonesian Government is 56 [D. Dapice 1991, personal communication]). This custom, which appeared to be positively adaptive to past conditions, also seems to adapt to current conditions. It may be that Javanese infant care cannot be fully explained in terms of requirements for infant survival. The Javanese emphasis on social and emotional ties and sharing also may shape the Javanese infant care system.

LeVine et al. (1991) take a new, more detailed, view of the precise mechanism through which female education influences mother–child interactions in their analysis of data from Mexico, as described in chapter 2. In our opinion, a similarly sensitive approach to the examination of specific pathways will lead to the understanding of family and parenting changes with socio-economic development in Java, where soothing behaviour may continue to coexist with high levels of conversational interaction between mother and infant and may actually be used to sustain in the infant a high level of attention to cognitive stimulation by the mother.

As Geertz noted, soothing and overprotecting infants, and inculcation of self-control after the age of five, are necessary ways in which the family enculturates the concepts of "respect," "obedience," and "maintenance of social harmony." The infant care pattern prepares a child for harmonious social relationships within the community that continue through adulthood. Perhaps this kind of parenting strategy is parallel to a nineteenth-century American Calvinist doctrine in child-raising. Sunley (1955) studied several magazines that were published between 1832 and 1876 (*Mother's Magazine, Mother's Assistance*, and *Parents' Magazine*), and noted that the doctrine showed the parents how to train obedience in children by "break[ing] the will" of the children, because complete submission was requisite if the child was to be protected from sin and evil. In the first three months of life, or even for the first year, infants should be tenderly cared for and their wishes granted. (For the Javanese children this lasts until the child has reached the age of five). However, after that, one should "Establish your will, as the law ... this would keep the child from experiencing all those conflicts of feeling of those doubtful as to their guide" (Sunley 1955, 160). This is similar to introducing self-control in Javanese children.

Given the Javanese and Japanese examples, we cannot totally accept the Western idea of independence as the best solution for facing "the new information-based society." We are apprehensive of the links that can be made between independence and the family's isolation from friends and neighbours. Garbarino (1982) noted that do-

135

mestic violence and neglect are indications of excessive stresses and strains associated with family isolation. Therefore, interventions to change maternal treatment of young children in Javanese culture (from high physical nurturance to independence) may not guarantee better results and could result in collapse of the long-standing social equilibrium. Koentjaraningrat (1985) indicates that self-reliance and independence cannot go hand in hand with the value of "mutual help" (*gotong royong*) and "mutual understanding" in the social relationships.

The need for more self-reliance and greater self-responsibility is, of course, a consequence of the general decline of the *gotong-royong* value. The national Indonesian state ideology, the *Pancasila*, on the other hand, capitalizes on the *gotong royong* ideal and stresses common endeavor, mutual help, mutual understanding, and tolerance as important principles in human relations and national life, and the insistence from above on maintaining these values will probably put restrictions on the development of a liberal individualistic outlook among most Indonesians in general and the Javanese in particular. (Koentjaraningrat 1985, 461)

None the less, the existence of these seemingly contradictory values of self-reliance and mutual help is not supported by ample empirical evidence. In contrast, cross-cultural studies show that strong feelings of mutual responsibility uniting members of extended kinsmen (e.g. in Papago [Rohner 1975], and in Fiji [West 1988]) coexisted with encouragement of self-reliance. In addition, despite migration, interconnectedness between kinsmen was still maintained. The Javanese emphasis on social bonds, introduced to children at an early age, does not separate self-reliance from social bonding. Jay's report (Jay 1969) indicates that children are encouraged but not pressured into doing adults' work. It seems that Javanese nurturing activities are well adapted to social expectations.

If we link the Javanese infant care system with the rejection–acceptance theory described by Rohner (1975), the Javanese children would be categorized as "accepted" children. Rohner defined "accepted" children as those who are loved, protected, and given full children's rights, resulting in positive personality functioning. In his cultural studies, he notes that:

The rejection–acceptance theory ... predicted that rejected children and adults the world over will be, in comparison to accepted persons, more hostile and aggressive or passive–aggressive (or have more problems with the management of hostility and aggression), will be more dependent, evaluate themselves more negatively, will be less emotionally responsive, less emotionally stable, and will have a more negative view. (Rohner 1975, 159)

Therefore, encouragement of self-reliance in children should not be at the expense of social bonding.

The increase in materialism may change parent–child relationships. One example is a move in language patterns towards less formally polite speech (Sosrodihardjo 1972). However, this change process may have been slowed down by the mixed feelings that many Indonesians have toward modernization (Hull 1986). Hull concluded that:

In Indonesia two terms which are often used interchangeably are *cara modern* (modern ways) and *tingkat Internasional* (international standard), both of which imply that the essential characteristic of modern goods is that they are imported. Moreover, while the goods – jeans, cars, plastic buckets – are manufactured in Asia, the technologies are largely derived from Western industrial societies. In Indonesian thinking, then, modernization is sometimes regarded as synonymous to Westernization. Understandably, in a nation which fought to rid itself of Western colonialism, modernity is regarded with mixed emotions. On the one hand modern material life is pleasurable, convenient and comfortable; on the other, the goods are symbolic of a form of neocolonial domination and loss of hard-won independence. (Hull 1986, 199)

Notes

1. "Unity in Diversity" is the major theme of the efforts of national integration in Indonesia. Therefore, any activities that lead toward the divisiveness of ethnic identity in Indonesia are prohibited.
2. Wolfe (1988) referred to a study conducted by Kung (1983).

References

Afonja, S. 1990. "Changing Patterns of Gender Stratification in West Africa." In: A. Tinker, ed. *Persistent Inequalities. Women and World Development.* New York: Oxford University Press.

Aina, T.A., M.F. Zeitlin, K. Setiolane, and H. Armstrong. 1992. Phase I Survey Results: Positive Deviance in Nutrition Research Project, Lagos State, Nigeria." Draft Report to UNICEF.

Bachtiar, H.S. 1973. "The Religion of Java: A Commentary." *Madjalah Ilmu-ilmu Sastra Indonesia* 1/V (January): 85–118.

Barnlund, D.C. 1989. *Public and Private Self in Japan and the United States: Communicative Styles of Two Cultures.* Tokyo: Intercultural Press (by arrangement with Simul Press).

Bary, H., III, I.L. Child, and M.K. Bacon. 1959. "Relations of Child Training to Subsistence Economy." *American Anthropologist* 61: 51–63.

Blumberg, R.L. 1984. "A General Theory of Gender Stratification." In: R. Collins, ed. *Sociological Theory*. San Francisco: Jossey-Bass, pp. 23–101.

Booth, A., and R.M. Sundrum. 1976. "The 1973 Agricultural Census." *Bulletin of Indonesian Economic Studies* 12: 90–105.

Bornstein, M.H., J. Tal, and C. Tamis-LeMonda. 1991. "Parenting in Cross-Cultural Perspective: The United States, France, and Japan." In: H.M. Bornstein, ed. *Cultural Approaches to Parenting*. New York: Lawrence Erlbaum Associates, pp. 69–90.

Boserup, E. 1970. *Women's Role in Economic Development*. New York: St. Martin's Press.

Caldwell, B.M., and R.H. Bradley. 1984. *Home Observation for Measurement of the Environment*. Little Rock, Ark.: University of Arkansas.

CBS. 1985. *Perkiraan Angka Kelahiran dan kematian: Hasil Survey Penduduk Antar Sensus 1985. Seri Supas No. 35*. Jakarta: Biro Pusat Statistik.

———. 1987. *Penduduk Indonesia 1987 Menurut Propinsi.* [Population of Indonesia in 1987 According to Province.] Jakarta: Biro Pusat Statistik.

Chomitz, V.R. 1992. "Diet of Javanese Preschool Children: Relationship to Household Environmental Factors and Stature." Unpublished doctoral dissertation, Tufts University School of Nutrition, Medford, Mass.

Colcutt, M. 1991. "The Legacy of Confucianism in Japan." In: G. Rozman, ed. *The East Asian Region: Confucian Heritage and Its Modern Adaptation*. Princeton, NJ: Princeton University Press.

Coltrane S. 1988. "Father–Child Relationship and the Status of Women: A Cross-Cultural Study." *American Journal of Sociology* 95: 1060–1095.

Community Systems Foundation. 1988. "Household and Community Indicators for Identifying Health and Nutritional Risk: An Analysis in East Java and Bali." Report submitted to Indonesian Ministry of Health and the World Bank, April 1988.

Crawfurd, J. 1820. *History of the Indian Archipelago, Vol. 1*. Edinburgh: Archibald Constable and Co. Cited in: Winzeler, R.L. 1982. "Sexual Status in Southeast Asia: Comparative Perspectives on Women, Agriculture and Political Organization." In: P.V. Esterik, ed. *Women of Southeast Asia. Occasional Paper No. 9, Center of Southeast Asian Studies*. Dekalb, Ill.: Northern Illinois University.

Dizard, J.E. and Gadlin, H. 1990. *The Minimal Family*. Amherst, Mass.: University of Massachusetts Press.

Doi, T. 1981. *The Anatomy of Dependence*. 2nd edn. Tokyo: Kodansha International.

Ebrey, P. 1991. "The Chinese Family and The Spread of Confucian Values." In: G. Rozman, ed. *The East Asian Region: Confucian Heritage and Its Modern Adaptation*. Princeton, NJ: Princeton University Press.

Garbarino, J. 1982. *Children and Families in the Social Environment*. New York: Aldine Publishing Company.

Geertz, H. 1961. *The Javanese Family: A Study of Kinship and Socialization*. New York: Free Press of Glencoe.

Haboush, J.K. 1991. "The Confucianization of Korean Society." In: G. Rozman, ed. *The East Asian Region: Confucian Heritage and Its Modern Adaptation*. Princeton, NJ: Princeton University Press.

Hoffman, L.W. 1988. "Crosscultural Differences in Childrearing Goals." In: R.A.

LeVine, P.M. Miller, and M.M. West, eds. *Parental Behaviors in Diverse Societies, New Directions for Child Development.* San Francisco: Jossey-Bass, pp. 99–122.

Hugo, G.J., V. Hull, T.H. Hull, and G.W. Jones. 1987. *The Demographic Dimension in Indonesian Development. East Asian Social Science Monograph.* Singapore: Oxford University Press.

Hull, T.H. 1986. "SocioDemographic Change in Indonesia." In: Mahadevan et al., eds. *Fertility and Mortality: Theory, Methodology, and Empirical Issues.* New Delhi: Sage Publications.

Hull, V. 1982. "Women in Java's Rural Middle Class: Progress or Regress?" In: P.V. Esterik, ed. *Women of Southeast Asia. Occasional Paper No. 9, Center of Southeast Asian Studies.* Dekalb, Ill.: Northern Illinois University.

Husken, F. 1991. "Power, Property and Parentage in a Central Javanese Village." In: F. Husken, ed. *Cognation and Social Organization in Southeast Asia.* KTLV Press.

Jay, R.R. 1969. *Javanese Villagers: Social Relations in Rural Modjokuto.* Cambridge, Mass.: MIT Press.

Ketcham, R. 1987. *Individualism and Public Dilemma.* New York: Blackwell.

Koentjaraningrat. 1957. *A Preliminary Description of the Javanese Kinship System. Southeast Asian Studies, Cultural Report Series.* New Haven, Conn.: Yale University.

———. 1984. *Kebudayaan Jawa. Seri Etnografi Indonesia. No. 2.* Jakarta: Balai Pustaka.

———. 1985. *Javanese Culture.* Singapore: Oxford University Press.

Kohn, M.L. 1969. *Class and Conformity: A Study in Values.* Homewood, Ill.: Dorsey Press.

Kung, L. 1983. *Factory Women in Taiwan.* Ann Arbor: University of Michigan Press.

LeVine, R.A. 1963. Child Rearing in Sub-Saharan Africa: An Interim Report. *Bulletin of the Menninger Clinic* 27: 245–256.

———. 1974. "Parental Goals: A Crosscultural View." *Teachers College Records* 76: 2.

———. 1988. "Human Parental Care: Universal Goals, Cultural Strategies, Individual Behavior." In: R.A. LeVine and P.M. Miller, eds. *Parental Behavior in Diverse Societies. New Directions for Child Development No. 40.* San Francisco: Jossey-Bass, pp. 3–12.

———, S.E. LeVine, R. Richman, F.M. Tapia Uribe, C. Sunderland Correa, and P.M. Miller. 1991. "Women's Schooling and Child Care in the Demographic Transition: A Mexican Case Study." In: *Population and Development Review, Volume 17.* New York: Population Council, pp. 459–496.

Magnis-Suseno, F. 1988. *Etika Jawa: Sebuah Analisa Falsafi Tentang Kebijaksanaan Hidup Jawa.* Jakarta: PT Gramedia.

Mangkuprawira, S. 1981. "Married Women's Work Pattern in Rural Java." In: T.S. Epstein and R.A. Watts, eds. *The Endless Day: Some Case Material on Asian Rural Women.* New York: Pergamon Press.

Megawangi, R. 1991. "Preschool-aged Nutritional Status Parameters for Indonesia and Their Applications to Nutrition-related Policies." Unpublished doctoral thesis, Tufts School of Nutrition, Medford, Mass.

———, U. Sumarwan, and Hartoyo. 1994. "Peran Suami Dalam Mejalankan Kedelapan Fungsi Utama Keluarga." [The Role of Husbands in fulfilling the Eight Familian Functions]. Report Submitted to the BKKBN Office (The National Family Planning Board of Indonesia), Bogor, March 1994.

Mulder, M. 1978. *Mysticism and Everyday Life in Contemporary Java: Cultural Persistence and Change.* Singapore: Singapore University Press.

Nag, M., N.F. White, and R.C. Peet. 1980. "An Anthropological Approach to the Study of the Economic Value of Children in Java and Nepal." In: H.P. Binswanger, ed. *Rural Household Studies in Asia.* Singapore: Singapore University Press.

Piwoz, E. 1986. "Assessment Field Activity: Ethnography Infant Feeding Practices in East Java and West Nusa Tenggara." *The Weaning Project: New Strategies to Improve Infant Feeding Practices.* Washington, DC: Manoff Group.

Richman, A.L., P.M. Miller, and M.J. Solomon. 1988. "The Socialization of Infants in Suburban Boston." In: R. LeVine and P.M. Miller, eds. *Parental Behavior in Diverse Societies, New Directions for Child Development No. 40.* San Francisco: Jossey-Bass, pp. 65–74.

Rohner, R.P. 1975. *They Love Me, They Love Me Not: A Worldwide Study of the Effects of Parental Acceptance and Rejection.* Washington, DC: Human Relations Area Files.

Rozman, G. 1991. "The East Asian Region in Comparative Perspective." In: G. Rozman, ed. *The East Asian Region: Confucian Heritage and Its Modern Adaptation.* Princeton, NJ: Princeton University Press.

Satoto, and N.D. Colletta. 1987. "Changing Caretaking Behaviors to Improve Child Growth and Development, An Action Research Proposal." Submitted to the Ford Foundation, New York and Jakarta (unpublished).

So, A.Y. 1990. *Social Change and Development: Modernization, Dependency, and World-System Theories. Sage Library of Social Research 178.* New Delhi: Sage Publications.

Sockalingam, S., M. Zeitlin, V.R. Chomitz, and Satoto. 1990. "Results of a Study of Positive Indigenous Caretaking Behavior in Child Nutrition and Health." Indonesian Positive Deviance in Nutrition Research Project. Phase I report, Tufts University School of Nutrition, Medford, Mass.

Sosrodihardjo, S. 1972. *Perubahan Struktur Masyarakat di Djawa: Suatu Analisa.* [*The Changing Social Structure in Java: An Analysis.*] Yogyakarta: Karya.

Stini, W.A. 1983. "Nutritional Stress and Growth: Sex Difference in Adaptive Response." *American Journal of Clinical Nutrition* 37: 645–651.

Stinson, S. 1985. "Sex Differences in Environmental Sensitivity During Growth and Development." In: R.M. Malina, ed. *Physical Anthropology Yearbook 28.* New York: Alan R. Liss.

Sunley, R. 1955. "Early Nineteenth-Century American Literature on Child Rearing." In: M. Mead and M. Wolfenstein, eds. *Childhood in Contemporary Cultures.* Chicago: University of Chicago Press, pp. 150–167.

Supas. 1987. *Ulasan Singkat: Hasil Survey Penduduk Antar Sensus 1985. Seri Supas, No. 4.* Jakarta: Biro Pusat Statistik.

Super, C.M., M.G. Herrera, and J.O. Mora. 1990. "Long-term Effects of Food Supplementation and Psychosocial Intervention on the Physical Growth of Colombian Infants at Risk of Malnutrition." *Child Development* 61: 29–49.

Tan, M.G., Djumadias, Suharso, Rahardjo, J. Sutedjo, and Sunardjo. 1970. *Social and Cultural Aspects of Food Patterns and Food Habits in Five Rural Areas in Indonesia.* Jakarta, Republic of Indonesia: National Institute of Economic and Social Research (LEKNAS), LIPI and Directorate of Nutrition, Department of Health.

UNICEF and Government of Indonesia. 1988 (December). *Situation Analysis of Children and Women in Indonesia.* Jakarta: UNICEF.

Warner, R.L., G.R. Lee, and J. Lee. 1986. "Social Organization, Spousal Resources, and Marital Power: A Crosscultural Study." *Journal of Marriage and the Family* 48: 121–128.

West, M.W. 1988. "Parental Values and Behavior in the Outer Fiji Islands." In: R.A. LeVine, and P.M. Miller, eds. *Parental Behavior in Diverse Societies. New Directions for Child Development, No. 40.* San Francisco: Jossey-Bass, pp. 13–26.

White, B. 1975. "The Economic Importance of Children in a Javanese Village." In: M. Nag, ed. *Population and Social Organization.* Chicago: Aldine Press, pp. 127–146.

Whiting, B.B., and J.W.M. Whiting. 1975. *Children of Six Cultures: A Psycho-cultural Analysis.* Cambridge, Mass.: Harvard University Press.

Whyte, M.K. 1978. *The Status of Women in Preindustrial Societies.* New Jersey: Princeton University Press.

Williams, L.B. 1990. *Development, Demography, and Family Decision Making: The Status of Women in Rural Java.* Brown University Studies in Population and Development. Rhode Island: Westview Press.

Winzeler, R.L. 1982. "Sexual Status in Southeast Asia: Comparative Perspectives on Women, Agriculture and Political Organization." In: P.V. Esterik, ed. *Women of Southeast Asia. Occasional Paper No. 9, Center of Southeast Asian Studies.* Dekalb, Ill.: Northern Illinois University.

Wolfe, D. L. 1988. "Female Autonomy, the Family, and Industrialization in Java." *Journal of Family Issues* 9: 85–107.

World Bank. 1983. *World Development Report 1983.* Washington, DC: Oxford University Press.

———. 1988. *Indonesia: Adjustment, Growth, and Sustainable Development.* Washington, DC: Oxford University Press.

———. 1992. *Indonesia: Growth, Infrastructure and Human Resources.* Report No. 10470-IND. Washington, DC: World Bank.

World Health Organization. 1985. *Energy and Protein Requirements. Report of a Joint FAO/WHO/UNU Expert Consultation. Technical Report Series 724.* Geneva: World Health Organization.

Zeitlin, M.F., H. Ghassemi, and M. Mansour. 1990. *Positive Deviance in Child Nutrition: With Emphasis on Psychosocial and Behavioural Aspects and Implications for Development.* Tokyo: United Nations University Press.

7

The Yoruba family: Kinship, socialization, and child development

Introduction to the Yoruba model

As noted in the chapter on Indonesia (ch. 6), our development of a model for testing the influences of family-level variables on child welfare uses data first analysed in relation to the child, bypassing family dynamics. In this chapter we orientate the reader to Yoruba concepts of family, kinship, and socialization and introduce the data, which we reanalyse in chapter 8 to explore the pathways through which family dynamics influence nutritional status and cognitive development and to test a model that brings these pathways together.

The survey data

The purpose of the Positive Deviance in Nutrition Research study, for which the data were collected, was to identify a wide range of factors that contributed to good growth and cognitive development under conditions of poverty in the greater Lagos area of Nigeria. Details of the methodology are reported elsewhere (Aina et al. 1992). The sample consisted of 211 two-year-olds, ranging in age from 22 to 26 months.

Three low-income locations were identified – the Makoko section of central Lagos, and a semi-rural area and a rural area, both in Ifo Ota. A sample of 181 children was recruited by taking the first eligible Yoruba children with birth certificates, discovered within walking radius of daily starting points that were systematically distributed in each location and selected on the basis of low-income housing. Eligible children were with their mothers, were 22–26 months in age, and had birth certificates. An additional purposive sample of 30 households was selected through screening for the presence of a malnourished child (mid-arm circumference less than 13.5 cm), to understand better the problems associated with malnutrition. This group was included in comparative analysis, not in descriptive statistics.

Survey instruments (see Appendix to chapter 8) were administered by a team of two university graduates in psychology during home visits of approximately three hours' duration. The instruments included the following:

1. Food frequencies, diet histories for infancy and weaning, questions about the family meal schedule, and maternal attitudes related to food beliefs and practices;
2. The Bayley scales of infant development (Bayley 1969), supplemented with interviewer-rated scales of behaviour and affect of the mother and child.
3. A sociodemographic questionnaire and a modified Caldwell HOME inventory (Caldwell and Bradley 1984);
4. Anthropometric measurements, including weights, heights, and mid-upper arm circumference of the children, and weights and heights of the mothers.

We used logistic regression to contrast children in the top one-third for both growth and cognitive development with those in the bottom one-third (n = 69 in each group); these groups are referred to below as the "high" and "low" developmental groups. Most of the high group were children whose Bayley mental development index (MDI) score was above the median of 91, whose height-for-age Z-score (HAZ) was above -2.25, and whose weight-for-height Z-score (WHZ) was above -1.25. All three scores were below these levels in the low group. A few children who had MDI scores above 100 but who had marginal nutritional indicators were placed in the high group. The children's HAZ scores were correlated to MDI at $r = .3$. (These Z-scores indicate how far below the norm these children fall, as measured against a well-nourished reference population measured in standard deviations based on the reference values.) The majority of mothers (76 per cent) were engaged in petty trade, while the fathers were mainly skilled labourers (39 per cent) or in farming or fishing (18 per cent).

The effects of social change on family dynamics

The rapid pace of change in Nigeria and the underlying assumptions of our research led us to deal explicitly with the effects of social change on family dynamics. Many of the variables that emerged as child-level correlates of good growth and high Bayley MDI scores of the two-year-olds in our sample appeared to reflect changes in traditional lifestyles and social values rather than differences in the family's psychosocial functioning or in economic resources. Our selection of families in low-income housing within low-income neighbourhoods eliminated major socio-economic distinctions.

In North America, in the context of therapeutic or remedial programmes, the mother's verbal responsiveness to her child tends to be interpreted as a measure of maternal competence and possibly mental health, following what has been termed a "deficit" model – i.e. the mother whose verbal responsiveness is low displays a deficit in competence. In Nigeria, in the context of the government's Early Child Care and Development Programs, we chose to view differences in verbal responsiveness as differences between traditional and modern strategies of child-rearing. This interpretation avoids casting negative value judgments on persons and makes it possible to appeal to the desire to be modern in order to motivate change. We made this choice knowing that any single interpretation oversimplifies a complex web of causality in which differences in social background (class or rural/urban location), individual temperament, mental health, and maternal competence probably all contribute to differences in variables such as the verbal responsiveness of the mother to her child. As an aside, the perception that it is necessary to contextualize and interpret variables in a linguistic structure that empowers the users of the information is in itself post-modern, as discussed in chapter 2, pages 32–34. The need for modernizing influences to be reinterpreted through "redescription" from within each culture is a recurrent theme of this volume.

Recent history has transformed the requirements for profitable employment in Nigeria. Above the subsistence level, earnings now are tied to competitive educational achievement. Lloyd (1974) calculated that the Nigerian university graduate earned on average three times the annual salary of the secondary school graduate, while Aronson (1980, 71; citing Teriba and Philips 1971, 99) stated that a secondary school graduate earned two to three times what a primary school leaver could expect. Although professionals have been marginalized by pay scales that have failed to keep pace with inflation, these differences in earning power remain. Unemployment is high and competition for advancement steep. New livelihoods tend to depend on technical skill and individual competition, whereas the old relied on social skill and group collaboration. Our focus groups with low-income parents in Lagos found them acutely aware of the high returns of education, to the extent that most had entered their children into preschool lessons by the age of three at a going rate as low as US$0.02 per hour.

We estimate that the disparities in standards of living between rural farmers and the urban employed continue to grow larger with increasing pressures on the land. The Federal Republic of Nigeria and UNICEF (1990) estimated that more than one-half of Nigerian land holdings now are of one hectare or less, creating a situation in which the majority of farmers are constrained by small farm size to grow cassava to feed their families.

As noted in chapter 2 on theories of social change and the family, we assume that parenting codes are evolving compromise formulas for the accomplishment of multiple goals (LeVine 1974; LeVine, Miller, and West 1988). In the design of our research on Yoruba mothers and children, we assumed that rapid social change would lead to a lag in adapting parenting codes to new livelihoods and new values, and that rapidly adapting parents would have better child outcomes than those who still applied codes based on traditional modes of employment. We hypothesized that changing codes would have culture-specific influences on certain cultural food habits that appeared to be uniquely West African, while at the same time showing similarities to other changes in parent–child relations that have been documented universally in response to modernizing influences.

From a nutritional perspective, we found that almost all parents still followed, to a greater or lesser degree, a previously rational formula of rather severely restricting the amount of high-quality foods of animal origin given to very young children, in order to develop the child's moral character. Through the visible sequence of serving these foods and the sizes of the pieces given to different persons, this restriction taught children the order of rank and privilege within the family and lineage, preparing them to become self-disciplined members of a hierarchically governed society. Our data confirmed that parents who believed in and practised lesser degrees of food restriction had both better-growing and higher-scoring children.

As noted in chapter 2, we sought and found evidence of relatively universal changes in parent–child interactions, in response to modernization, that had been summarized by Werner (1979). Moreover, in the Yoruba data set, we found that such changes, listed below, were linked to superior child outcomes:

1. A change in discipline away from physical punishment and harsh scolding or threats that lead to immediate unquestioned obedience. In our sample, the mothers of children in the top developmental group displayed significantly less hostility (slaps, shouting, and threats) towards misbehaviour than those of children in the low group.
2. Acceptance of the child's dependency up to an older age. Our high-group two-year-olds were more likely to stay in sight of their mothers in safe play environments. While learning self-help skills, they were not yet expected to sweep, or wash clothes or dishes.
3. More affection and intimacy and a more personal relationship with the father. Mothers of high-group children were more often seen caressing and kissing their two-year-olds. These children more often ate with their mothers and their parents together and spent more time with their fathers and other male relatives than did children in the low group.
4. A more verbally responsive and a more school-like way of speaking and using explanations to teach the child. High-group mothers spoke to their two-year-olds slowly, in simple language, rather than rapid adult speech. Parents of high scorers in the ethnographic study explained many things to their children.

The debate in the sociological literature regarding the impact of modernization of industrial production and employment on the extended family system and, conversely, the effects of the extended family system on industrialization and socio-economic development, has been applied to Nigeria (Goode 1963; Gugler and Flanagan 1978). Whether or not industrial production reaches high levels, individualized urban employment has led gradually to the formation of small, self-contained families and to a reduction in the areas of life covered by extended family support. Lloyd (1972) documented ways in which traditional Yoruba lineage structures, inheritance laws, occupations, and social values worked against both the accumulation of capital and the establishment of family businesses. These ways were consistent with the conclusion by Dizard and Gadlin (1990, 27) that traditional precapitalist family networks in Europe and the United States were well suited to the *dispersal* but not to the *concentration* of surplus.

Several writers of the 1970s (Fadipe 1970; Lloyd 1974; Gugler and Flanagan 1978) demonstrated, however, that certain new and old social roles tended to be complementary rather than conflicting. Extended family support facilitated rather than hindered individual educational attainment, and repayment of these benefits to the extended family was important to the development of rural areas. Fadipe (1970, 315–316) concluded that kinship solidarity remained strong but expressed itself not in physical presence so much as in financial assistance, advice, and guidance, through which educated members of the family tended to assume an importance greater than that of the official lineage head.

These observations are once again concordant with the view of Western development, noted by Dizard and Gadlin (1990, 29), that "the traditional family, even as it was slowly being transformed, subsidized a considerable portion of the bill for industrialization." More recently, Guyer (1990) has suggested that a fundamental reorientation is occurring *away* from cross-generational and *towards* within-generational flows of resources, resulting in a change in the structure of kinship networks.

Focus group and ethnographic research

The above discussion sidesteps the specific skills, attitudes, and world views taught by old versus new parenting codes and the mechanisms through which specific new and old ways are adapted to their respective socio-economic climates. The high psychological costs of social change make it reprehensible to promote change without clearly understanding the ways in which change would be beneficial, even when the changes are statistically linked to positive outcomes. Therefore, we conducted an ethnographic substudy of the families of six of the highest and four of the lowest scorers on the Bayley MDI. We also used focus groups to explore the nature of old versus new parenting styles and family structures and to determine how well these styles adapted to the prevailing transitional economy and to the need to prepare children to compete on the world market.

These focus groups on child development and nutrition themes took place in the form of a periodic ongoing dialogue with members of urban communities neighbouring our sample area and among faculty members of the University of Lagos. These groups also explored ways in which socio-economic development could be accelerated by changes at the micro level of child care and by social programmes that promote child development. We looked for skills and attitudes that enable children to master technologies that are valued on the world market, and for family-level variables that are determinants of child development, and hence of socio-economic development. Findings from this dialogue and from the ethnography enter into our discussion of changes in Yoruba family life.

The Yoruba family

Geographical background

South-western Nigeria is home to about 20–25 million Yoruba (figures projected from the Nigeria Fertility Survey 1984), who inhabit an area that stretches about 120 miles along the coast of the Gulf of Guinea, east from the Benin border, to about 200 miles inland into the savannah belt of West Africa. The Yoruba are the most urbanized and possibly the most industrialized ethnic group in sub-Saharan Africa. About 20 per cent of Nigerians and 10 per cent of West Africans are Yoruba. Yorubaland has at least nine cities with populations of more than 100,000, and has a 60–70 per cent rate of urbanization overall. Lagos, the home of our urban sample children, is the centre of a greater metropolitan area with a projected population in 1991 of 10 million (Federal Republic of Nigeria and UNICEF 1990). South-western Nigeria has the country's highest concentration of industries, with more than 50 per cent of the country's manufacturing output, predominantly in light industrial manufacturing products such as furniture, textiles, clothing, plastics, paper, leather goods, foodstuffs, confectionery, beverages, and tobacco products.

The Yoruba had a complex precolonial system of urban residence, economic production, and trade (Bascom 1969). Their precolonial town crafts, dating from the Middle Ages, were among the earliest developed in Africa. Yoruba towns are mentioned in written records of the sixteenth century (Gugler and Flanagan 1978). These towns were composed of enclosed compounds, with descent groups varying in size from 20 to 2,000 persons living together in each compound. The towns had divine kings who were selected from a royal lineage by governing bodies of chiefs and elders, who represented the different wards and constituencies of the town. Originally, most towns had

members. Lineages typically manage land allocation among their members, while competing with other lineages for tracts of land. According to Eades (1980, 60), it appears likely that the degree of corporate identity is correlated with the control of resources.

In addition to lineage membership, Yoruba town dwellers belong to many traditional community associations based on age, religion, and occupation. As the more traditional versions of these associations have fallen into decline, new associations take their place, based on such alliances as modern religious groupings, neighbourhood friendships, occupational associations, rotating credit associations, and town improvement unions (Aronson 1980; Eades 1980, 61).

Seniority system

Inherent in the concept of lineage structure is the system of seniority, which establishes a single hierarchy of reciprocal obligations in all situations (Aronson 1980, 93–94). Traditionally, any senior had a right to unquestioned service, deference, and submissiveness from any junior (Lloyd 1974, 35–36). Traditional rules assign age seniority according to order of entry into the lineage, either by birth or by marriage. Seniority also is derived from gender, hereditary titles, designated leadership roles, physical ability, and supernatural endowment (as in the case of the priesthood).

Seniority traditionally determined task allocation and resource distribution in the labour system of the household production unit. Distinctions defining seniority were, of necessity, elaborate and were expressed in the myriad terms by which individuals greeted and addressed each other (Fadipe 1970). Distinctions among these titles and greetings might claim in the old production system the same importance now attached in the modern sector to job grades and job descriptions.

By 1988, however, commercialization of the rural economy had led to major shifts in production systems such that seniority no longer entitled the senior party to significant productive labour, such as farm work, for example, from the junior party (Guyer 1990). According to Gugler and Flanagan (1978), the unrelated members of city housing and neighbourhoods re-create and make use of the seniority system in social discourse and in requests for minor errands or services. While Aronson (1980, 94) claims that the importance of seniority for purposes of social etiquette has not diminished in new urban areas, the modern employment structure introduces a time-bounded se-

151

niority system with new rules, sometimes creating uncomfortable conflicts in seniority, as, for instance, when a young, highly educated female supervises an older male driver or secretary. Overall, although seniority still is much honoured, the resources that flow through the system are more and more supplemental rather than crucial, except in providing access to such things as job opportunities that are not awarded on the basis of money or merit.

Living arrangements

The typical traditional Yoruba compound contains a large patrilineal and patrilocal extended family. The head of the family is usually the most senior male member, and the men are normally polygamous, with each wife having a separate room. Most houses are rectangular single-story buildings, with either a traditional central compound or a central corridor and a yard at the back (Eades 1980, 40). With the reduction of courtyard space, doors and windows have become larger. Before European contact, the rooms had no windows (Fadipe 1970, 98).

In our study population, fewer than 10 per cent lived in traditional compounds, whereas 74 per cent lived in the more compact style with the narrow central corridor, referred to as "face-to-face" housing; 71 per cent of families occupied one room. This distribution of living arrangements contrasts with data from 799 families of slightly higher socio-economic status in the Ebute-Metta section of Lagos studied by Olusanya (1981). In this sample, only 1.6 per cent lived in "face-to-face" flats and only 59 per cent in one room in a house. Of Olusanya's (1981) élite sample of 1,002 families in Suru-Lere, Lagos, 63 per cent had self-contained flats, and 27 per cent lived in single-family houses.

A major difference between low-income urban dwellings and traditional compounds is the predominance of unrelated families, often of different ethnic groups, living together within the urban buildings on a rental basis. In studying Ijebu immigrants to the city of Ibadan, Aronson (1980) found that very few lineage members lived in the same urban compounds or housing complexes, although they often accommodated each others' children in their urban residences and automatically would have lived in the same compound in their own home towns.

The average family size in Olusanya's lower-income sample in Ebute-Metta was 6.5 persons, consisting of 87 per cent nuclear families (mother, father, and children); 6.6 per cent polygynous families (two wives under the same roof); and 6.5 per cent modified–extended families (including one or more grandparents). All of these types of households could include house help and fostered children. For the élite in Suru-Lere, these figures were 7.5 persons per family, with 86 per cent nuclear, 2 per cent polygynous, and 11.2 per cent modified–extended (Olusanya 1981).

In our groups who were poorer than Ebute-Metta residents, average household size of the rural, semi-rural, and urban subsamples were 4.5, 5.6, and 5.6 persons, respectively. Although we did not ask whether co-wives lived under the same roof, indirect measures suggest that about 6 per cent of families had two or more wives living together under the same roof. The small household size of our poor samples confirms Olusanya's assertion that extended family members, who live separately under conditions of urban poverty, tend to regroup somewhat as socio-economic level rises. Aronson (1980), however, made a marked distinction in Ibadan between the highly educated élite, who continue to maintain small monogamous nuclear families, and the more traditionally affluent urban dwellers, whose households expand with co-wives and extended family members.

Sleeping arrangements also have changed. In the past, the husband and each of his wives had his or her own separate room. Female children slept with their mothers until adulthood, as did male children during early childhood, after which time they moved onto the veranda or into a separate boys' room (Fadipe 1970, 98). Now, when finances permit, husband and wife share a room, and the children sleep in the parlour (Aronson 1980, 34). If only one room is affordable, husband and wife share the bed and the children sleep on mats on the floor. The opening of these single-room dwellings onto a narrow central hallway may accentuate crowding. Fadipe (1970, 101–102) described the intense interaction of the kinsmen and co-wives of the traditional compound:

A large part of the day is spent in the open ... everyone eats and drinks and talks in the full view of everybody else; and as the rooms are hot in the daytime ..., most of the life of the compound has to be passed on the open veranda [now, in the yard] ... quarrels and rebukes take place within the full hearing of neighbors ... each individual's weaknesses and vices are open to the observation of other[s] ... People outside the immediate family are interested in its members and their welfare ... This makes exclusive family life in the Western sense impossible. Only a limited amount of privacy is possible.

According to Aronson (1980, 52) and Gugler and Flanagan (1978), the same lack of privacy tends to prevail in urban households with unrelated occupants, although larger windows and amenities such as electric fans make it more comfortable to seek seclusion behind closed doors. Aronson (1980) asserts that a major change associated with urbanization is the *possibility* of privacy, even if it is rarely realized. Olusanya (1981, 23) studied both low- and upper-income neighbourhoods in Lagos. In quoting a lament from a column in the newspaper *Lagos Weekend*, he notes a trend towards privacy and seclusion when it is affordable:

Once in the city of Lagos, this virtue [of openness, and being one's brother's keeper] is no longer to be found. This is because there has been a cold craze ... branded "fenceophobia" ... and its symptoms include a tendency for seclusion. Many people are getting secluded in Lagos and one cannot even know his neighbors again. This is all part of being Westernized.

As indicated in the column, the communal quality of life is a social value, extending to the traditional town quarter or ward, and to the low-income urban neighbourhood. Gugler and Flanagan (1978, 76–78) quoted an elder in a Mushin, Lagos, neighbourhood:

The action of a man cannot be hidden. If you are living in the neighborhood and you are bad, before you speak your neighbors will know what kind of man or woman you are ... If you go to them for help, they will pity you and help you. They may help you settle a quarrel.

The status of women

Yoruba women are both autonomous and subordinate to men. Autonomy arises through a fairly rigid sexual division of labour, which excludes women from most agricultural work, and means that traditional women work independently of their husbands and not jointly or cooperatively with them (Lloyd 1974, 37–38). Although a woman traditionally expects her husband to provide her with capital to start trading or to establish her craft, she is her own supervisor. Income derived from her labour is her own – to spend on herself and her children, after fulfilling her obligations to share in purchasing food, clothing, and sundries.

An aspect of the division of labour that is often ignored but which puts women at some economic advantage in Yorubaland is that, except in the case of cash crops, Yoruba social expectation and conjugal etiquette forbids the farmer to carry his own farm products to the

154

market to sell. Any man who does is regarded as a miser. Since it is the wife who sells these items, whatever she declares as a sales profit is what the man will accept. It is not unusual for women to use some of such funds to begin petty trading in other goods as well.

The Western concept of the full-time housewife, who earns no income, is alien to Yoruba tradition, although women in urban areas who cannot find employment do become housewives, and the concept itself has been introduced by Christianity and Islam. In our sample, 10 per cent of mothers of two-year-olds described themselves as "housewives," but only 1 per cent reported earning no income. In Olusanya's study (1981), 34 per cent of the low-income and 15 per cent of the élite group described themselves as full-time housewives (after reassigning women who identified themselves as both housewives and income earners to a non-housewife category).

In our sample, the mean ratio of father's contribution to food expenditure to the mother's income was 1:8 for the urban, 1:3 for the semi-rural, and 1:17 for the small rural sample. The lower contribution of women among the semi-rural may reflect their separation from rural agricultural production and from the major urban markets. Husbands and wives traditionally do not pool their finances. On the death of spouses, their individual property does not pass to each other, unless they have been married in the church (Fadipe 1970, 140–146). In everyday life, each spouse comes and goes by himself/ herself, without necessarily telling the other one where he or she is going, although wives are expected to announce their intentions more frequently than husbands (Aronson 1980, 115).

Despite women's autonomy, however, many aspects of the social system give men greater seniority and control than women. Men are permitted several wives, but women may have only one husband. According to the terms of traditional agriculture, the man controlled the farm labour of his sons by all wives until the time of their marriage. Moreover, according to traditional marriage conventions, a new wife was junior not only to her husband but to all of his lineage members born before the date of her marriage (Fadipe 1970, 114). She was also a subordinate in the domestic domain, where much unpaid labour was expected of her from her husband and his extended family. Young urban wives now prefer living away from their husbands' families because they no longer are willing to take so subservient a part in family life – being subject to running errands at any time, and shopping, fetching water, and cooking for the older women. Urbanism, education, and adherence to Christianity – with monogamy as its marriage tenet – have given women some measure of freedom from the control of the extended family.

Women's economic enterprises typically have been smaller in scale and subordinate to those of men. Despite very high female participation in petty trade, the trading structure has always been stratified to the relative disadvantage of women, with men in charge of most major long-distance trading enterprises. In addition, women were traditionally excluded from most, but not all, traditional political offices (Afonja 1990).

According to Afonja (1990), the Yoruba ideology of kinship and marriage, which operates to the disadvantage of women and which is relatively impervious to change, has greatly influenced the effects of modernization. Women have been denied access to, or control of, the new means of earning income introduced through contact with the West, and their relative position has deteriorated progressively since this contact began. Proportionately fewer girls than boys have attended school or studied to the higher levels. In our sample, the mean years of schooling for the fathers was 6.7, with 25 per cent having completed secondary and 10 per cent not having attended school. Corresponding figures for the mothers were 4.3 years, and 11 per cent and 35 per cent. Beginning with the slave trade, and increasingly thereafter with the introduction of coffee and cocoa, gender inequality among the Yoruba was intensified through increased male control over critical resources. Yet there have been counter-currents to this trend during the giddy years of the petroleum "oil boom," in which women competed and sometimes succeeded in landing bigger oil contracts than did men (Babatunde 1992).

Men used precapitalist systems of control to monopolize the technology, the new knowledge, and the products of capitalistic production of export commodities (Afonja 1990). Women were easy targets for "peasantization" and "proletarianization." With cash cropping, some women have entered commercial farming, but more have been co-opted to work on their husbands' cash crops, to their husbands' financial benefit and to the disadvantage of their own income-generating activities. Children's school attendance increases the women's work and financial burden. In short, Afonja states that the rubric of joint financial support for the household remains superimposed on a structure that denies women control of the most critical resources in modern capitalist society.

According to Afonja (1990), the nature–culture mystique for explaining gender inequality is relevant to the Yoruba view of women.

This model holds that women are closer to nature by virtue of biological reproduction and that men, as creators of culture, are inherently superior because culture is superior to nature. Babatunde (1992) does not hold this view that procreation becomes the justification for women's inferiority. He demonstrates, instead, that the relatively lower status of females in day-to-day life is reversed in the symbolism of the fertility-enhancing Gelede cult, which honours the powers of older women who are believed to hold control over fertility. These women, past the age of menopause, have the right to speak their minds freely (Fadipe 1970, 116) and potentially are to be feared if they misuse their powers over nature.

Virtue in the form of "good character" also is idealized as female. In myth she was the Supreme Diety's granddaughter, given in marriage to the oracle divinity. When, after some time, he mistreated her, she returned to her father's house. When the oracle divinity traced her to her hiding place and begged her to return, she refused to return in physical form but promised to abide with him in the invisible form of a helper – i.e. "good character." Good character brings success in life to a man who treats his wives with kindness and affection, takes care of his children, and does what is good (Babatunde 1992, 214).

The Yoruba value of children

Yoruba culture places extremely high value on children. It is safe to say that children are the *summum bonum* – the highest good – of the Yoruba. An economic rationale underlies this value, as has been pointed out by Caldwell (1976) and other "price tag theorists" (Olusanya 1987), who imply that parents bear many children because they profit from them financially. According to Olusanya (1987), these writers miss the point of the Yoruba experience and are in error regarding the profits as well.

When taken literally, arguments that parents bear children because of crude economic incentives are demeaning and inaccurate. The value of children to their parents may better be expressed in spiritual terms. A spiritual view explains why women, whom Olusanya (1987) refers to as "fertility martyrs," continue to bear children when further child-bearing is not only unprofitable, but also places women's health and financial security at risk. According to Babatunde (1992) and Hallgren (1991, 120–122), the very nature of the immortality of the soul flows cyclically through the lineage through the birth of children, and not primarily through the type of afterlife pictured by Christianity or Islam.

In traditional Yoruba religion, the various component parts of the soul can continue the good life eternally in a cycle of three states – the living, the ancestors, and the unborn awaiting reincarnation. Children reincarnate ancestors of their own lineage. Continuing participation in this cycle depends on bearing children, living a long, full life, and being venerated by one's descendants. Although the majority of Yoruba now belong to the major world religions, their feelings about the value of children engendered by the earlier belief system do not appear to be greatly altered by new beliefs.

The old religious beliefs supported the old economic order. As discussed by Zeitlin et al. (1982), the traditional flow of investment, not only in Africa but in earlier decades in industrialized societies, was from child to parent, not from parent to child. This direction of flow could still be observed in the United States as late as 1907, when many children lived at home and contributed their incomes to their parents until they were married, and when children's earnings were more important than a wife's earnings in supplementing family income, as documented by Hogan (1985, 107) in Chicago. Over the course of economic development, the direction of investment reversed.

Surveys conducted by Caldwell and Caldwell (1977) indicated that Nigerian children began to contribute substantively to the family's subsistence by the age of five or six. The parents estimated that each child born would remit an amount of money to the parents equivalent to 10 per cent of household income, in addition to providing child care for younger children and old-age and disaster security. Children also benefited the family materially at the lineage level. The larger the population of the lineage, the greater its claims on land and other resources, and the greater its chances of surviving in perpetuity (Lloyd 1974).

According to Guyer (1990), however, even in rural areas the direction of intergenerational transfer has changed since the 1960s. At the time of Guyer's first field work in rural Oyo in 1968, sons already were ambivalent about working on their fathers' farms, as tradition demanded, because their fathers were not under obligation to share any given amount of the farm proceeds with them. But a young man had few personal needs in those days, except the bride-wealth for a first marriage, for which the cash component accounted for over half a year's income from an average adult man's farm. The father was obligated to pay this sum. When Guyer returned to the same area in 1988, she found that teenaged and young adult sons no longer worked on their fathers' farms: on the one hand, a higher level of commercialization allowed the sons to earn ready cash; on the other, the custom of paying bride-wealth was less mandatory. Guyer states that while lineal identity and loyalties continue, the only material transfers that parents claim they can now rely on from their children are burial rites, nursing through their final illness (by daughters), and some crisis assistance.

The fact that bride-wealth has been commuted to cash payments denies the philosophy behind bride-wealth, which had to do with testing the endurance and patience of men who take daughters into marriage and keeping husbands in close touch with the wife's family. Although not all parents count on their children's support, the obligation for adult children to provide it is still strong. In fact, two factors that have made corruption a problem are the need to satisfy acquired expensive tastes and the need to keep up with the never-ending entitlements of the extended family.

To support her observations on the changing economic value of children and hence changing family priorities, Guyer quotes a statement from Berry (1985), in *Fathers Work for their Sons*, regarding productive assets: "Low and uncertain returns to most forms of productive and commercial activity do not slow things down; rather they reinforce the impetus to keep moving, if only to avoid falling farther behind in the economic and political lottery of accumulating good connections (Berry 1985, 192)." Guyer (1990, 5) proposes that children now are valuable for the lateral networks of kin relations which they establish between a mother and the father(s) of her children, in a shift "from longer term to shorter term logic, on the part of both men and women." The parents provide support and a network of kin connections and opportunities to each of their biological children and the child's other parent during the present generation. A new survival strategy for women, therefore, becomes one of bearing children by several fathers in serial relationships. This pattern is similar to that described by Gussler (1975) among low-income mothers on St. Kitts.

In support of the hypothesis that survival hinges on lateral networking, Guyer noted a marked increase in ceremonial celebrations for professional launchings, such as freedom from apprenticeship or book publication, that create opportunities for occupational, political, and other forms of entrepreneurial networking by attracting heterogeneous crowds. With respect to lifestyle rituals, she found marriage

159

less formal, naming ceremonies for babies much more lavish, and apprenticeship "freedom" ceremonies second only to funerals in expense.

Marriage and the husband–wife relationship

Marriage typically is prohibited between partners who can trace a blood relationship. The normal age of marriage is between 25 and 30 for men and between 17 and 25 for women (mean age 20 in our sample). A man's father traditionally was, and often still is, responsible for arranging and financing his sons' marriages. Although today the majority of young people choose their own partners, most obtain their parents' consent. Lengthy, discreet inquiries and introductions may still be made through a female intermediary who belongs to the groom's side of the family by marriage (Eades 1980, 56–59).

Modern forms of marriage vary from the English-style weddings, under the Marriage Ordinance, to marriage by Yoruba customary law, to simple parental consent and blessing, down to casual and temporary mutual consent. Of our sample mothers, 75 per cent claimed to be married by customary law; 6 per cent had been married under the Marriage Act; 13 per cent were cohabiting, 2 per cent each were single and divorced, and 1 per cent were widowed. One pattern is for men with monogamous homes to have "outside wives" (Aronson 1980, 113–114). While the existence of these women may not be known to the "inside" wife, the outside wives consider the man their husband and consider their children entitled to share in his inheritance. Another common pattern is for urban polygynous men to divide their time between wives and children living at different addresses.

In the traditional division of labour, the husband provides capital with which his wives trade or engage in crafts. With their profits, the women cover many of the costs of food, clothing, and sundry needs for themselves and their children, and take turns feeding the husband (Aronson 1980, 132–135). The husband provides housing, staple foods, and some money for education and children's clothing; the wife provides her own clothes, the rest of the children's clothes, and other items of food (Eades 1980, 68). In rural areas, the wives have a share of farm products. A farmer and his wife have a commercial arrangement whereby she markets his crops. When game was available, the husband provided meat by trapping or hunting. Housekeeping chores were the responsibility of the wife, who could delegate them to children and others junior to her in rank. Husbands disciplined their wives without the intervention of neighbours, unless the neighbours judged that the punishment exceeded the crime (Aronson 1980, 52).

As part of the proliferation of new arrangements, urban husbands and wives, according to Aronson (1980, 53), may operate more as a team than they would in the rural areas, where gender roles are more rigidly defined. In the city, as mothers work at greater distances from the home and as the costs of children's schooling increase, the father may look after the children more directly, and the couple may share expenses more cooperatively. As noted by Olusanya (1981), higher-status urban husbands might prefer that their wives did not work, if her work were not needed to cover extended-family obligations from the wife's side.

Polygyny and the relationship between co-wives
While polygyny was necessitated by the traditional structure of the economy, not all men can afford more than one wife, and it is questionable whether the majority of husbands ever had more than one wife (Aronson 1980, 115). In our sample, 33 per cent of our urban, 47 per cent of the semi-rural, and 89 per cent of the small rural sample of families were polygynous. Olusanya's estimates of 7 per cent polygynous families in Ebute-Metta and 2 per cent in Suru-Lere (Olusanya 1981) apparently counted only those cases of polygyny where co-wives lived together under the same urban roof.

In traditional rural conditions, acquisition of a co-wife adds to the prestige of the household and of other wives living in the same compound, who are entitled to assistance with chores from the newcomer according to their seniority. According to Fadipe (1970, 115ff.), the socially approved young wife is extremely deferential to senior compound members for at least a year after her marriage, or until the arrival of her first child, after which time she can pay more attention to her own immediate business. Among other things, the new wife is a useful standby for children in trouble with their parents, rushing forward to plead for a child she hears crying under punishment. Wives of the compound, individually or collectively, ideally should never lose their role as a peacemaking force in the compound.

In rural areas polygyny remains profitable. Polygynous men have been found to have larger farms. More wives enable a man to manage scattered landholdings, which, traditionally, their sons would farm for their father. By helping with child care and household duties, junior wives in rural areas free the senior wife to trade (Eades 1980, 69).

Polygyny has been linked to a number of drawbacks, particularly in urban areas. As Aronson (1980) notes, if any misfortune befalls a child, the jealousy of a co-wife may be suspected as the cause. In addition, polygynous marriages in Ibadan were found by Olusanya (1970) to be less stable than monogamous marriages. Co-wives tend to compete through bearing children. In our study, the greater her number of co-wives, the higher the mother's stated ideal number of children. Sembajwe (1981) provides evidence from several studies that Yoruba women in polygynous unions have the same high fertility rates as those in monogamous unions. This occurs in spite of the fact that reduced coital frequency and greater age differences between spouses tend to make polygynous women less fertile. De facto or temporary unions, however, were less fertile than formal unions.

Bledsoe (1990) claims, based on field work in Liberia and Sierra Leone and a literature review that includes Nigeria, that female education exacerbates inequities between polygynous women who previously would have lived together. A man can now at almost any point marry a new wife who is more educated and more socially presentable than his earlier one(s), at which point he can effectively cut off, or greatly reduce support to, children by the previous unions. The previous laws that would have given an older wife seniority, regardless of education, no longer apply. Bledsoe states that men now sustain the costs of polygyny and high fertility by marginalizing low-status women, usually those with the least education, as outside wives and their children as outside children.

In our study, children from monogamous unions were significantly more likely to be in our high developmental group, even after controlling for rural–urban location, presence of the father, and economic and educational variables. After controlling for monogamy, children whose fathers lived with their mothers all or most of the time, rather than less than half of the time or never, were also significantly better in growth and cognitive scores. Fathers and mothers who had never attended school, and hence probably followed the rules of traditional polygyny, had children with marginally higher growth and development indicators than did parents with some primary or secondary education. At the other extreme, the 28 children with parents who were married under the Marriage Ordinance or listed "professional" occupations, or with fathers with more than 12 years of schooling, had significantly better status than all others.

Divorce and other forms of family stress

Traditionally, a Yoruba woman had only one marriage ceremony, without rituals to mark remarriage after being widowed or divorced (Eades 1980, 58–59). Her husband's death did not mark the end of her marriage, which would continue according to the levirate system with a junior member of his descent group. Now, the ease of divorce varies with the legal status of the marriage. While English-style ordinance marriages can be dissolved only in the High Court, marriages contracted under customary law, which permits polygyny, easily can be dissolved in the local courts. Yoruba men rarely sue for divorce, and only on grounds of adultery. More commonly, wives leave husbands who have stopped supporting them, move in with a lover or with their parents, and start divorce proceedings from there. The main issue in these proceedings is repayment to the husband of marriage presentations and trading capital. Fathers traditionally have the right to keep the children, but do not usually do so.

It is easy for a woman to remarry, in part because it costs less to marry a divorcee than a first-time bride. In a study by the Okedijis (Okediji and Okediji 1966) in Ibadan, cited by Eades (1980, 58), the most common reasons given by women for divorce were non-support by the husband (71 per cent), trouble with co-wives (32 per cent), trouble with in-laws (20 per cent), and lack of children (20 per cent).

In the old days, when marriages dissolved, the parent generation apportioned blame and dictated conditions of settlement according to custom. Their role now is more and more limited to giving advice. In court cases, custody of children is increasingly awarded to the mother, and instead of receiving refunded bride-wealth, the husband may find that urban courts require him to provide child support (Gugler and Flanagan 1978). According to Guyer (1990), casual, easily broken alliances are increasing, although almost one-half of the men in her 1968 sample still had the same wives 20 years later. She states that women increasingly are able to keep the children after divorce and to maintain their claims on the father.

The changing pattern, according to which it is common for men to require girls to prove their fertility by becoming pregnant before they marry them, starts a chain reaction of marital dysfunction. The girl who proves herself in this manner enters into a depreciated role as wife and, hence, continues a demanding rather than a respectful relationship with her husband. She judges him on his ability to prove himself to her by providing support. Lacking emotional satisfaction, he then courts other women. His wife accepts his infidelity as the price she pays for sexual abstinence during breast-feeding. Her main concern is that he does not give the new woman too much money. Aronson (1980, 45), however, reports that urban women may also prefer to be pregnant before marriage to avoid the many problems that a childless married woman encounters, and therefore the woman also may initiate this process.

Both husbands and wives suffer from the fact that the urban environment tends to reduce women's earning capacity in comparison with the costs of living. Both expect, as under rural conditions, that she will be economically independent and able to contribute substantially to the family income. Yet she may not be able to find a paid job, sufficient capital, or sufficient child-care assistance to trade profitably in the urban setting. The husband is then forced into the unfamiliar role of breadwinner for his wife and children, and is alone held responsible for their financial support. He, meanwhile, may not regard his wife and children as having first claim on his wage or salary, often feeling that his mother, siblings, or cousins have prior claims.

Babatunde (1992) notes that difficult economic circumstances and the new value placed on consumer goods tend to make women value men for their money, rather than for traditional virtues. The breaking and the forming of marital ties is less regulated than before. Husbands may simply turn away a barren wife who earlier would have been kept on, although, according to Guyer (1990), the wife might leave first to attempt to bear a child by another man. Wives also may leave a husband who cannot pay the rent. A man may bring a new wife into the home without prior warning, and wife-beating may ensue from these stresses. This sequence of observations highlights the preoccupation with lateral transfers of support noted by Guyer (1990).

Modes of conflict resolution
According to Fadipe (1970, 307–308), anger is given very little overt expression or is expressed diplomatically in noncommittal sarcastic words whose literal meaning is the opposite of the true meaning of the speaker. Personal problems of all kinds commonly are believed to be caused by the jealousy of enemies within the family, whose identity may be secretly revealed through divination, and against whom religious protection is needed.

When conflict is overt, according to Aronson (1980, 115–116), Yorubas externalize it by direct and indirect insult and resolve the issue by involving outsiders. He claims that the first of three phases is an outburst of hostility, usually in the form of insults, ridicule, or, most seriously, imprecations or curses. The second phase brings an audience of friends and supporters for both sides of the issue. Resolution, the third phase, results from mediation by neutral parties, during which responsibility for the conflict is fairly apportioned to both sides. The above process is very public.

Relationships in the family

Personal success among the Yoruba ultimately was defined in terms of family relations. According to Babatunde (1992, 236–237):

The successful "good person" was cautious, respectful of elders and committed to and persistent in hard work. He (she) took family responsibilities seriously and understood that obligations to the family included those to the extended family. In behavior to and treatment of relations he operationalized the communitarian principle of shared responsibility inherent in the concept of classificatory kinship terms. He was loyal to relations, accountable to the members of the kinship group, and a good father and husband. Whatever his success in life, it was subordinated to how he proved himself as the head of his extended family. If he behaved in an exclusivist manner, treating his children with preference to those other children of the extended family, he was regarded as mean and unworthy of the responsibilities of success. If he accumulated resources and used them on himself and his immediate compound family, he forfeited having the group of dependents which was part of the consequences of success.

Parent-and-child relationships

Yoruba tradition stresses that the parents are the first teachers of their children, instructing them in the "proper" way of relating to their elders and people of the same age group. In the communal atmosphere of the traditional family, parents of children who behave in approved ways are approved as successful; parents whose children misbehave are shamed and advised to "put their houses in order" (Babatunde 1992, 8–10).

According to traditional Yoruba religion, it is the duty of parents to bring up their children ethically and in the knowledge of God (Adewale 1986). From the beginning, children are made to believe in reward and punishment and, accordingly, in the potency of blessings and the efficacy of curses of spiritual beings. Parents' role in training is reflected in the verse from the Ifa divinatory corpus (Odu):

> If one trains one's children,
> They will be perfectly wise
> As Ire, the daughter of Olokun.
> If one does not train one's children,
> They will be stupid and foolish
> Like Ibawini, the son of Otu Ife.

Parents also must love their children and not be harsh to them or selfish. The lesson of generosity towards children is expressed in the following verses:

> An elder who consumes everything without leaving a remnant will himself carry his calabash home.
>
> The dove eats and leaves a remnant for the pigeon.
> The green wild pigeon eats and leaves a remnant for the mocking bird.
> I will leave a remnant for my children when I eat.

These verses pertaining to child training and to child feeding and care have divergent implications for teaching the modern concepts of child stimulation and nutrition. While perception of the need for the special training of children is rooted in traditional culture, the fact that children need special feeding to promote their development – rather than mere "remnants" from the adult meal – is a new concept.

From the start of training, as early as the age of two years (but often later), the child destined to become a priest was given the honorary status of an elder, so that all information and explanations could be made available to him or her. A rule of training was that the apprentice's questions were answered truthfully in full. One chief illustrated this point with the story of his own eight-year-old son who had been apprenticed to the Ifa from early childhood. The boy approached the headmaster of his elementary school and informed him that he was a *babalawo*, or Ifa priest, and that therefore the teachers had to answer all his questions and treat him with respect. The headmaster's response was to send round to the house to find out if this were true, and then to inform the teachers that they must accord the boy the seniority he requested.

This seniority status accorded to child apprentices to the priesthood was not extended to food distribution. As stated by the father of the boy in the previous story, "We don't spoil them with food." The frequent animal sacrifices to the Ifa, however, assured a meat supply to priestly households. Some ceremonies for child apprentices also required them to eat the flesh of the animals whose powers they were to incorporate by ritual means.

A major way in which parents teach their children is by sending them on errands (Akinware et al. 1992), and their performance of errands was found by Lloyd (1970) to be the most valued. The two-year-olds in our sample already had been taught to bring or deliver needed items or information to the mother, or from the mother to another destination. Two-year-olds observed in the ethnography often were given small amounts of money and sent to purchase items. Errands school the child in following sequential instructions, carrying objects, and finding neighbourhood locations, and also teach the social skills needed for verbal and commercial transactions (Timyan 1988). Other caregivers are less likely than the mother to create and reward errands for preschool children (Akinware 1992).

Children are taught to report to their parents any kind gestures of others and to show them any gifts received, and must gradually learn how to be honest without being a tattle-tale (Babatunde 1992, 95).

PHYSICAL DISCIPLINE. Early cross-cultural comparisons (LeVine 1963; Doob 1965) characterized African parenting practices as emphasizing obedience and responsibility (Doob 1965, cited by Lloyd 1970, 83) and obedience and corporal punishment (LeVine 1963, as cited in Lloyd 1970, 83). According to Babatunde (1992, 91), when Yoruba children fail they are often flogged. The flogging is seen as an act of kindness aimed at preventing the child from becoming a difficult person, or at protecting them from true danger. This attitude is expressed in the proverb, "When the child behaves foolishly, one prays that he may not die; what kills more quickly than foolishness?"

Our study of two-year-olds found that parents used mild forms of physical punishment, such as flicking the fingertips against the child's arm, more often than the Caldwell HOME inventory provided for. The HOME item II.15: "No more than one instance of physical punishment during the past week," was modified as follows with the bracketed response rates, "Child needs spanking: never (20%); more than once a week but less than daily (75%); many times a week, can't remember exactly (8%)." Focus groups disclosed a "Spare the rod and spoil the child" attitude, and mothers in one group expressed the opinion that spanking was acceptable, but that ignoring or refusing to speak to the child was an inhumanely cruel form of discipline. Anecdotal reports of children's experiences at school (e.g. Awolowo's autobiography [Awolowo 1960]), leave no doubt of the value attached to physical punishment.

DIFFERENCES IN THE MOTHER'S AND FATHER'S PARENTING ROLES. Proverbs quoted by Babatunde (1992, 8–12) regarding the differences between the mother's and the father's relationship to the child include the following: "The mother is gold, the father is glass," which means that the affection of the mother is as durable as fine gold, whereas the father's affection, like glass, can be splintered, never to be restored; "No matter how terrible the mouth is, the owner will always lick it," refers to the mother's unending love for her child; "When the child is good it belongs to the father; if it is bad, it is the mother's," reflects the patrilineal point of view according to which the normal, well-behaved child belongs to the father, whereas the abnormal or poorly behaved child is left to its mother.

After the early period of indulgence, the father must be a keen disciplinarian and keep a cool formal relationship with the child. Dignity must be maintained by seniors to preserve their moral authority. The mother provides a gentle refuge from the father's firm discipline. One proverb, "When we use the right hand to flog the child, we use the left hand to draw him back to ourselves (make him comfortable)," expresses the two divergent parental roles.

LeVine, Klein, and Owen (1967, 239) reported that fathers in a low-income compound in Ibadan did not participate directly in childbirth or infant care, and that they ate separately from their wives and children. By contrast, élite fathers believed a man should be present at the delivery of his child, had participated in infant care, and believed that eating together as a family was important.

Our own research did not inquire into childbirth. We did, however, find a greater tendency for educated fathers in low-income neighbourhoods to eat together with their wives and children and to be listed as their two-year-olds' primary caretaker than was true for less-educated fathers. The percentages of two-year-olds eating together with their fathers and mothers three or more times a week were 45 per cent in rural areas, 53 per cent in semi-rural, and 61 per cent in urban areas. Percentages of two-year-olds having an adult male as primary caretaker were 5 per cent in rural areas, 12 per cent in semi-rural, and 18 per cent in urban areas. Almost all two-year-olds (95, 88, and 94 per cent for the three subgroups), however, played daily with their father or another adult male relative. There also was a close traditional style of father–child interaction around food: although the young child officially was served by his mother and ate separately, he would then join the father during the father's meal, during which time the father would indulge him with meat or other delicacies. Mothers verbally stated their disapproval, but also appeared proud of this "spoiling" of their children.

Relationship with other relatives and household members
In traditional compounds, the compound head had wide disciplinary responsibilities (Fadipe 1970, 108–109). Disrespect to elders, theft, disturbing the peace, or sexual impropriety usually were punished by flogging and warnings against recurrence. Repeat misbehaviour brought red pepper rubbed into flogging wounds or knife slashes on the back of the hand. In describing traditional Yoruba life, Fadipe (1970, 312–313) writes:

It is chiefly within the extended family – that is, from members of his compound – that a child obtains the bulk of his education as a member of society. Since the child cannot be continuously under the eyes of his parents and elder brothers and sisters, various members of the extended family take a hand in his education at one time or another.

But the indirect education the child receives in the compound is almost as important as the direct. In the extended family the child is afforded frequent opportunities of various experiences not only of the practical effects of many items of the social code but also of the unpleasant consequences attending their infraction. The handling and punishment of such offenses as theft or incest which occur within the household and the opinion of members on such crimes are all impressive object lessons to him.

Now, because extended families do not live together in the city, the family and community play a smaller role in training of children. Beyond the boundaries of the small urban household, 46 per cent of Olusanya's Ebute-Metta sample and only 25 per cent of his élite Suru-Lere sample said that they regularly entrusted their children to their co-tenants/neighbours (Olusanya 1981).

Our child-care findings clearly indicate trends with urbanization away from community and extended family care towards nuclear family and commercialized care, with more reliance on adult males and female friends for regular care in the urban sample, as shown in table 7.1. Mothers were read the list of caretakers in the table and asked if the child was "not left with," "usually left with," or "sometimes left with" each category. Mothers gave multiple responses; therefore, the percentages of mothers mentioning each caregiver in

169

Table 7.1 **Sources of child care by rural–urban location**

(a) Percentages of mothers mentioning each caregiver

Caretaker	Frequency of caretaking	Rural ($n = 20$)	Semi-urban ($n = 74$)	Urban ($n = 86$)
Child is own caretaker	Sometimes	15	3	3
	Usual caretaker	15	3	3
Grandmother	Sometimes	65	49	22
	Usual caretaker	35	38	19
Female relative	Sometimes	55	44	31
	Usual caretaker	15	17	11
Female friend	Sometimes	50	38	46
	Usual caretaker	5	13	18
Adult male	Sometimes	65	56	54
	Usual caretaker	5	13	18
Housemaid/foster child	Sometimes	30	11	9
	Usual caretaker	5	5	5
Older sibling	Sometimes	75	62	60
	Usual caretaker	30	28	33
Lessons or daycare	Sometimes	0	0	8
	Usual caretaker	0	0	8

(b) Frequency of caretaking according to relationship of caregivers and location of mothers

Frequency of caretaking	Relationship	Mothers (%)		
		Rural	Semi-urban	Urban
Sometimes	Total	340	260	230
	Total non-family	80	49	48
	Total nuclear family[a]	140	118	114
	Total paid	30	11	9
Usual caretaker	Total	90	101	112
	Total non-family	10	18	31
	Total nuclear family	30	28	51
	Total paid	5	5	13

a. Siblings and adult males. Most adult male caretakers were fathers. Although some undoubtedly were grandfathers and other relatives, this information is not available.

each category add to more than 100, and this total is an indicator of the amount of care available and used. The rural mothers mention more than one-third more persons with whom they sometimes leave their two-year-old than do the urban or semi-urban mothers, but fewer persons with whom they usually leave him/her. Greater casualness – and, perhaps, greater safety – of rural life is indicated by the fact that 15 per cent of rural mothers claim that their two-year-old is usually his own caretaker, compared with 3 per cent for each of the other groups. Almost twice as many rural as urban mothers sometimes leave their children with non-family (community or lineage) members, but only one-third as many rely on non-family members for usual care.

The child's more intensive reliance on fewer individuals may tend to forge the more intimate bonds expected in the urban family. Further analysis of both our child-care data and our ethnography found that children who were developing well were, indeed, in closely bonded, highly interactive families, whereas those who were developing poorly had mothers who appeared to rely on community care structures that were no longer functional in the city.

According to Fadipe (1970, 316), at least among Christians, a form of compensation for the loss of extended family structures occurs in the extension of kinship titles and principles to church members and other close friends, ranking them closely as parents and older siblings, and thereby restoring some community control.

Brothers and sisters have traditionally regarded each others' children as their own. A sister's children, who belong to another lineage or patriclan, are made welcome by their mother's brother should they wish to resettle with him (Babatunde 1992, 12). The relationship between the child and its grandparents is one of overpampering; nevertheless, it is traditional that Yoruba grandparents raise some of their grandchildren. The proverb, "the child of the elderly one is as spoiled as the left hand" (Babatunde 1992, 11), refers both to grandparent care and to the care by the mother of her last-born child.

Fostering of less well-to-do and rural children with wealthier and more urban relatives in exchange for child care and housework, has become common. Olusanya (1981) claims that this practice had mixed origins in the traditional pawning of children to work off debts as servants in the creditor's house, and in sending a young girl of the family to accompany and help a new bride at her husband's house.

Commonly, the young relative both attends school and works for the family. The distinction between such a relative and a hired nurse-maid, who also may be a distant lineage member, may be blurred.

In Olusanya's Suru-Lere sample, 31 per cent had housemaids, compared with 8 per cent in Ebute-Metta. In addition, young female relatives not attending school were present in 10 per cent of Suru-Lere and 11 per cent of Ebute-Metta families. The mean age of maids was 14.1 years in Suru-Lere, compared with 10.5 years for maids in Ebute-Metta (Olusanya 1981). Of our urban, semi-rural, and rural two-year-olds, 9 per cent, 11 per cent, and 30 per cent, respectively, were sometimes in the care of a housemaid, although only 5 per cent in each group "usually" were left with a housemaid. The average age of the eight housemaids with whom the mothers "usually" left the children was 12.3 years, compared with 11.6 years for housemaids overall. The average age of older siblings with whom the mother "usually" left the child was 10.5 years, compared with 8.8 years for siblings who sometimes cared for the child.

In our low-income sample, increased formal employment appeared to lead to greater use of paid outside day care or lessons rather than to more maids. The maids apparently served the mother more in trading and other activities than in child care, since their presence appeared highest among the rural mothers who were engaged in relatively large trading operations.

Olusanya (1981) documents that the women in his two samples who engaged in formal employment requiring separation from their children had low fertility and a high frequency of severe family stress. Much of this stress centred around the nursemaid, who was considered unreliable and a source of family conflict. Rates of formal employment away from home were 58 per cent in his Suru-Lere sample and 14 per cent in Ebute-Metta. Although different questions were asked in our study, about 20 per cent of mothers had employment to which they did not take the child, and reported leaving the child for more than six hours per day. Women who worked as skilled labourers, clerks, shopkeepers, professionals, and other higher occupational categories had higher rates of leaving the child for more than six (53 per cent) or more than eight (39 per cent) hours per day, compared with traders and vendors, for whom these figures were 28 per cent and 15 per cent. Given the much higher numbers of traders and vendors, however, the majority of children left for six or more hours belonged to these mothers.

Transitions of childhood and characteristic child-care practices
Traditionally, a woman's own mother might spend as long as a month caring for her after the birth of a baby (Fadipe 1970, 128). Divination on the third day after birth commonly set the elders' perceptions of, and expectations of, a child. While this practice has declined, divinatory revelations regarding the child's nature and destiny are not uncommon.

Frequent contact with the mother or another caretaker, often from riding on the back, diminishes as the child learns to walk. Traditionally, this close adult supervision ended at about the age of two years, when the child was weaned from the breast and joined a group of siblings for much of the day. From this time on, the child in the old-style compound was in the direct care of senior siblings, as well as adults, and in the indirect care of the entire adult community.

High priority was placed on the infant's motor development, and traditional stimulation activities promoted early attainment of motor milestones. Focus groups with Yoruba mothers and grandmothers found a preference for babies who were wiry and agile – children who learned to walk early without long remaining a burden to be carried. Walking was a major indicator of development. Folk wisdom relates that girls and later-born children walk earlier than boys and the first-born, and that spoiled children and children who are carried walk later. It was a disciplinary imperative for the child to begin to walk. The child was coaxed to start walking and was rewarded with singing and clapping. He might be given objects to hold so that he did not realize he was walking without support.

Heavy staple foods, such as cassava meal and pounded yam, tended to be withheld until the Yoruba child could walk, out of fear that he would become *wuwo*, a word applied to immobile older infants. This folk diagnosis of the "heavy or clumsy child" applied both to fat but normally nourished lazy babies and to malnourished starch-fed babies with enlarged stomachs and swelling from *kwashiorkor.*

Caretakers also promoted early standing, sitting, and crawling. Babies were encouraged to stiffen their legs to support their weight from birth. From birth, infants also were carried upright on the back, usually supported by a cloth that was not firmly fastened but that needed to be frequently retucked (like a bath towel), entailing repeated moments during which the caretaker and infant coordinated their alignment and during which the infant was momentarily exposed to the free-fall sensations of gravity. From the age of three months for girls and five months for boys, babies were propped in a sitting position in a hole in the ground or with cushions. The reason for the later age for boys was fear of crushing the testicles.

Agiobu-Kemmer (1984) observed that the Yoruba mothers trained their infants to crawl by repeatedly placing objects just beyond their reach, while Scottish mothers in her comparison study did not do so. Yet, in response to interview questions, the Yoruba mothers claimed they had done nothing special to train their children. The Yoruba parents engaged their infants in social play and motor training for a greater percentage of the time, while the Scottish mothers spent more time involving their infants in technical play.

Whiten and Milner (1984) analysed information from the same children as Agiobu-Kemmer and observed that the Yoruba infants spent about twice as much time as the British in physical contact with a caretaker. The British infants, however, were more frequently handled and positioned in a manner that enabled them to pay attention to the technical flexible manipulation of objects. British mothers scored three times higher than the Yoruba on a scale that measured the amount of time the caretaker spent structuring the infant's immediate posture and environment so that the child could manipulate and explore the uses and properties of objects.

In a preliterate society, as Nigeria used to be, memory was a prized form of intelligence. For brainpower, children were given a powdered concoction called *isoye*, which was believed to supplement the intelligence and ensure a good memory. The *isoye* ordered by one of the authors to improve the memory of her eight-year-old son came as eight paper-wrapped doses of black powder to be taken at periodic intervals. The boy was to dip his finger first in highest-grade red palm oil, then into the powder, which he should lick from his finger, continuing this process until the powder from the packet was finished.

Focus group discussions on the definition of the child revealed that Yoruba parents in Lagos most commonly defined childhood in relation to the self-reliance and autonomy of the growing person. According to some of those interviewed, once a child could talk, walk, dress him- or herself, and do certain other things around the house, he or she was no longer referred to as a child. Others defined childhood as the period prior to puberty. Childhood was further defined in terms of economic independence: once a person began to earn a living, he or she ceased to be called a child. The common element expressed in these definitions of childhood was dependency on others for care, protection, and development, as a result of age.

Relationships among siblings

The bond between siblings of the same mother is closer than between half-siblings of the same father only, although good fathers and good co-wives consciously minimize these differences by scrupulous fairness and equal displays of affection. In the previous century, the only form of inheritance was between full siblings, a custom that has long since changed to inheritance passing from parents to children (Fadipe 1970, 140–146), with half-siblings inheriting from the same father but only from their own mothers.

Ranked by seniority in age, more than by gender, older siblings supervise and care for younger ones. According to Fadipe (1970, 130ff.), a child in a strictly regulated family had to obey the orders of older siblings as soon as he was past the infancy stage. Families who were lax in this respect were reproached by relatives and neighbours if a younger child asserted himself against his older brother or sister. The practice of handing a whip to the older child and instructing him to use it on his junior whenever the latter first became offensive and insubordinate towards him was very commonly used to instil respect and obedience in a rebellious junior. Even the most tolerant families could not permit insubordination of a child towards another who was six years his senior, as a difference of six years was the basis for exclusion from membership in a traditional age-set system that has fallen into disuse.

Social network and family support system

Lineage membership guarantees an extended social welfare system not provided by the state. In fact, loyalty to one's kinship group rather than to the state is viewed as a major problem for development (Babatunde 1992).

Yoruba concept of life

The cultural context

Family goals as well as parenting practices are shaped by cultural concepts of the good life. Although Yoruba cultural ideals are in transition, it is important to understand the world view in which they are anchored. Traditionally, the good life is realized materially in this world as part of the eternal revolving cycle, from the living, to the ancestors, to the unborn. Earthly success is a main feature of traditional religion; death and diseases must be defeated, and virility and fertility must be supported. According to Hallgren (1991, 120–122), the key statement from the Yoruba religious tradition regarding the nature of the good life is, "Wealth, wives, and children will keep us from obscurity." The person who leads a good life attains wealth and transfers this to the next generation in a virtuous manner. Money is needed to obtain wives, and wives are necessary for the birth of children. Children are most important of all, as they are the forward-flowing stream of immortality.

Traditionally, in a manner consistent with the fact that the family acted as both a production and a consumption unit, prestige was not tied to individual occupational categories – the prestige of the individual was not a function of his occupation as it is in the West (Aronson 1980, 94–96). In colloquial Yoruba, occupations were classed together in two categories – "clerk" and "trader" – neither with status implications. Now, however, these views appear to be changing, as parents have strong opinions about the high-status occupations they desire for their children.

"Children, money, and health/prosperity/authority ... I want it so" is possibly a more modern proverbial formulation of traditional values, quoted by Aronson (1980, 156–257). In Yoruba, this quotation uses the word *alafia*, which comes from the Arabic word for health, and which perhaps replaces the Yoruba words for wealth and for honour (both pronounced "ola" but with different tonal accents). According to Aronson (156–157), *alafia* is a word for well-being that combines physical health, peace of mind, material prosperity, harmonious relationships, and a reputation for wisdom. The goal of achieving *alafia* has implications for the lifestyle of the self-actualized individual, according to this ideal.

Lloyd (1966, 332) has described traditional Yoruba society as one in which wealthy and powerful men did not stand apart as a separate class, but were at the "apices of groups consisting of kin and followers." Lloyd (1972) has also noted that the demands of such leadership roles diverted successful older men away from further accumulation of wealth through businesses, the management of which they would then delegate to others. At the apex of a large compound and a wide group of followers, the successful leader led a life of relative leisure and sedentariness (Aronson 1980, 159), holding court to supervise household management, mediate problems, and advise on business activities, and participating in day-to-day politics in the offices of more powerful patrons. This pattern may be compared to the pre-industrial use of capital in Europe (Dizard and Gadlin 1990, 27), whereby the upper classes spent their surplus in sumptuous leisure, viewing work as a curse rather than a virtue.

This role provides for those who become revered ancestors to continue as the most senior members in the social structure of the lineage after death, as the dead continue their earthly roles as long as they remain in the memory of their descendants (Hallgren 1991, 68). According to traditional religious beliefs, however, those who lead bad or childless lives and die without funeral rites are like broken crockery and at death are thrown onto the rubbish heap of the "heaven of potsherds," where they cease their participation in the eternal cycle of rebirth, or may be reborn as animals.

Ethics and values
While most of the Yoruba now are Christian or Muslim (in our sample, 40 per cent were Muslim, 58 per cent Christian, and 2 per cent traditional), the similarity between the value systems of the world religions and those of Yoruba traditional religion must have facilitated conversion. Adewale (1986) reviews traditional Yoruba religious values as embodied in the extensive oral texts (Odu) of Ifa divination. He claims, "There are only two questions for Yoruba moralists: what conduct do the gods command and what conduct do the gods forbid? Why the gods sanction or disapprove one or another line of conduct does not matter much." The core values expressed in Ifa are first of all respect, loyalty, and devotion to one's parents. The ethical person must not tell lies, be a talebearer, or break contractual agreements. Faithfulness and loyalty are also due to one's lineage members, to one's government, and to one's friends.

Traditional Yoruba values presented by Babatunde (1992, 83–115) include kindness/goodness/moral power for effecting good, bravery, respect for seniority, truthfulness, reliability, diplomacy, and the art of dissembling for the greater good of the whole. The Yoruba word for "kindness/goodness" literally means a good "inside" (stomach and heart, or the totality of the physical substance within the person). A cruel person has a bitter inner self, and someone so kind as to ignore his own needs has a distorted stomach or inner self. A kind person redistributes wealth to others, but not at his own expense. Acts of kindness should begin at home in the immediate and extended family.

Bravery is viewed in terms of physical, metaphysical, medicinal, and moral power, and is an essential attribute for both males and females. Use of wisdom is superior to use of physical strength, and foolhardiness is not permissible. Women are praised for showing courage in childbirth. The Yoruba word for "kindness/goodness" noted above also implies moral courage. Endurance also is associated with bravery.

The moral obligation to tell the truth is tempered by the fact that "the truth is bitter," and must be spoken with regard to context and consequences, as reflected in the proverb, "It is not all that the eye sees that the mouth speaks." Moreover, "obligations of seniority institutionalize telling lies in order to give the impression that the system works" (Babatunde 1992, 114). This statement refers to contingencies when neither the junior nor the senior person can live up to the expectations of the seniority system – when it works better to maintain appearances by lying than to expose discrepancies. Verbal contracts, however, must be kept, and failure to do so reliably may be punished by Ogun, the divinity of iron and patron of first-born sons.

Diplomacy includes the gift for communication through gesture and innuendo, combining wisdom with a capacity to be devious and to keep the inner self hidden in the interests of the whole. Quoting Lienhardt (1980, 71, as cited by Babatunde 1992):

... from childhood the Yoruba are not only supposed to have an idea of a hidden, private self (an inner "activity" or thought process) ... but to understand that it may ultimately be more important than the outer activity, the persona, or mask ... presented to others.

Linked to skills of diplomacy is the overarching value of protecting the survival and unity of the social group, by dissembling as necessary. A leader is expected to put the good of the group above the expression of lesser values, and is expected to be his or her own judge of occasions on which such dissembling is needed.

TEACHING MANNERS AND VALUES. According to Adewale (1986), there are no separate teachers of moral education. All adults inculcate moral values in children to ensure a healthy and disciplined society.

SOCIAL EXPRESSIONS OF THE YORUBA VALUE SYSTEM. The "man of principle" (Bascom 1969) is gentlemanly, fearless, socially responsible, and generous. Social responsibility is elaborately articulated through the etiquette of greetings and exchange of resources. As noted earlier, the Yoruba language has a salutation for every conceivable occasion, situation, and human relationship – while sitting or standing;

when overtaking another on the road, at work, or at play; while carrying a load; in cold or in warm weather; for relatives, friends, and strangers. On the first meeting of the day for people from different compounds, general and specific inquiries must be made about all close relatives (Fadipe 1970, 301–302). An extension of the greeting code is the obligation to offer condolences or sympathy to anyone who is bereaved, ill, injured, or even momentarily indisposed. Hospitality is emphasized, with older and wealthier persons expected regularly to express their generosity through giving. Warmth, a spirit of fun, cooperation, trust, and mutual help are core values expressed through these practices. Unsympathetic and covetous attitudes breed distrust and could lead to suspicion of witchcraft.

References

Adewale, S.A. 1986. "Ethics in Ifa." In: S.O. Abogunrin, ed. *Religion and Ethics in Nigeria*. Ibadan, Nigeria: Daystar Press, pp. 60–71.

Afonja, S. 1990. "Changing Patterns of Gender Stratification in West Africa." In: A. Tinker, ed. *Persistent Inequalities. Women and World Development*. New York: Oxford University Press.

Agiobu-Kemmer, I. 1984. "Cognitive and Affective Aspects of Infant Development." In: H.V. Curran, ed. *Nigerian Children: Developmental Perspectives*. Boston: Routledge and Kegan Paul, pp. 74–117.

Aina, T.A., M.F. Zeitlin, K. Setiolane, and H. Armstrong. 1992. "Phase I Survey Results: Positive Deviance in Nutrition Research Project, Lagos State, Nigeria." Draft Report.

Akinware, M., E.B. Wilson-Oyelaran, P.A. Ladipo, D. Pierce, and M.F. Zeitlin. 1992. *Child Care and Development in Nigeria: A Profile of Five UNICEF-Assisted LGAs*. Lagos: UNICEF.

Aronson, D.R. 1980. *The City is Our Farm*. Cambridge, Mass.: Schenkman.

Awolowo, O. 1960. *Awo: The Autobiography of Chief Obafemi Awolowo*. Cambridge (UK): Cambridge University Press.

Babatunde, E.D. 1992. *Culture, Religion, and the Self: A Critical Study of Bini and Yoruba Value Systems in Change*. Lewiston, NY: Edwin Mellen Press.

Bascom, W.A. 1951. "Yoruba Food." *Africa* 21: 40–53.

Bascom, W.A. 1969. *Ifa Divination; Communication Between Gods and Men in West Africa*. Bloomington, Ind.: Indiana University Press, pp. 493–497.

Bayley, N. 1969. *Manual for the Bayley Scales of Infant Development*. New York: Psychological Corporation.

Berry, S.S. 1985. *Fathers Work for Their Sons: Accumulation, Mobility and Class Formation in an Extended Yoruba Community*. Berkeley, Calif.: University of California Press.

Bledsoe, C. 1990. "Transformations in Sub-Saharan African Marriage and Fertility." *Annals, AAPSS* 510: 115–125.

Caldwell, B.M., and R.H. Bradley. 1984. *Home Observation for Measurement of the Environment*. Little Rock, Ark.: University of Arkansas.

Caldwell, J.C. 1976. *The Socioeconomic Explanation of High Fertility. The Changing African Family Series. Monograph No. 1.* Canberra: Australian National University Press.

———, and P. Caldwell. 1977. "The Economic Rationale of High Fertility: An Investigation Illustrated with Nigerian Survey Data." *Population Studies* 31: 5–27.

Dizard, J.E., and H. Gadlin. 1990. *The Minimal Family.* Amherst, Mass.: University of Amherst Press.

Doob, L.W. 1965. "Psychology." In: R.A. Lystad, ed. *The African World: A Survey of Social Research.* New York: Praeger, pp. 373–415.

Eades, J.S. 1980. *The Yoruba Today.* Cambridge (UK): Cambridge University Press.

Fadipe, N.A. 1970. *The Sociology of the Yoruba.* Ibadan: Ibadan University Press.

Federal Republic of Nigeria and UNICEF. 1990. *Children and Women in Nigeria: A Situation Analysis.* Lagos: Federal Republic of Nigeria and UNICEF.

Goode, W. 1963. *World Revolution and Family Patterns.* Glencoe, Ill.: Free Press.

Gugler, J., and W.G. Flanagan. 1978. *Urbanization and Social Change in West Africa.* New York: Cambridge University Press.

Gussler, J.D. 1975. "Adaptive Strategies and Social Networks of Women in St. Kitts." In: B. Bourguigno, ed. *A World of Women.* New York: Praeger, pp. 185–209.

Guyer, J.I. 1990. *Changing Nuptuality in a Nigerian Community: Observations from the Field. Working Papers in African Studies, No. 146.* Boston, Mass.: African Studies Center, Boston University.

Hallgren, R. 1991. *The Good Things in Life. A Study of the Traditional Religious Culture of the Yoruba People.* New York: Plus Ultra.

Hogan, D. 1985. *Class and Reform.* Philadelphia: University of Pennsylvania Press.

LeVine, R.A. 1963. "Child Rearing in Sub-Saharan Africa: An Interim Report." *Bulletin of the Menninger Clinic* 27: 245–256.

———. 1974. "Parental Goals: A Cross-Cultural View." *Teachers College Records* 76: 2.

———, N.H. Klein, and C.R. Owen. 1967. Father–Child Relationships and Changing Lifestyles in Ibadan, Nigeria. In: H. Miner, ed. *The City in Modern Africa.* New York: Praeger, pp. 215–255.

———, P.M. Miller, and M.M. West, eds. 1988. *Parental Behavior in Diverse Societies: New Directions for Child Development, No. 40.* San Francisco: Jossey-Bass.

Lienhardt, R.G. 1980. "Self: Public, Private. Some African Representations." *J.A.S.O.* 11(2): 69–82.

Lloyd, B.B. 1966. "Education in Family Life in the Development of Class Identification among the Yoruba." In: P.C. Lloyd, ed. *New Elites of Tropical Africa.* London: Oxford University Press, pp. 163–183.

———. 1970. "Yoruba Mothers' Reports of Child-rearing, Some Theoretical and Methodological Considerations." In: P. Mayer, ed. *Socialization, The Approach from Social Anthropology.* New York: Tavistock Press, pp. 75–108.

Lloyd, P.C. 1972. *Africa in Social Change.* Baltimore, Md.: Penguin.

———. 1974. *Power and Independence, Urban Africans' Perception of Social Inequality.* London: Routledge and Kegan Paul.

Mabogunje, A.L. 1968. *Urbanization in Nigeria.* London: University of London Press.

Nigeria Fertility Survey, 1981/82. 1984. *Principal Report. World Fertility Survey International Statistical Institute.* Lagos: National Population Bureau.

Okediji, O.O., and F.O. Okediji. 1966. "Marital Stability and Social Structure in an African City." *Nigerian Journal of Economic and Social Studies* 8(1): 151–163.

Olusanya, P.O. 1970. "Notes on Some Factors Affecting the Stability of Marriage among the Yoruba of Western Nigeria." *Journal of Marriage and the Family* 32: 150–155.

———. 1981. *Nursemaids and the Pill: A Study of Household Structure, Female Employment, and the Small Family Ideal in an African Metropolis. University of Ghana Population Studies No. 9.* Lagos: Tyburn Enterprises.

———. 1987. "Human Reproduction in Africa: Fact, Myth and the Martyr Syndrome." Lecture, Department of Sociology, University of Lagos.

Sembajwe, I.S.L. 1981. *Fertility and Infant Mortality Amongst the Yoruba in Western Nigeria. Changing Family Project Series, Monograph No. 6.* Canberra: Australian National University Press.

Teriba, O., and O.A. Philips. 1971. "Income Distribution and National Integration." *Nigerian Journal of Economic and Social Studies* 13: 77–122.

Timyan, J. 1988. "Cultural Aspects of Psycho-Social Development: An Examination of West African Childrearing Practices." Report Prepared for the Regional UNICEF Workshop, "Toward a strategy for enhancing early childhood development in the West and Central Africa region," Abidjan, 18–22 January 1988.

Tuden, A., and L. Plotnicov. 1970. *Social Stratification in Africa.* New York: Free Press.

Werner, E.E. 1979. *Cross-Cultural Child Development: A View from the Planet Earth.* Monterey, Calif.: Brooks Cole.

Whiten, A., and P. Milner. 1984. "The Educational Experiences of Nigerian Infants." In: H.V. Curran, ed. *Nigerian Children: Developmental Perspectives.* Boston: Routledge and Kegan Paul, pp. 34–73.

Zeitlin, M.F., J.D. Wray, J.B. Stanbury, N.P. Schlossman, J.J. Meurer, and P.J. Weinthal. 1982. *Nutrition and Population Growth: The Delicate Balance.* Cambridge, Mass.: Oelgeschlager, Gunn, and Hain.

8

Structural models of family social health theory

Conceptualization of the family system model

In this study we have used data from Indonesia and Nigeria to develop an exploratory empirical model of family-level characteristics that determine child welfare and development. Through this model we hope to improve our understanding of the ways in which family resources influence family management, beliefs, and caring behaviours, including emotional climate and child-care quality within the home, and through which family management, beliefs, and caring behaviours influence the development of the children. Because child development is measured multidimensionally, this model integrates several family components that potentially influence each dimension of child development. Although we have conducted this analysis with respect to child outcomes, we believe that the well-being of other family members is similarly determined. We used structural equation modelling with latent variables (Bollen 1989), also known as LISREL (Jöreskog and Sörbom 1989).

Myers (1992) distinguished between the definitions of child growth and child development. He defined growth as "a change in size," whereas development was defined as "changes in complexity and function." For practical purposes, we use the term "child development" to refer to both child growth (as measured by anthropometric indicators) and child mental development (characterized by the mental development index or IQ, the physical development index for younger children, and the social development index for older children). The terms are separated for measurement and analysis purposes, however.

The general family functioning model is presented in figure 8.1. In this general conceptual form, the model is applicable to both Nigerian (the Yoruba) and Indonesian (the Javanese) cultures. The overall set of variables and the indicators designed to measure each factor may vary between the Yoruba and the Javanese (see Appendix to this chapter) because the same type of data were not always available for both cultures, and some factors that influence family management, beliefs, and caring behaviours are culturally specific.

The first level of this model, "Family Resources," includes both material (no. 1) and social (no. 2) resources. Many factors at this level of the model are measures of socio-economic status, such as housing, food budget, literacy and educational level, and media use. These factors feed into the next level of the model, "Family Management, Beliefs, and Caring Behaviours." These encompass measures of hygiene (no. 3) and feeding practices (no. 4), parents' caregiving behaviours (affection and attention, no. 5), and academic stimulation (no. 6). These factors, in turn, determine the child's growth and development (no. 7).

Figure 8.2 presents a more detailed version of the model. Additional factors not listed in figure 8.2 are community endowment and support from within the family. These two factors are conceptually related to sociocultural support and are tested only in the Javanese models (fig. 8.3–8.7). We hypothesize that sociocultural support influences family management and caring behaviours. Sociocultural support includes support from the family and other kin (the father's involvement in child care and the mother's satisfaction from support received from family and relatives) and community support/endowment (the number of health facilities and community health indicators). We do not have information on maternal satisfaction and community endowment in the Nigerian data set; therefore, the role of these factors is tested in the Javanese data set only. Our literature review on Javanese families indicates that fathers also are involved in child-care activities, especially after the child has begun to walk; therefore, it is culturally appropriate to test this aspect in the Javanese setting with samples of older children. The father's involve-

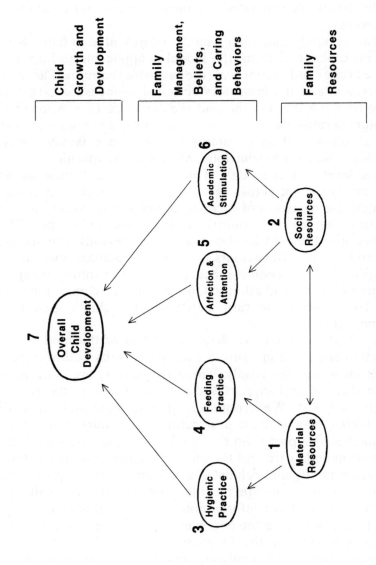

Fig. 8.1 **Simplified conceptual family functioning model, based on Nigerian data**

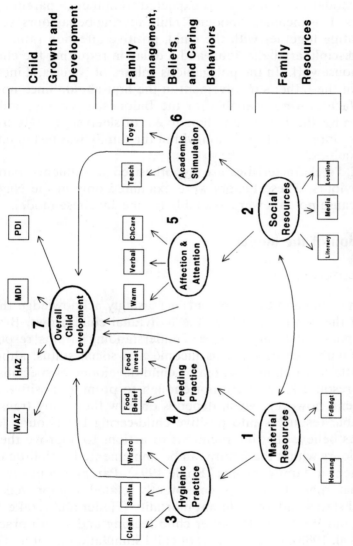

Fig. 8.2 Detailed conceptual model, based on Nigerian data. See Appendix for full explanation of abbreviated terms

ment in child-rearing in Yoruba families is less clear and, therefore, was not tested.

Two other factors not listed in figure 8.2 are modernizing lifestyle and child personality; these are included in figures 8.8–8.10 (Nigerian models). Modernizing lifestyle is expected to influence parental care behaviours. This includes "modern" child-rearing behaviours, such as parents eating together with the child, positive affection rather than negative disciplinary behaviour, and a delay in requiring the child to perform housework. In the polygamous culture of Nigeria, it includes the level of the father's involvement in the household. Since no data on these factors were available for the Indonesian sample, and it is uncommon for the Javanese fathers to eat or sleep separately from a wife and children, modernization within the family was tested only in Yoruba families.

The child's characteristics are hypothesized to influence parental care behaviours. These factors were examined only in the Nigerian model because no data were available for the Javanese model.

Justification of the model

Family resources

Professionals in child development increasingly acknowledge the influence of the context in which the individual child grows. Bradley (1989) emphasized the importance of understanding parents' responses to other family factors, such as income and social status, although there is little research in this area by child development specialists.

Family resources alone are not enough to promote positive child development, however. Much depends on how the family translates the available resources into positive child-caring behaviours. Many researchers believe that interventions or actions to improve the caring behaviours within the family can be implemented with little or no improvement in family income (Engle 1992). Parental education, especially maternal education, is consistently related to improved child nutritional status and lower infant mortality (Heller and Drake 1979; Behrman and Wolfe 1984), better child feeding and health practices (Zeitlin et al. 1988), a higher level of child stimulation (Zeitlin, Ghassemi, and Mansour 1990), greater use of health care services (Grant 1984), lower fertility, and more child-centred care behaviours (Ware 1984). Some researchers argue that the positive association between mother's schooling and child health is not due primarily to the effect of schooling *per se*; instead, schooling serves largely as a proxy for unobserved characteristics related to her childhood background. A study in Nicaragua that controlled for the heterogeneity in unobserved maternal endowment through the shared childhood experience of adult sisters found that the impact of the mother's education declines substantially. Behrman and Wolfe (1987) also found that maternal schooling effects evaporate when the maternal endowment (abilities, habits, and health status related to childhood family background) is controlled for, thus raising doubts about standard estimates of the impact of maternal schooling on child welfare.

A study of infant development in South India confirms the argument that maternal childhood experience is related to positive caring behaviour. Landers (1989) found adequate growth and cognitive performance among three-month-old babies despite the poor environment and high biological risks. In this case, cultural patterns of child care, such as maternal proximity and a high degree of psychosocial commitment of the mothers, supported positive child development during infancy.

In our Javanese model we used measures of the social network to represent family social resources. The social network provides families with a sense of integration in the community and an opportunity to obtain interpersonal gratification and material resources. In the industrialized world, social isolation has been associated with child abuse (Belsky 1984). Women of higher social class in Java were found to interact less often with neighbours and, in Nigeria, to exchange child care less often with neighbours (Olusanya 1981). In the United States, low-income families in Detroit viewed neighbourhood friends as more intimate than non-neighbourhood friends, whereas high-income families described their neighbourhood friends as less intimate than non-local friends (Fischer 1977); non-local friends can be part of the social network too, however.

Family management, beliefs, and caring behaviours

Our measures of "Family Management, Beliefs, and Caring Behaviours" are similar to "family climate" (Schneewind 1989) and "parental personality" (Belsky 1984) and include feeding and hygiene behaviours along with other factors in child caregiving noted by Engle (1992) in her definition of "care." In our own case, these measures rely on the mother's report of family practices and on observations of the mother–child dyad and the home environment. Family climate or parental personality imply a human locus of control or executive function with values operated by the family as a unit. The term "Family Management and Caring Behaviour" in this study is defined as (1) the extent to which decisions to allocate family resources are made and monitored by a central executive function for the achievement of a rational optimization strategy, (2) health and hygiene behaviours, as determined by cultural norms, and (3) parental personality.

Family climate, or "inner-family socialization activity" (Schneewind 1989) or "parental personality" (Belsky 1984), is a transactional relationship between parents and children. It determines to what extent the family's potential resources can be transformed for the benefit of family members. Family climate includes maternal affection and environmental stimulation.

Belsky (1984) asserts that parental personality is the most influential factor in determining child outcome. Optimal child development is promoted by parents whose caregiving is attentive, physically demonstrative, stimulating, responsive, and non-restrictive. Based on a literature review, Belsky, Lerner, and Spanier (1984) found that a high level of overall maternal attentiveness at five months (as measured by the frequency with which the mother looked at, touched, held, or spoke to the baby) predicted high levels of infant exploratory activity. Attentiveness may be a proxy for other maternal qualities and behaviours that facilitate the infant's intellectual growth because other positive caregiving personality traits are also able to predict the intellectual and emotional development of infants (Belsky, Lerner, and Spanier 1984). A review of the positive deviance literature found that caregiver–child interactions associated with adequate growth and development included a high degree of physical interaction (holding and hugging), speaking and responding to a child's vocalizations, establishing frequent eye contact, responding to the child's needs, creating a stimulating physical environment for the child, and enhancing the child's initiative and creativity (Zeitlin, Ghassemi, and Mansour 1990).

Studies of family ecology (e.g. the amount and availability of toys and rooms) did not support the assumption that the physical environment was important for development of cognitive skills (Hwang, Lamb, and Broberg 1989; Kreppner 1989). When the quality of mother–child interactions was added to environment variables, a greater association was found (Wachs 1984). Family interactions, such as the involvement of fathers in child care, seemed more significant for child development than the physical environment (Hwang, Lamb, and Broberg 1989).

We do not have direct measures on family cohesion. We postulate that families with a high degree of paternal involvement are more cohesive. The pattern of fathering also reflects the quality of the marital relationship. Belsky, Lerner, and Spanier (1984) pointed out that marital quality can be a powerful predictor of fathering. We assume that fathers who are involved in child care are not in conflict with their spouses or are at least available to care for their children. When considering family variables that affect children's mental health, enduring family conflict is seen to have the most negative impact (Colletta 1991).

Support and community endowment

Sociocultural support determines the quality of care the mother is able to give her infant. "Intimate" support is provided by the immediate family, and "community" support comes from neighbourhood and workplace associations (Zeitlin, Ghassemi, and Mansour 1990).

Bronfenbrenner, Moen, and Garbarino (1984) reviewed the significance of health services in the community in the context of family well-being and concluded that the use of health services is influenced by access to services, their availability and quality, and the orientations of service providers to the clients. They also noted that the provision of health services to individuals rather than to the family is a major source of inefficiency and inequities. The disorganization of health services in the United States, for example, in which different services are provided in different locations, creates logistical difficulties for families seeking multiple services. This has led to efforts to develop a new model of comprehensive health care along neighbourhood lines.

The idea of *posyandu* services (integrated health care services, family planning, nutrition education, immunization, prenatal care, supplementations, and oral rehydration therapy) in Indonesia provides one-stop multiple services for the family rather than for individuals. There is ample evidence that this kind of service has positive effects on child welfare in Indonesia.

Grandmothers in both Nigeria and Indonesia provide child care and emotional support (See chs. 6 and 7). Rohner's cross-cultural study (Rohner 1975) found that mothers who are unable to get away from the burden of child care from time to time are more likely to withdraw warmth and affection and to reject their children than mothers who have another adult to help them with child care. When grandparents are present, children are more likely to receive adequate warmth. Similar findings also were observed in some African cultures (Minturn and Lambert 1964) and in developed countries (Bengston and Robertson 1985; Hwang, Lamb, and Broberg 1989).

Alternate caregivers, especially grandparents, not only assume some of the burden of child care, but also serve as additional teachers of social skills and models for adaptive behaviour. Moreover, they can improve the quality of parental behaviours by providing emotional support and advice.

In Nigeria, fathers enjoy playing with their young children and may be alternative caretakers, but only if they regularly live with the child. In our sample, most fathers (74 per cent) always live in the same house as their wives and children but might occupy a separate bedroom. This pattern also has been documented in Kenya (Whiting and Whiting 1975). The intimacy of the father's role in child care is also determined by the degree of modernization (Caldwell and Caldwell 1977).

In Java (ch. 6), fathers can be secondary caregivers even before the children reach the age of five. Usually, husbands live in the same house as their wives and children. This conforms to the Whitings' findings that when a father shares a room with his wife, he is more likely to become involved in child care.

Community endowment is defined structurally. The community is

... a territorially bounded social system or set of interlocking or integrated functional subsystems (economic, political, religious ...) serving a resident population, plus the material culture of physical plant through which the subsystems operate. The community concept does not include such characteristics as harmony, love, or intimacy ... but it does include a minimum of consensus. (International Encyclopedia of Social Sciences 1968, 3: 163)

Modernizing lifestyle

Kohn's work (Kohn 1969) showed that working-class fathers, whose jobs require compliance and obedience, tend to hold values that stress obedience in their children, whereas middle-class fathers, whose jobs require effective intellectual functioning and self-direction, value intellectual development and independence in their children (Kohn 1969). Our literature review on Javanese families shows that there is little class difference with respect to child obedience and compliance: child obedience is still preferred by the majority of Javanese parents, even among the professional parents (about 50 per cent, according to Hoffman's study [Hoffman 1988]). However, LeVine, Klein, and Owen (1967), Lloyd (1970), and our own study found in Nigeria that élite and modernizing parents appeared to be less restrictive of their children's aggressive behaviour, and to value self-reliance and responsibility more than traditional parents.

In the case of Nigeria, modernization within the family can be partially characterized by the living arrangements. The norm for the traditional family is usually polygamy, when a man can afford more than one wife. This means that the same family may be more "modern" in its early phases and more traditional in later phases when affluence permits the acquisition of more than one wife. In monogamous families, the father lives in the same house all the time.

Child's characteristics

In Nigeria, the child's characteristics of individuality are assumed to be related to parental care. Belsky's literature review (Belsky 1984) cited several studies that linked the child's temperament with parenting and concluded that a difficult temperament, especially in infancy, can undermine parental functioning. The relationship between a child's personality and parental care behaviours can be reciprocal, however (Morris 1969). Parental personality, such as responsiveness and the ability of the mother to form a strong bond with her child, also can shape the child's personality.

The synergistic relationship between child growth and child development

Child growth and child mental development are mutually related. The synergistic relationship between these factors has been noted by several authors (Zeitlin, Ghassemi, and Mansour 1990; Myers 1992). Zeitlin and co-workers (Zeitlin, Ghassemi, and Mansour 1990) reviewed numerous studies to examine the link between psychosocial well-being, nutritional thriving, and health. They concluded that psychological stress has a detrimental effect on the use of nutrients, whereas psychological well-being enhances growth.

Myers (1992) also reviewed the literature to establish the link

191

between growth and mental development. He offers the following summary:

... satisfying psychosocial needs can have an effect on nutritional status through its effect on metabolism linked to stress reduction, and by helping to produce changes in the care demanded and provided. At the same time, nutrition is seen to have an effect on psychosocial development, operating primarily through its impact on attention, responsiveness, independence, irritability, and affect. Nutrition is one of a complex of factors operating to influence that development and associated behavior. (Myers 1992, 188)

An application of structural modelling

Quantitative estimates of the relative strength of pathways between elements in the family behaviour model are obtained by specifying and estimating several structural equation models. Structural equations with latent variables permit the analyst to join all the important theoretical relationships in a data set together in the same comprehensive mathematical model. The term "structural" refers to the assumption that the parameters both are descriptive measures of association and reveal an invariant "causal" relation (Bollen 1989). In fact, this technique does not prove causality, but rather tests whether the causal assumptions defined in the model match the associations "found" in a sample of data. The use of structural modelling may be thought of as an attempt to represent explicitly both the direct influence of one variable on another, and the indirect influence that may occur through a third variable. An advantage of structural modelling is that it allows for separate estimates of these direct and indirect effects.

"Path" diagrams, such as those in figures 8.3–8.10, are a convenient way of visualizing these effects. The overall theory is used to specify a set of pathways between a set of idealized variables. Idealized variables are usually abstract concepts that cannot be precisely measured in practice. These idealized variables are referred to as "latent variables" and are shown as ovals on the path diagram. A latent variable is understood to be an underlying cause that influences a set of measurable outcomes, or "measured variables," represented by rectangles. We infer the values of the latent variable indirectly by measuring the outcomes it causes, and by entering these measured variables into factor analysis. The factor on which they load is a mathematical representation of the latent or idealized variable. Paths from each oval latent variable link it to its rectangular measured (or "proxy") variables. A single path from one variable to another represents a single direction of causation. When two paths link a pair of variables, they represent the simultaneous influence of the variables on each other.[1] For example, in the Javanese growth model (fig. 8.3), growth is a latent variable that explains some of the variation of two measured variables – weight-for-age Z-score (WAZ), and height-for-age Z-score (HAZ).

Prior to estimating a structural model, it is necessary to choose a scale for the latent variables, and to make sure that all of the paths can be identified with the available information. Following common practice, we have allowed each latent variable to have the same scale as one of the measured variables it determines. Our figures present the standardized values of all path coefficients for easy comparison. Estimating a structural model involves estimating the path coefficients and the error variances. The estimates presented here are maximum likelihood estimates generated by the CALIS procedure of the SAS statistical program.[2] The path coefficient, like a standardized regression coefficient, can be thought of as a measure of the strength of a relationship (or the percentage of variance in the dependent variable explained by the independent variable).

The coefficients show the relative importance of the pathways. The asterisks reflect the significance levels at which we can reject the hypothesis that the true path value equals zero (* represents p-value between .05 and .025 level, ▲ represents p-value between .025 and .01 level, and # represents < 0.01 level).

There is no measure for the overall fit of a system of equations that is as simple to interpret as the R^2 measure used for a single regression equation. Two descriptive goodness-of-fit measures are the Bentler–Bonnet statistic (BB fit index) and the adjusted GFI (goodness-of-fit index): the BB fit index gives the change in the value of a test statistic as a proportion of its value in a baseline model; the adjusted GFI gives the explained proportion of variances and covariances with an adjustment for degrees of freedom.

The total effects of each independent variable of interest can be broken down into direct and indirect effects. While the path coefficients shown in the figures represent the direct effects of one variable on another, the total effects represent both the direct and indirect effects. Both effects are of potential interest for policy purposes.

Technical limitations of the current model

The structural equation modelling technique provides promise for future use because of its comprehensiveness in covering different techniques such as factor analysis, regression, and other econometric procedures. This study is an exploratory analysis to illustrate a technique that will become increasingly important in the areas of family and child development research. Given the exploratory nature of this study, there are some limitations that should be mentioned. We hope that our descriptions of model limitations will give insights for other researchers who will use similar techniques in the future. The limits of this study originated from both the modelling process and the state-of-the-art of the techniques that are not yet well developed. We developed complicated models with very limited sample sizes. We took into account all factors in the family simultaneously in order to eliminate some variable omission bias. This is like a correction for widely used simple techniques such as ANOVA, ANCOVA and other simplistic statistical tools that do not take into account other potential confounding factors simultaneously; therefore, despite the limitations mentioned further below, we consider this to be less biased. Also, the directions of the associations and the significance levels of parameters in this study are consistent with the theory of the family, and other empirical findings using different techniques.

A major problem in the application of maximum likelihood estimation to structural models is that most of the current theory and software is based on the assumption of multivariate normality. In practice, it is not unusual for measured variables to be ordinal scales, even when the latent variables are normally distributed.

Bollen (1989) summarizes some consequences of using categorical variables in estimating these models: first, non-normality can influence the values of test statistics; second, the coefficient estimates for the paths may be attenuated. Despite non-normality, if there is no restriction on the variances and covariances imposed in the exogenous variables, we still can get consistent estimates, and significant tests (K. Bollen 1992, lecture note). Little is known about the robustness of structural equation techniques when categorical variables are used.

Many of the variables in this study are ordinal indices based on responses from survey questions. Because of the uncertain impact of using ordinal data, we do not rely on the commonly used chi-square statistic to evaluate the overall goodness-of-fit of the model. We also are inclined to be cautious about accepting or rejecting paths based solely on the conventional significance levels of test statistics.

Although theoretical results on the impact of using categorical variables are incomplete, simulation studies suggest that the attenuation of coefficients is smaller when ordinal variables include more categories. Since all but two of the variables used in this study have more than five categories, we felt that the known gains from an explicit modelling of the measurement errors would outweigh the possible losses due to the categorical nature of many of the variables.

One suggestion for the treatment of correlations involving categorical data has been to model the categories as representing measures of underlying continuous variables. The correlations of these underlying continuous variables can then be estimated with polychoric or polyserial correlations.[3] The usual Pearson correlation tends to understate these correlations by a substantial amount when there are few categories in the ordinal variables.

Since neither SAS nor other software at our disposal computes polychoric and polyserial correlations, we conducted a simple ad hoc test to see if our results were likely to be sensitive to the use of Pearson correlations. Each Pearson correlation value for continuous–ordinal variable pairs and ordinal–ordinal variable pairs was increased by 25 per cent and the model was re-estimated. About 90 per cent of the *t*-statistics of estimated parameters became more significant with the modified correlations, but the basic conclusions did not change. Therefore, we have elected to present results based on the Pearson correlations with the understanding that the path coefficients may be underestimated.

The presence of multivariate outliers can cause the convergence problem, because of negative error variance. We experience a high degree of difficulty in getting the program to converge. One suggestion from the SAS manual (SAS Institute Inc. 1989) was to impose a boundary statement that forces the error variance to be 0. This can affect the parameter estimates of certain observed variables to be 1. At the time of this study, there is no correctional procedure established in the program to deal with this problem. However, this does not influence the other parameter estimates in the models. Future development of this technique is needed.

Convergence problems forced us to eliminate some covariance pathways between exogenous variables. We had too many parameters to be estimated, given the small sample sizes. For future use of this technique with similar models, larger sample sizes are needed to satisfy all the required assumptions.

Yet another weakness in this form of modelling is the underlying assumption that all relationships can be expressed in linear form. Although transformations of variables may be used to introduce some non-linearities, it is possible that non-linear effects are not fully captured. Progress on this problem awaits new developments in structural modelling.

Finally, since this study tries to explain the outcome indicators with a fully elaborated model of family dynamics, there are many parameters to be estimated with a relatively small number of observations. A standard check to determine whether the sample is likely to generate precise estimates of coefficients is to look at the ratio of sample size to free parameters (Bentler 1985). Bentler's standard cut-off point is $5:1$. In this study, the total complete sample size in both data sets is less than 200 and there are more than 50 free parameters to be estimated, which makes the ratio less than the standard cut-off. While this does not make the model or the estimates invalid, it becomes more likely that the coefficient estimates will have high standard errors and low t-values.

Javanese family models

In the Javanese models (figs. 8.3–8.7), separate versions of the model were estimated using growth, the Vineland social quotient (SQ), and mental development (IQ) as outcome variables. Although these variables could be treated as alternate measures of a more general index of development, it is useful to examine first the size and significance of the paths in the separate models before making a decision on whether they are similar enough to be combined. Descriptions of the measured variables may be found in the Appendix to this chapter.

The latent variables in the models can be divided into three groups. The first group consists of family dynamics variables which we call "family management, beliefs, and caring behaviours": they are Academic Stimulation, Parental Affection, Feeding Practices, and Health Practices. The second group consists of resource variables and includes Social Resources, Material Resources, Support, and Community Endowment. The third group of latent variables represents outcomes such as Growth and Mental Development.

Each path between a pair of latent variables represents a conjecture about the causal relationships between these variables. For example, Social Resources (measured by literacy and mother's years of education) is postulated to affect directly Academic Stimulation and expression of Affection. Material Resources (measured by household possessions and housing quality) directly affects only Feeding Practices and Health Practices.[4] If Material Resources affects Academic Stimulation and Affection, we postulate it is through a covariance pathway to Social Resources.[5]

The indirect pathways between Material Resources and Academic Stimulation and Affection are explained by the assumption that wealthier people are more literate, more educated, and more inclined to stimulate their children. The links between the expression of Affection and Family Resources (Social and Material), however, are less well established. We have little hard evidence that Social and Material Resources affect Parental Affection, although such influences are documented in the cross-cultural literature.

The measured variables that we have available are strongly identified with the latent variables they represent. For example, household possessions and quality of house are strongly related to the Material Resources of the household. The only weak measure is the measure of protein adequacy for the Feeding Practice latent variable in the SQ and IQ models.

Growth model

In the growth model (fig. 8.3), Social Resources are strongly linked to Academic Stimulation; however, Social Resources surprisingly are not linked to the expression of Affection. The insignificant linkage between Social Resource and Affection may reflect cultural norms in Java, or behaviour that was learned by mothers during their own childhood; therefore, there is little variation in the degree of maternal affection with respect to their social status. The degree of Support, however, reflecting the mothers' emotional satisfaction and fathers' involvement in child care, is strongly associated with Affection, and in turn is strongly linked to Growth. Affectionate mothers (measured by warmth and hours spent with children – HrsWkd) had a positive impact on the growth of their children.

Academic Stimulation is not found to affect Growth directly. This result seems plausible for children between the ages of two and five years, and suggests that the pathway linking Academic Stimulation to Growth might not be part of models for older children. Previous

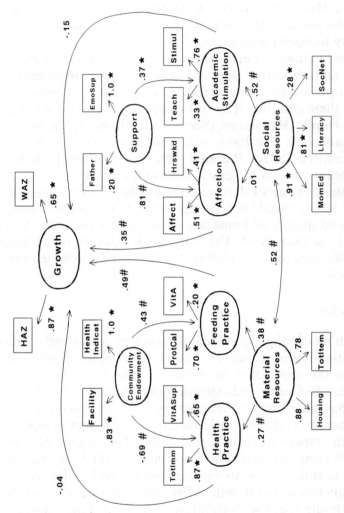

Fig. 8.3 **Path diagram of growth, Java. N = 185 2- to 5-year-old children and their families. GFI (adjusted) = 0.668; BB Index = 0.738; BB Index = 0.668. Ovals: latent variables; rectangles: measured variables; statistical significance of path coefficients:** * 0.025 < *p* < 0.050; ▲ 0.010 < *p* < 0.025; # *p* < 0.010

findings using ANOVA (Chomitz 1992) show that some components in Academic Stimulation are strong predictors of the child's diet. Parents who stimulate their children are likely to be those who also provide good diets; therefore, the link between Academic Stimulation and Growth is probably through its association with Feeding Practice. This hypothesis was investigated by including a covariance pathway between Academic Stimulation and Feeding Practice, but it showed insignificant association. This insignificant association may be due to the ages of the children in this study. Since only older, more active children are included in this data set, the more stimulated children might also have a higher energy expenditure, so that no direct effect on growth would be expected. Also, Academic Stimulation could be a source of stress in the absence of physical and emotional nurturance and hence could negatively influence growth if the malnourished child underwent pressure to perform. The insignificant association also may be due to the large number of alternate paths of influence included in the structural model.

Feeding Practice is strongly determined by Material Resources and Community Endowment, and showed a strong effect on Growth. This comes as no surprise, given the use of direct information on the child's diet.

The link between the Health Practice variable (measured by total immunization and vitamin A tablets) and Growth does not have the expected sign and is statistically insignificant. It may be that a simultaneity problem exists between Health Practice and Growth, in which malnourished children were more likely to be exposed to the health centre, and more likely to receive immunizations than healthier children. If this is so, a return pathway from Growth to Health Practice should show a negative sign, and may alter the path from Health Practice to Growth. When the model was estimated with this modification, no real support for the hypothesis was found. Even though Growth showed a negative effect upon Health Practice, the coefficient was not significant, and the effect of Health Practice on Growth remained the same. Since this result is counter-intuitive, it is likely that there is some other error in the specification that explains the findings. A possible non-linear effect may cause the insignificant negative effect of Health Practice on Growth: the nutritionally worse-off children may be brought to the health centre more often than the better-off children. Beyond some point, however, an improvement in nutritional status would not increase the child's presence in the health centres, and as the level of nutritional status is higher, the participation in the nutrition and health programme increases.

The significant negative link between Community Endowment (measured by the community health indicators – crude birth rate and children-under-five mortality rate) and Health Practices is also puzzling and may relate to the negative effect of Health Practice on Growth. It is possible that in villages where the quality of health facilities are low, mothers (or enumerators) tend to overreport the immunization information, or that immunization is conducted through highly memorable campaigns. If this is so, then there is a systematic bias in the data that cannot be eliminated by reformulating the model.

Mental development model

Two observed variables are used to measure the Mental Development construct: these are the Vineland SQ and the Stanford Binet IQ. Before we combined the two variables into a single Mental Development index, we estimated separate models with each variable. Except for the pathway linking Health Practice and Child Developmental outcome, the coefficients estimates are very similar for these two forms of the model (figs. 8.4 and 8.5). This stability supports the belief that the two measured variables represent a single concept, which we call Mental Development. This construct was used in subsequent work.

The relationship between Social Resources and Academic Stimulation (.68#), and Academic Stimulation and Mental Development (.48#) are both strong in the Mental Development model (fig. 8.6). This result conforms to the widely held belief that more-educated parents provide more academic encouragement to their children, and that children respond with greater performance.

The latent variable, Support, also is found to have an effect on Academic Stimulation (.41#). It seems that stimulation for their children is more likely to come from mothers who are emotionally satisfied and whose husbands are involved in child-care activities.

None of the other pathways into Mental Development appear to be significant in this model. This could be due to misspecification, measured variables that poorly represent the latent variable, too little variation in the data, or too few observations. Affection and Feeding Practices may affect Mental Development in more complex ways than can be represented as direct pathways in the model. Growth could be

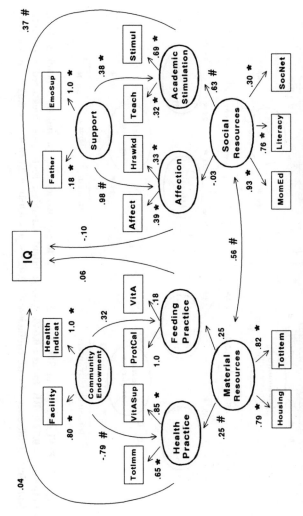

Fig. 8.4 Path diagram of IQ, Java. N = 185 2- to 5-year-old children and their families. GFI (adjusted) = 0.725; BB Index = 0.639. Ovals: latent variables; rectangles: measured variables; statistical significance of path coefficients: * 0.025 < *p* < 0.050; ▲ 0.010 < *p* < 0.025; # *p* < 0.010

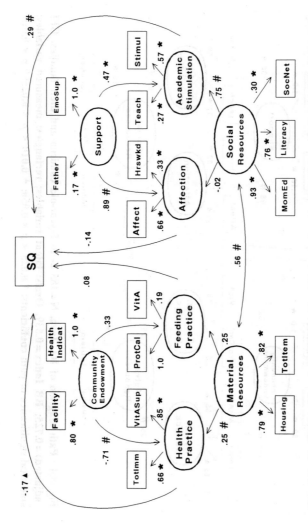

Fig. 8.5 **Path diagram of SQ, Java. N = 185 2- to 5-year-old children and their families. GFI (adjusted) = 0.727; BB Index = 0.640. Ovals: latent variables; rectangles: measured variables; statistical significance of path coefficients: * 0.025 < p < 0.050; ▲ 0.010 < p < 0.025; # p < 0.010**

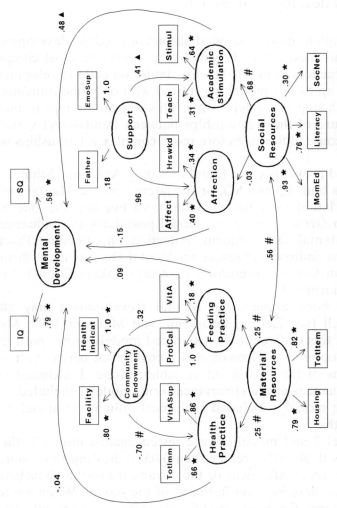

Fig. 8.6 **Path diagram of mental development, Java. N = 185 2- to 5-year-old children and their families. GFI (adjusted) = 0.731; BB Index = 0.639. Ovals: latent variables; rectangles: measured variables; statistical significance of path coefficients: * 0.025 < p < 0.050; ▲ 0.010 < p < 0.025; # p < 0.010**

an intervening factor in the underlying relationships, since it is expected that Growth will affect Mental Development, as discussed in the following section.

Overall child development model

The most complete model included all outcome (child development) indicators. This model was designed to provide the most complete test of the influences of family-level variables on child development.

In building up to this model we started with only one outcome indicator in each step of model testing. This was an attempt to understand the nature of the relationships between family-level variables and each outcome indicator before more complex relationships were explored.

As discussed previously, we found that only Academic Stimulation directly affects both IQ and SQ, or the latent variable Mental Development. The latent variables Affection and Feeding Practice have direct links to Growth. Since the model postulates the influence of Growth on Mental Development, Affection and Feeding Practice may have some indirect influences on Mental Development through their effects on Growth; therefore, pathways linking Growth to IQ and SQ were included.

It also has been argued that Mental Development may affect Growth as well (see Zeitlin, Ghassemi, and Mansour 1990; Myers 1992). To test this conjecture we examined models with a path from Mental Development to Growth, and a covariance between the disturbance terms of the two latent variables: model 1 included both reciprocal influences and a covariance term; model 2 included a covariance term; model 3 included reciprocal influences; model 4 did not include either.

When model 2 and model 3 were tested against model 1, the p-values were both slightly greater than 0.05, indicating that omitting either the reciprocal influences or the covariance of the disturbances cause very little deterioration in the fit of the model. When model 4 was tested against the other models, the p-values were all greater than 0.05, which indicates that the combined effect of the reciprocal influence and the covariance of the disturbance terms is statistically not significant; therefore, we could omit either reciprocal influence or covariance terms, and eliminate both at the same time. For this reason, the model shown in figure 8.7 does not include covariance terms

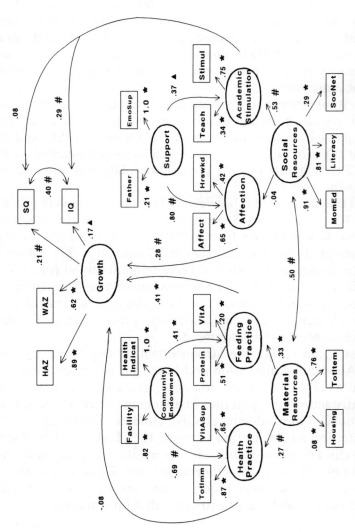

Fig. 8.7 **Path diagram of overall development, Java. N = 185 2- to 5-year-old children and their families. GFI (adjusted) = 0.740; BB Index = 0.650. Ovals: latent variables; rectangles: measured variables; statistical significance of path coefficients: * 0.025 < *p* < 0.050; ▲ 0.010 < *p* < 0.025; # *p* < 0.010**

nor reciprocal influence in older children's development model (see Nigerian model, chapter 8, pages 214–17, for explanation).

In another variation of the basic model, we treated IQ and SQ as separate variables. This allowed us to see if their relationship to Growth and other outcome indicators will differ. A covariance term was added to take into account the reciprocal relationship between the two variables. This model variant yielded coefficients and significance levels similar to those in the previous models. This model also revealed some interrelationships between the Growth and Mental Development indicators.

Academic Stimulation had a strong effect on IQ, and a less strong effect on SQ. Its effect on SQ differs from the previous model (fig. 8.5). After taking into account the effect of Growth on SQ and the covariance of IQ with SQ, the effect of Academic Stimulation on SQ evaporated. This suggests that Academic Stimulation is affecting SQ through Growth.

Notice that the relationships between Affection and Growth (.28 #), Growth and IQ (.17 ▲), and Growth and SQ (.21 #), are all strong; in fact, the two-link pathways from Affection to IQ and SQ through Growth are about .05, respectively (.28 × .17 and .28 × .21). This is in contrast to the finding in the Mental Development model (fig. 8.6) in which the effect of maternal Affection was negative and insignificant. This model confirms our expectations about the role of Growth as an intermediary element connecting Maternal Affection (also Feeding Practice) to child Mental Development.

This model again shows the strong effect of the latent variable Support on Academic Stimulation and Maternal Affection. It clearly indicates that a stable family environment, as measured by maternal emotional satisfaction and paternal involvement in child-rearing activities, is beneficial in producing positive child development.

We failed to find an association between the Health Practices variable and the child outcome indicators. As mentioned previously, this may be due to bias in the data-gathering process. Establishing precise estimates of this linkage may require more information on Health Practices and better methods of gathering that information.

We conclude that after controlling for socio-economic status (SES), Maternal Affection and Feeding Practice positively affect Growth. Given the interrelationships between Growth and Mental Development indicators, Maternal Affection and Feeding Practice also positively affect mental development. Academic Stimulation showed a direct and positive effect on IQ in older children; however, its effects on SQ and Growth are much less certain. It appears that a stable family environment helps to generate positive maternal attitudes towards the children, which in turn promotes positive child development.

Total effects of indicator variables

Tables 8.1–8.4 present a summary of the findings from the model by showing the total effects of each latent variable that could be considered an "input" on the variables that could be considered an "output." The total effects summarize the individual effects of all possible pathways connecting the input indicators to the output indicators. Since the entries are scaled in standardized units, they show the relative strengths of the influences of the input variables on the output indicators and intervening variables.

Table 8.1 **Total effects in Javanese growth model**

	Stimulation	Affection	Feeding	Health	Growth
Social	.191	.006	—	—	−.053
Material	—	—	.347	.225	.146
Stimulation	—	—	—	—	−.294
Affection	—	—	—	—	.445
Feeding practices	—	—	—	—	.451
Health practices	—	—	—	—	−.045
Support	.609	2.061	—	—	.737
Community endowment	—	—	.365	−.545	.189

Table 8.2 **Total effects in Javanese mental development model**

	Stimulation	Affection	Feeding	Health	MD[a]
Social	.275	−.015	—	—	.248
Material	—	—	.057	.206	.009
Stimulation	—	—	—	—	.893
Affection	—	—	—	—	−.216
Feeding practices	—	—	—	—	.275
Health practices	—	—	—	—	−.035
Support	.128	.384	—	—	.032
Community endowment	—	—	.075	−.579	.041

a. Mental development (IQ and SQ).

207

Table 8.3 **Total effects in Javanese overall child development model**

	Stimulation	Affection	Feeding	Growth	IQ	SQ
Social	.230	−.025	—	−.008	.198	.095
Material	—	—	.076	.079	.021	.024
Stimulation	—	—	—	—	.871	.427
Affection	—	—	—	.335	.089	.101
Feeding	—	—	—	1.248	.332	.337
Health	—	—	—	−.080	−.021	−.024
Support	.117	.409	—	.137	.139	.092
Community endowment	—	—	.099	.167	.044	.051

Table 8.4 **Legend for Javanese models**

Variable code	Description
MOMED	Mother's education
LITERACY	Reading and writing Bahasa Indonesian
SOCNET	Mother's involvement in social organization
HOUSING	Housing quality
TOTITEM	Total household possessions
TEACH	Learning and teaching environment
STIMUL	Academic stimulation and physical environment
AFFECT	Maternal affection
HRSWKD	Length of time a mother spent with her child per day
PROTCAL	Child's protein adequacy
VITA	Child's vitamin A adequacy
TOTIMM	Total immunization score
VITASUP	Vitamin A tablets
EMOSUP	Mother's emotional satisfaction with family support
FATHER	Father's involvement in child care
IQ	Stanford Binet Index
SQ	Social Quotient Index
WAZ	Weight-for-age Z-score
HAZ	Height-for-age Z-score

The coefficients of most variables are relatively stable from one model to the next. One exception was the impact of Affection on Mental Development: Affection was negative in affecting Mental Development (table 8.2); in the overall model, however (table 8.3), the effect of affection was positive. This provides an example of how ignoring the indirect effects of a variable through other variables may give a very different picture of its overall effect. One of the benefits of using structural equation analysis is that we can obtain an estimate of the indirect effect of a variable, which cannot be done by using a reduced-form model for each variable of interest.

Social (literacy and years of education) and Material Resources are usually the strongest predictors of Growth and other child developmental outcomes in other studies that do not control for the effect of family dynamics variables. When some intervening proximate "family management and caring behaviour" factors are added to the model (table 8.3), Stimulation, Affection, and Feeding Practice emerge as the dominant factors. This demonstrates the importance of the dynamics within the family, a point often overlooked by those interested in child welfare.

Nigerian family models

As in the Javanese model, separate versions of the Yoruba model were tested in separate steps to examine the size and significance of the linkages in the separate models before the outcome variables were combined. The outcome variables are Growth (WAZ and HAZ), Mental Development Index (MDI), and Physical Development Index (PDI). In the Nigerian models, two-year-old children were examined (figs. 8.8–8.10); SQ was not measured in these children.

The general measurements of family-level functioning are comparable to the Javanese model. The family dynamic variables (family management and caring behaviour variables/parental care) consist of Academic Stimulation (measured by "teach" and "toys" observed variables); Affection and Attention (measured by "warm," "verbal responsiveness," and "index of child care support"); Feeding Practices (measured by "index of food investment" and "food belief"); and Hygienic Practices (measured by "index of sanitary practices," "water source," and "cleanliness of the environment"). All of these latent variables are hypothesized to influence outcome variables such as Growth and Mental Development directly.

Resource variables include Material (measured by "housing quality" and "food budget") and Social Resources (measured by "maternal literacy," "exposure to media," and "rural–urban location"). The way that these two latent variables affect parental care variables is postulated to be the same as those in the Javanese models. The assumptions made in the Javanese model also apply to the Nigerian model. For example, if Material Resources affects Academic Stimulation and Affection, it is postulated to be through a covariance pathway to Social Resources. Another resource variable is a latent variable, Modernization within the Family (measured by "modern behaviours" and "the intensity of the father's living in the house"). This variable is assumed to affect Feeding Practice and Affection. A covariance pathway was made between Material Resources and Modernization within the Family to allow a certain degree of association between these two latent variables.

Parental Care variables affecting child developmental outcomes are influenced by the characteristics of the child. The latent variable Child Personality is included in the model to control for this effect. Note that only covariance pathways link Child Personality and Parental Care variables (i.e. Academic Stimulation, Affection, and Feeding Practice); this means that Child Personality and Parental Care variables can be thought of as mutually related. Drawing pathways would produce too many paths to estimate precisely with the data available.

Almost all of our measured variables are strongly identified with the latent variables they represent. Weak measures include the measure of Hygienic Practices and Material Resources in all models. These are indicated by the high coefficients (from "housing" and "water source") that are not significant, indicating that their standard errors are high and the measurements unreliable. The latent variables, Material Resources and Hygienic Practices, are complex variables unlikely to be characterized easily by such relatively simple indicators.

Growth model

In the growth model (fig. 8.8), Social Resources are linked strongly to Parental Care variables, Affection, and Academic Stimulation. The significant effect of Social Resources on Affection contradicts our findings in the Javanese setting. This suggests that the expression of maternal affection and attention behaviours towards infants in Yoruba society shifts with formal education, whereas, in Java, affectionate behaviour is internalized early during the mothers' childhood; therefore, education may have little impact on this behaviour in the Javanese society. Our finding is also consistent with the findings of LeVine, Klein, and Owen (1967) in Nigeria, that more-educated parents are more friendly and demonstrate more affection towards their children. The expression of Affection and Attention is strongly ($\#$) linked to Growth. Academic Stimulation, however, only marginally

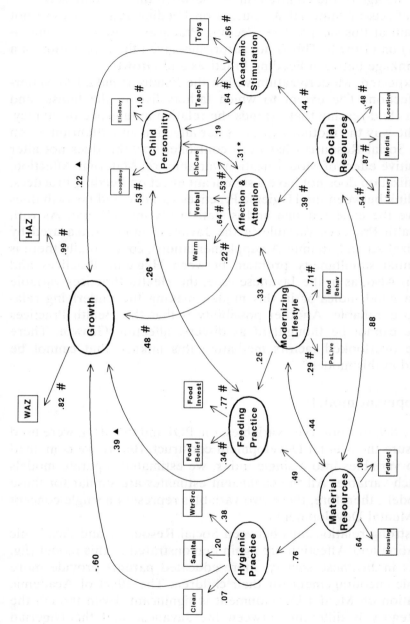

Fig. 8.8 Path diagram of growth, Nigeria. N=170 2-year-olds and their families. GFI (adjusted) = 0.754; BB Index = 0.641. Ovals: latent variables; rectangles: measured variables; statistical significance of path coefficients: * 0.025 < p < 0.050; ▲ 0.010 < p < 0.025; # p < 0.010

211

affects Growth. This is consistent with our findings in Java, even though the age of the children differs between the two data sets.

The effects of Material Resources on Feeding Practices were not significant at this sample size. Feeding Practices showed a strong effect ($\blacktriangle$) on Growth. This is not surprising, given the supposition of a direct linkage between Feeding Practices and Growth.

As expected, Modernization within the Family is linked to Maternal Affection. The extent to which fathers live in the house, and modern child-rearing that extends the relative indulgence of infancy, affect the way the mother expresses her affection and attention. Even though Social Resources has been controlled for, this does not alter the positive effect of Modernization variables on Maternal Affection. Modernization does not have a significant effect on Feeding Practices.

The link between the Hygienic Practices variable and Growth does not have the expected sign and is statistically insignificant. As with the Health Practices variable in the Javanese model (measured by immunization and vitamin A supplementation), conceptually there is a potential simultaneity problem between Hygienic Practices and Growth. Also, as in the Javanese case, the Health Practices variable is not a good indicator in this model, making the underlying relationship unreliable. Another possibility is that the Health Practices variable cannot be thought of as directly affecting Growth. There may be overlooked factors mediating this linkage that cannot be included in this model.[6]

Development model

In figure 8.9, two observed variables, the PDI and the MDI, were used to measure the Mental Development construct. Before we combined the two variables into a single index, we estimated separate models with each variable. All the coefficient estimates are similar for these two models; therefore, these two variables represent a single concept called Mental Development.

The strong relationships between Social Resources and Academic Stimulation and Affection are again demonstrated in this model (fig. 8.9). As in Javanese society, more-educated parents provide more academic encouragement for their children. The effect of Academic Stimulation on Mental Development is significant. Even though the age category is different between the Javanese and the Nigerian samples, Academic Stimulation in both data sets appears to be important. The latent variables Affection and Attention and Feeding

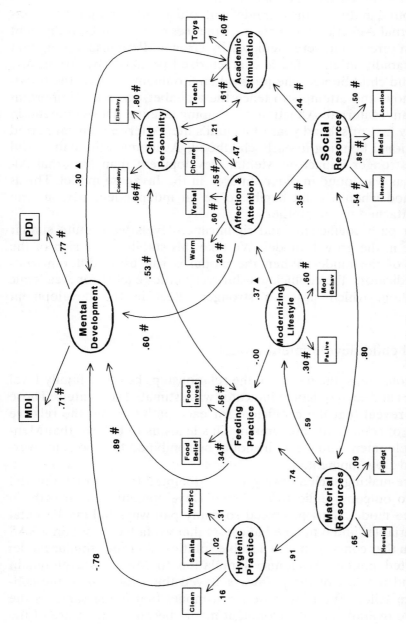

Fig. 8.9 Path diagram of mental development, Nigeria. N = 170 2-year-olds and their families. GFI (adjusted) = 0.736; BB Index = 0.569. Ovals: latent variables; rectangles: measured variables; statistical significance of path coefficients: * $0.025 < p < 0.050$; ▲ $0.010 < p < 0.025$; # $p < 0.010$

Practice turned out to be the most important factor in determining the child's Mental Development (#).

We found in the Javanese model with older children that the effects of Maternal Affection and Feeding Practices on Mental Development were not direct, but were mediated by Growth. Perhaps learning that occurs rapidly in early life is characterized primarily by strong maternal and child bonds. The physical environment, such as the provision of toys and attempts to teach the alphabet, has a less important role than Maternal Affection in shaping Mental Development in the early first or second year of a child's life. After the critical period of emotional bonding in early childhood, Academic Stimulation will have a stronger impact on Mental Development than Maternal Affection, as was found in older children in the Javanese model. This is the period when a child begins to be an independent person, and is less attached to the mother.

Other path coefficients and significance levels were quite similar to those in the growth model. We take this stability as a sign of the validity of the model. When the model is run using different outcome indicators, the coefficients shift very little (except for Academic Stimulation, which shows a stronger effect in the development model).

Overall child development model

In previous steps, the nature of the relationships between family-level variables and each outcome indicator was estimated separately. Those models reveal that the coefficient for each pathway and the relative ranking of coefficients are similar. This leads us to believe that Mental Development and Growth should be combined to represent overall Child Development.

Before making such a decision, we attempted to construct a model with two outcome indicators, Mental Development and Growth, in the same model. This produced so many pathways linking Parental Care variables and outcome indicators that we failed to obtain a SAS program that converged into a stable solution. Another similar model was tested linking Academic Stimulation to Mental Development only, and the rest of the pathways stayed the same: again, the convergence failed. We cannot design a model that is the same as the Javanese overall child development model because the nature of the linkages differs between the two settings.

Examination of the Pearson correlation coefficients between all outcome indicators (WAZ, HAZ, MDI, and PDI) reveals that they are highly correlated (more than .33). The correlations among outcome indicators in older children (in Java) are weaker (HAZ and SQ, and HAZ and IQ are .24 and .26, respectively), and are not significant between WAZ and SQ or IQ. Perhaps, in a rapid growth period, Growth and Mental Development are strongly mutually related: the development of each will reinforce the development of the other. This pattern seems to be less clear in older children, in which it appears that each outcome indicator becomes a more separate entity, although they may be mutually related. In addition, based on our analysis in the Javanese model, some Parental Care variables behave differently in each child development model. Therefore, we believe that Growth and Mental Development represent a single concept in younger children, which we call Overall Child Development. This construct was used in subsequent work.

This model (fig. 8.10) again shows the strong effect of the latent variable Affection and Attention on Overall Child Development. It indicates that a warm and attentive mother is clearly beneficial in producing positive child development. The latent variable, Academic Stimulation, had significant effect but was weaker than the effect of Affection and Attention and Feeding Practices in this model.

The effect of the latent variable Feeding Practices is very strong (#), and stronger than in the older children's model in Java (*). This suggests that good feeding practices are important in rapidly growing children.

The latent variable Modernization within the Family behaves in relatively the same way as in the previous model, but has a weaker effect in the overall model (*).

There is a strong reciprocal influence between Child Personality and Maternal Affection (and also Feeding Practices). This association appears consistent in all models. Affectionate mothers are associated with good Child Personality (measured by such factors as smiling and ease of handling), and vice versa. A smiling baby may be attractive to the mother, encouraging her to stay with the infant and play with it. This interlude may help to cement the bond between the child and its mother, producing a powerful reciprocal attachment that further affects positive child development outcomes.

Besides the strong effect of maternal affection on child development, its strong effect on maternal bonding also can influence the

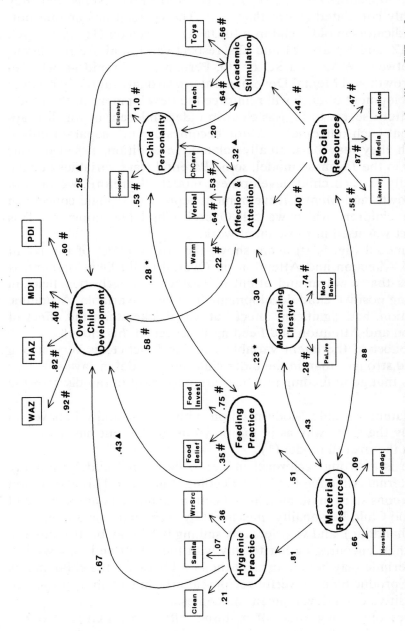

Fig. 8.10 Path diagram of overall development, Nigeria. N=170 2-year-olds and their families. GFI (adjusted) = 0.754; BB Index = 0.641. Ovals: latent variables; rectangles: measured variables; statistical significance of path coefficients: * 0.025 < p < 0.050; ▲ 0.010 < p < 0.025; # p < 0.010

216

child's personality later in life. According to Morris (1969), this bond is extremely important. A bond developed in the first year of life will imprint a large capacity for making strong bonds during adult life.

As in the Javanese model, we failed to find an association between the Hygienic Practices variable and all outcome indicators. Future efforts to improve methods of gathering Health and Hygienic Practices information are needed.

We conclude that after controlling for SES, the quality of care including Maternal Affection (which includes verbal responsiveness), Feeding Practices and Academic Stimulation positively affect all outcome indicators. Even though Academic Stimulation shows a relatively strong effect on all outcome indicators in younger children, its effect is weaker than the effect of Maternal Affection and Feeding Practices.

Total effects of indicator variables

A summary of the findings from the models is presented in tables 8.5–8.8. The coefficients of most variables are relatively stable from one model to the next.

Note that three factors emerged in all models as having the greatest effect: they are Maternal Affection, Feeding Practices (and Academic Stimulation in the mental development model), and Social Resources. The negative effect of Material Resources is unreliable in this model because we do not have good measures of this factor. Also, Material Resources are hypothesized to influence outcome indicators through Hygienic Practices. Since we could not obtain a good indicator of Hygienic Practices, and its effect is negative on

Table 8.5 **Total effects in Nigerian growth model**

	Stimulation	Affection	Feeding	Hygiene	Growth
Social	.286	.235	—	—	.268
Material	—	—	.201	.606	−2.630
Stimulation	—	—	—	—	.320
Affection	—	—	—	—	.751
Feeding practices	—	—	—	—	.928
Hygiene practices	—	—	—	—	−7.449
Modern family	—	.585	.298	—	−.716

Table 8.6   **Total effects in Nigerian mental development model**

	Stimulation	Affection	Feeding	Hygiene	MD[a]
Social	.331	.223	—	—	.306
Material	—	—	−.325	.284	−.481
Stimulation	—	—	—	—	.384
Affection	—	—	—	—	.835
Feeding practices	—	—	—	—	.549
Hygiene practices	—	—	—	—	−20.565
Modern family	—	.004	2.845	—	2.184

a. Mental development (MDI and PDI).

Table 8.7   **Total effects in Nigerian overall child development model**

	Stimulation	Affection	Feeding	Hygiene	All dev[a]
Social	.288	.240	—	—	.362
Material	—	—	1.880	.604	−3.169
Stimulation	—	—	—	—	.406
Affection	—	—	—	—	1.023
Feeding	—	—	—	—	1.136
Hygiene practices	—	—	—	—	−8.792
Modern family	—	−.136	.291	—	.900

a. Overall development.

child developmental outcomes, the total effect of Material Resources through Hygienic Practices became negative.

This study again demonstrates the importance of the dynamics within the family in promoting positive development. Improving family resources alone, a point that is often emphasized by the economist and by those involved in development, cannot guarantee improvements in child welfare unless Family Management, Beliefs, and Caring Activities are favourable for this purpose.

Compared with the Javanese model, in which Social Resources has a small effect on the expression of Maternal Affection, this factor also is dominant in affecting positive child developmental outcomes. This suggests that, in the Javanese society, improvements in maternal education cannot be relied upon to change maternal expression of affection because of maternal childhood experience in adopting this attitude (ch. 6); this is not true in Yoruba society. Improving maternal attitudes and behaviours should go hand in hand with the improve-

Table 8.8 **Legend for Nigerian models**

Variable code	Description
LITERACY	Mother's last year of schooling and her literacy (reads Yoruba and reads English)
MEDIA	Mother's exposure to media
LOCATION	Location (rural, semi-rural, and urban)
HOUSING	Housing quality
FDBUDGT	Total food budget
FOODINVEST	Food investment score for the child
FOODBELIEF	Food belief
MODBEHAV	Modern behaviour score
PALIVE	Father lives with mother
TEACH	Teach child
TOYS	The amount of toys score
WARM	Maternal affection
VERBAL	Maternal verbal responsiveness
CHCARE	Child-care arrangements
CLEAN	Cleanliness of the environment
SANITA	Hygiene practices
WATERSRC	Water source
ELICBABY	Eliciting baby
COOPBABY	Easiness to be handled
MDI	Bayley mental development index
PDI	Bayley physical development index
WAZ	Weight-for-age Z-score
HAZ	Height-for-age Z-score

ment of the educational level of the family; however, improving social resources is very important in order to increase the awareness of parents to stimulate their children academically, in both cultures.

Notes

1. Error terms commonly represented by Es and Ds have been removed from our diagrams for simplicity of visual representation, but are taken into account in the analysis.
2. The RAM specification of the PROC CALIS was used from SAS Version 6.01. The documentation for this procedure is available on pp. 292–365 of the *SAS/STAT User's Guide* (SAS Institute Inc. 1989).
3. Polychoric correlation would be used to estimate the correlation based on a pair of categorical variables, and polyserial correlation would be used when one variable was continuous and the other was categorical.
4. Some of our original analysis attempted to link the Material Resources and Social Resources variables with all aspects of parental care. Since there is some correlation between these variables, this approach produced too many pathways to estimate precisely with the data available.

5. A pathway between two variables with arrows at each end represents correlation between the two variables.
6. A trial was made to include morbidity variable as a mediator variable. This produced too many factors to estimate precisely with the data available. Also, the simultaneity problem between growth and morbidity needed to be solved, making the model too complicated, given the limited sample size.

Appendix: Variable description and composite index construction

Indonesia

The variables presented here were based on a subset of data from the Ford Foundation-funded intervention project, Changing Caretaking Behaviors to Improve Child Growth and Development (Satoto and Colletta 1987). The project consisted of three phases: (1) sample selection (including both intervention and control groups) and collection of baseline information in 1987; (2) 18 months of in-home intervention with the *kaders* and mothers, and (3) follow-up data collection and analysis in August–November 1989. The data used in this study were based on the follow-up data. A total of 304 children over two years of age were selected for this study (Chomitz 1992).

Social resources

MOTHER'S YEARS OF EDUCATION (MOMED). This variable referred to the total years of mother's education (value ranged from 0 to 16). A summary of descriptive statistics is as follows:
– No education (0 years)   1.0%
– Primary school (2–6 years)   73.1%
– Secondary school (7–9 years)   12.9%
– High school (10–12 years)   12.3%
– College (13–16 years)   1.7%

MOTHER'S LITERACY (LITERACY). This variable was composed of two survey questions (coded from 1 to 4):
1. Reading abilities of mothers (MOMREAD)
    – Very fluent   0.8%
    – Fluent   16.2%
    – Slow   61.8%
    – Cannot read   21.2%

2. Writing abilities of mothers (MOMWRITE)
   - Very fluent   22.5%
   - Fluent   54.3%
   - Slow   22.5%
   - Cannot write   0.7%

The definition of LITERACY is: LITERACY = SUM (MOM-READ, MOMWRITE).

Mother's social network (SOCNET). This variable was composed of two survey questions:
1. Number of organizations mother joins (MOMNOORG) ranged from 0 (none) to 5
2. How frequently mother meets friends (ISOLATE) ranged from 1 to 4:
   - Never   1.2%
   - 2–4 times monthly   6.2%
   - 2–3 times weekly   18.2%
   - Every day   74.4%

The definition of SOCNET is: SOCNET = SUM (MOMNOORG, ISOLATE).

Material resources

Quality of house (HOUSING). This variable was composed of three survey questions (value ranged from 1 to 4):
1. Building material of front of house (HOUSE1)
   - Not brick/stone   49.8%
   - Half brick   17.4%
   - Brick without windows   9.3%
   - Brick with windows   23.5%
2. Floor of living room (HOUSE2)
   - Earth   71.1%
   - Half earth/half cement   7.4%
   - All cement   4.7%
   - Tiles   14.1%
3. Lighting in living room (HOUSE3)
   - Nothing, or *sentir*   2.4%
   - Kerosene lamp   30.3%
   - Petro Max/City electricity   59.8%
   - Diesel: own generator   7.5%

The definition of HOUSING is: HOUSING = SUM (HOUSE1, HOUSE2, HOUSE3).

WEALTH POSSESSIONS (TOTITEM). This variable was composed of household possessions (nine items). The nine items were added up to form a single variable (TOTITEM) weighted by factor scores based on ranks of status of each item (Chomitz 1992) (0 = no, 1 = yes). The percentages of "yes" scores for each item were as follows:

1. Car ownership   0.8%
2. Motorcycle ownership   21.4%
3. Sewing machine ownership   12.8%
4. TV ownership   30.0%
5. Sofa ownership   17.2%
6. Radio-cassette ownership   65.7%
7. Bicycle ownership   56.0%
8. Petro Max ownership   58.1%
9. Mattress ownership   95.7%

The definition of TOTITEM is: TOTITEM = (ITEM1*3) + (ITEM2*3) + (ITEM3*3) + (ITEM4*3) + (ITEM5*2) + (ITEM6*2) + (ITEM7*2) + (ITEM8) + (ITEM9*2).

Health practices

TOTAL IMMUNIZATION (TOTIMM). TOTIMM refers to total immunization received by the child during his/her entire life. It is composed of three immunization types: diphtheria/pertussis/tetanus (DPT), polio, and bacillus Calmette-Guérin (BCG). DPT and polio have three boosters from which the total shots were added into TOTDPT and TOTPOLIO. TOTDPT and TOTPOLIO have values ranging between 0 and 3 (0 means no immunization at all and 3 means a complete course was received). For BCG, 0 means no immunization and 1 means immunization received. Scores were as follows:

TOTDPT
0: 8.1%
1: 15.4%
2: 10.4%
3: 56.3%
TOTPOLIO
0: 24.7%
1: 5.8%
2: 6.9%
3: 62.5%

BCG
0: 6.3%
1: 93.7%

The composite index TOTIMM is defined as follows: TOTIMM = SUM (TOTDPT, TOTPOLIO, BCG).

VITAMIN A SUPPLEMENTATION (VITASUP). VITASUP is defined as the total number of vitamin A tablets received by the child over his/her entire life. The values ranged between 0 (none) and 6 (six tablets received). The percentages of children scoring 0–6 were as follows: 0, 7.3%; 1, 2.7%; 2, 10.8%; 3, 14.3%; 4, 13.1%; 5, 10.8%, and 6, 40.9%.

Community endowment

HEALTH INDICATOR (HLTHIND). The HLTHIND variable consisted of community-level indicators on crude birth rate (CBR) and under-five mortality rate (U5MR). These variables were expected to reflect the quality of programme or facility available in the community. The CBR (per 1,000 population per year) was 39 (35.7%), 67 (56.1%), and 120 (8.2%). CBR was transformed into 0 (if above the mean) and 1 (if below the mean).

The U5MR (per 1,000 population) was 3 (35.7%) and 4 (56.9%). U5MR was recorded as 0 and 1 (0 = 4; 1 = 3).

The HLTHIND variable was defined as follows: HLTHIND = SUM (CBR, U5MR).

HEALTH FACILITIES AVAILABLE IN THE COMMUNITY (FACILITY). FACILITY is composed of three information variables: the number of traditional birth attendants (TBA), nutrition groups (NUTGRP), and health facilities (HLTHFAC) available at the community level. The descriptive statistics of these variables are presented below. Since each variable has a different scale measurement, they were transformed into 0 and 1 values (1 = higher than average; 0 = lower than average).

The TBA scores (per 1,000 population) were 6.6 (56.1%), 18.30 (35.7%), and 27.80 (8.2%).

The NUTGRP scores (per 1,000 population) were 6.3 (56.1%), 9.50 (35.7%), and 10.40 (8.2%).

The HLTHFAC scores (per 1,000 population) were 2.2 (49.7%), 4.1 (35.7%), and 6.0 (7.2%).

The FACILITY variable was defined as follows (after all variables were transformed): FACILITY = SUM (TBA, NUTGRP, HLTHFAC).

Feeding practices

PROTEIN ADEQUACY (PROTEIN). Protein adequacy is also a measure of energy adequacy, which is why we call this term ProtCal. We used protein as a proxy for protein and energy because it was more highly correlated with child developmental outcomes than was caloric adequacy. Protein adequacy was calculated by Chomitz (1992) based on the total portions of foods per day collected by the food frequency questionnaire (FFQ) developed by Chomitz (1992). The protein intake was adjusted downward to correct for the digestibility of the diet and quality of protein consumed, in order to represent the estimated biological value of the diet. A Filipino mixed diet (digestibility relative to reference proteins = 93) was chosen as the most similar diet for which information was available (for detailed description see Chomitz 1992, 113). The percentage recommended dietary intake (%RDI) was calculated, in order to present the data in a more readily interpretable manner and to control analytic variables for age, weight, and characteristics of the diet.

The protein intake value collected by the FFQ was compared with estimated requirements for actual weight and US National Center for Health Statistics (NCHS) weight for age and sex. Thus, PROTEIN was defined as follows: ProtCal = (Available Protein/RDI of Protein)*100. The mean and the median of this variable were 255 and 234%, respectively.

VITAMIN A ADEQUACY (VITA). Total vitamin A intake was calculated by Chomitz (1992) based on 24-hour recall information. The RDI of vitamin A was based on the United States Recommended Dietary Allowance (National Research Council 1989) estimate (RE/day) according to age categories. The %RDI of vitamin A (VITA) was estimated as follows: VITA = (available vitamin A RE/RDI of Vitamin A)*100. The mean and the median of this variable were 269 and 187%, respectively.

Affection

MATERNAL AFFECTION (AFFECT). Factor analysis was used as the basis of creating the AFFECT scale using the US-based Caldwell

HOME inventory of mother-and-child interaction. Two factors related to warmth and affection emerged from the factor analysis (WARMTH and ACCEPT). Since these factors were highly correlated, they were combined into a single factor called AFFECT.

The percentages of positive responses for the WARMTH and ACCEPT factors were as follows:

WARMTH

– **Home 26.** Parent holds child close for 10–15 minutes per day   70%
– **Home 30.** Parent praises child's qualities twice during visit   49%
– **Home 31.** Parent caresses, kisses, or cuddles child   49%
– **Home 40.** Parent introduces visitors to child   73%

ACCEPT

– **Home 54.** Parent does not slap or spank child   95%
– **Home 55.** No physical punishment used during past week   88%.

The AFFECT variable is defined as follows: AFFECT = SUM (WARMTH,ACCEPT).

MOTHER'S TIME SPENT WITH CHILD (HRSWKID). The total amount of time the mother spent with the child per day (HRSWKID) consisted of five items: (1) mother out of home with the child (HRS1); (2) mother doing housework with the child (HRS2); (3) mother sleeps with the child (HRS3); (4) mother feeds the child (HRS4); (5) mother plays with the child (HRS5).

The variable HRSWKID is defined as: HRSWKID = SUM (HRS1, HRS2, HRS3, HRS4, HRS5).

The mean and median hours per day the mother spent with the child were 14.6 and 15, respectively.

Academic stimulation

ACADEMIC STIMULATION AND PHYSICAL ENVIRONMENT (STIMUL). Factor analysis was used to create a STIMUL scale using the US-based Caldwell HOME inventory of mother-and-child interaction. Two factors related to learning and teaching environment emerged from the factor analysis (EDUPLAY and VARIETY). Since these factors were highly correlated, they were combined into a single factor called TEACH.

The percentages of positive responses for the EDUPLAY and

VARIETY factors were as follows:

EDUPLAY
- **Home 3.** Child owns five tapes   16%
- **Home 8.** Books visible in home   65%
- **Home 7.** Child owns books   63%
- **Home 10.** Magazine subscription   7%

VARIETY
- **Home 43.** Child has real or toy musical instruments   22%
- **Home 45.** Child has been on trip more than 50 miles in past year   34%
- **Home 46.** Child has been to museum during past year   9%
- **Home 49.** Child's art work   9%.

The STIMUL variable is defined as follows: STIMUL = SUM (EDUPLAY, VARIETY).

LEARNING AND TEACHING ENVIRONMENT (TEACH). The same procedure as before was used to construct the TEACH variable. Based on factor analysis loading factors using Caldwell's HOME inventory for measurement of the environment for preschool children, three related factors emerged, namely LEARN, LANGUAGE, and DISCIP. Some items in LANGUAGE are not culturally appropriate (see section on Javanese family literature review): for example, a child is not supposed to talk to parents in the presence of visitors (e.g. interviewers); therefore, **Home 27** (parent converses with child twice during visit), **Home 28** (parent answers child's questions verbally), and **Home 29** (parent responds verbally to child's speech) were eliminated. This elimination improved the correlation of LANGUAGE variables with some child developmental outcome.

The percentages of positive responses for the LEARN, LANGUAGE, and DISCIP factors were as follows:

LEARN
- **Home 13.** Encouraged to learn alphabet   78%
- **Home 37.** Encouraged to learn to read a few words   72%

LANGUAGE
- **Home 14.** Parent teaches verbal manners   97%

DISCIP
- **Home 38.** Child must wait for mealtime   22%
- **Home 39.** TV is used judiciously   45%.

These three variables were conceptually related and were highly correlated. Therefore, they were combined into a single variable called TEACH: TEACH = SUM (LEARN, LANGUAGE, DISCIP).

Support

EMOTIONAL SUPPORT RECEIVED BY THE MOTHER (EMOSUP). This variable was the sum of the following responses. Each response was coded between 0 and 2 (0 = not happy; 1 = happy; 2 = very happy):
1. Is mother satisfied with family help caring for the house?
2. Is mother satisfied with family help in child rearing?
3. Is mother satisfied with moral support she received from others?
4. Is mother satisfied with frequency of meeting with relatives and friends?

FATHER'S INVOLVEMENT IN CHILD CARE (FATHER). This variable was made by using the information on substitute caretakers. If the father was the first substitute caretaker, a value of 3 was assigned; if he was the second substitute caretaker, a value of 2 was assigned; if he was the third substitute caretaker, a value of 1 was assigned; if the father was none of those, a value of 0 was assigned. A percentage of 49.4% of the Javanese fathers were involved in child-care activities. FATHER: no involvement, 50.6%; SUB1, 17.4%; SUB2, 14.3%; SUB3, 17.8%.

Growth
A child's growth was determined from repeated measures of weight (kilograms) and height (centimetres), converted to ratios of weight-for-age (WAZ) and height-for-age (HAZ) and compared with the US NCHS reference population data according to procedures recommended by WHO. The means of WAZ and HAZ were − 1.53 and −2.24, respectively.

Mental development
Stanford Binet IQ scores (IQ) and Vineland's Social Quotient scores (SQ) were computed. The means of these scores were 89.1 and 102.7, respectively.

Nigeria

The variables presented here were based on a subset of data from the Positive Deviance in Nutrition Research Project funded by UNICEF, New York, conducted in Lagos, Nigeria (Aina et al. 1992). This project focused primarily on urban and semi-rural children in Lagos State, south-western Nigeria, with a small rural subsample. A total of 211 two-year-old children were chosen.

Social resources variables

MOTHER'S LITERACY (LITERACY). Literacy refers to the mother's last year of school completed (LSTYR), and the literacy of the mother (reads Yoruba and reads English). The definition of LITERACY is LITERACY = LSTYR + RDENGLSH + RDYORBA. The results were as follows:

1. LSTYR (coded from 0 to 5)
   - No formal education   (35%)
   - Some primary   (17%)
   - Primary completed   (27%)
   - Some secondary   (11%)
   - Secondary completed   (11%)
2. Literacy of mother (1 = yes) (0 = no)
   - Reads Yoruba   (56%)
   - Reads English   (37%).

MOTHER'S EXPOSURE TO MEDIA (MEDIA). Mother's media exposure consisted of three questions:

1. Number of states in Nigeria correctly identified (STAT), coded from 0 to 2:
   - None   4%
   - One to three   22%
   - Four or more   74%
2. Names of radio programmes identified (RADPGMM), coded from 0 to 3:
   - None   36%
   - One to two   38%
   - Three   21%
   - Four or more   6%
3. Numbers of TV programmes identified (TVPGM), coded from 0 to 3:
   - None   13%
   - One   13%
   - Two to three   45%
   - Four or more   30%.

The composite variable MEDIA was computed as follows: MEDIA = STAT + RADPGM + TVPGM.

LOCATION (LOCATN). The location variable consisted of three categories (coded from 0 to 2):

1. Rural   11%
2. Semi-rural   41%
3. Urban   48%.

Material resources

Two variables, HOUSING and LFDBUDGE, were chosen to measure the latent variable Material Resources. These two variables were significantly correlated.

HOUSING. The quality of house composite index consisted of the following information:
1. Housing type (TIPE) coded from 1 to 3
   - Face-to-face   74%
   - Compound or flat   9%
   - Detached   17%
2. Wall construction (WALLS) coded from 1 to 3
   - Mud   13%
   - Corrugated iron   9%
   - Cement blocks   79%
3. Roof construction (ROOF) coded from 1 to 4
   - Thatched   2%
   - Asbestos sheets   32%
   - Corrugated iron   65%
   - Concrete   1%
4. Floor construction (FLOOR) (1–4)
   - Mud   2%
   - Wood   2%
   - Cement   80%
   - Linoleum   15%
   - Tiles   1%
5. Number of rooms (RMS) (1–3)
   - One   71%
   - Two   19%
   - Three to four   10%
6. Housing condition (CONHOU) (1–4)
   - In very bad shape   13%
   - In need of repairs   51%
   - In good repair   33%
   - Paint, furniture looks new   3%
7. Electricity in house (ELECTR) (1–2)
   - No   25%
   - Yes   75%.

HOUSING = SUM (TIPE, WALLS, ROOF, FLOOR, CONHOU, RMS, ELECTR).

FOOD BUDGET (LFDBUDGE). Food budget consisted of the mother's contribution for food (CASH1), the father's contribution for food (CASH2), and the total amount all others contributed for food (CASH3): FDBUDGE = sum (CASH1, CASH2, CASH3); LFDBUDGE = ln(LFBUDGE).

Feeding practices

FOOD BELIEF (FDBELIEF). Meat was chosen in order to investigate the mother's perception of the proportional reward function. Meat was selected because it was the food most frequently and emotionally referred to when parents articulated the traditional value system with regard to children, food, and spoiling.

The question investigating belief towards meat was, "Is there any reason why you don't think a child of this age should have more meat?" The percentages of positive responses (coded as 0) were as follows (a code of 1 means negative response):
1. Spoil child's moral character   66%
2. Cause a child to steal   31%
3. Can spoil the child   46%.

The composite index of FDBELIEF is defined as follows: FDBELIEF = SUM (1,2,3)

FOOD INVESTMENT (FDINVEST). The food investment variable consisted of two questions:
1. Imagine that you have plenty of money for food. How big a piece of meat do you think is the right amount for a two-year-old child for one meal?
2. Imagine this is a piece of meat enough for one meal, and the child's father were eating with you. Please show how much meat each person in the family would receive. Be sure to indicate how much the two-year-old child will get compared to the other children.

An 11 × 9-inch board, one-third of an inch thick and varnished a beefsteak brown colour was developed to represent a slab of meat. This meat-board was deliberately made rather large in size to convey the notion that plenty of meat was available. It was marked by a grid of lines forming 396 half-inch squares, which represented pieces of meat. Mothers were asked to indicate their answers to questions about meat distribution by drawing on this board with chalk.

These two components were combined into the right amount of meat for a two-year-old. The composite variable is right amount of meat for two-year-old times sums of weekly frequencies of snacks, fruits, and other animal foods. The formula is: sum of the weekly frequency of intake of animal food, snack, and fruit, weighted by the portion size of meat appropriate for a two-year-old child. Sum (TOTANI, TSNACK, NFRUITOT) * (MTWOYRS). This variable is transformed into a natural logarithmic transformation.

Hygiene practices
The cleanliness of the environment consisted of three indicators – Cleanliness, Hygienic information, and Water source.

CLEANLINESS (CLEAN).
1. Debris on floor, inside or out.
2. Animal faeces (ANIMFC) (no = 1) (yes = 0)
   – No   87%
   – Yes   13%
3. Human faeces (HUMFC)
   – No   99%
   – Yes   1%
4. Spoiled food (SPLFD)
   – No   94%
   – Yes   6%
5. Dirt or other (DIRT)
   – No   33%
   – Yes   67%.
   CLEAN = SUM (ANIMFC, HUMFC, SPLFD, DIRT)

HYGIENIC INFORMATION (SANIT). Hygienic information refers to the following (yes = 1) (no = 0):
1. Was bowl cleaned before using (BWLCL)?
   – Yes   98%
   – No   2%
2. Were the utensils clean (UTENSCL)?
   – Yes   97%
   – No   3%
3. Did mother clean hands (HNDCLN)?
   – Yes   90%
   – No   10%

4. Did mother clean her hands (MOMHND)?
 - Yes 81%
 - No   19%.
SANIT = SUM (BWLCL, UTENSCL, HNDCLN, MOMHND).

WATER SOURCE (WATERSC). The water source variable has five categories ranging from 1 to 5:
1. Stream   9%
2. Well   9%
3. Rain or tank 6%
4. Borehole   12%
5. Tap   64%.

Affection

MATERNAL AFFECTION (WARM). This variable (WARM) consisted of a sum of interviewer rating of maternal behaviour and affection towards her child during the Bayley test situation. WARM is the sum of eight variables (each variable was coded from lowest to highest, or 1–5). The percentages of positive responses for each category are shown in table 8.1A.

MATERNAL VERBAL RESPONSIVENESS (VERBAL). This variable (VERBAL) is a sum of observed maternal verbalizations with her child. Each was coded from 0 to 2.
1. Simple words that child could repeat
 - Never   53%
 - Sometimes 35%
 - Usually   10%

Table 8.1A **Percentage of mothers scoring one (lowest) to five (highest) on eight variables of Maternal Affection (WARM)**

| Variable | Percentage of mothers with score | | | | |
	Lowest	Low	Average	High	Highest
Comfort	2	14	29	46	8
Encouragement	2	12	26	55	3
Eagerness	1	7	25	57	9
Emotional	1	7	17	64	10
Visible signs	1	13	19	66	10
Responsiveness	1	6	28	61	5
Response to mother	2	16	20	53	8

2. Were sounds without meaning
   - Never   89%
   - Sometimes   7%
   - Usually   4%.

CHILD-CARE ARRANGEMENTS (CHCARE). This variable included the quality of primary caregivers, secondary caregivers, total number of regular caregivers, and mother's proximity to the child when she worked. They were ranked using criteria consistent with the Caldwell HOME inventory. The Z-scores with these separate indicators were summed. In this sum, full weight was given to primary care and number of caregivers and half to secondary care and proximity to the mother.

Academic stimulation

TEACH CHILD (TEACH). The TEACH variable consisted of seven variables that related to the following questions (each was coded 1 = yes; 0 = no):
1. Do you teach your child the ABC? (ABC) (69% yes);
2. Does anyone in the family ever read him/her stories? (RYES) (25% yes);
3. Does anyone read stories? (STY) (38% yes);
4. Mother's play with child – social play (SOCT) (25% yes);
5. Mother's play with child – technical play (TPLA) (9% yes);
6. Do you teach child to put away toys? (90% yes);
7. Do you teach child to wash hands? (90% yes).
TEACH is the sum of these variables.

AVAILABILITY OF TOYS (TOYS). This variable is the sum of variables that relate to the following questions:
1. Does your child have any of the following toys? (yes = 1; no = 0):
   - Football, plastic ball, toys with wheel, rocking horse, toy airplane, wind-up toy, plastic rattle, plastic dolls, plastic building toys, puzzles, crayons, jewellery (not including earrings), stuffed animal, other toys
2. What other things does he/she like to play with? (yes = 1; no = 0):
   - Bottle covers, special stones (sticks), empty tins, plastic containers, school box, papers or newspaper, plastic bag, special cloth, sand, and water.

Modernizing lifestyle

MODERN BEHAVIOURS (MODBEHAV). This variable was the sum of variables relating to the following information (coded as 1 = yes and 0 = no). These variables loaded onto a single factor in factor analysis:
1. Eats with mum and dad at least twice a week (78% yes);
2. Caresses the child (48% sometimes = 0, 52% usually = 1);
3. Uses modern medical treatment (35% yes);
4. No safety hazard (28% yes);
5. No physical punishment, shouting, or threats observed toward the child during three-hour home visit (55% yes);
6. No housework required from two-year-old (83% yes).

FATHER LIVES WITH MOTHER (PALIVE). PALIVE consisted of four categories (coded from 1 to 4):
Father lives with mother:
1. Rarely or never   10%
2. Less than half-time   11%
3. More than half-time   5%
4. All the time   74%.

Child's personality

ELICITING BABY (ELICBABY). ELICBABY consisted of observer ratings of infant behaviour and affect during the Bayley test. ELICBABY is the mean of five components. Each component was coded from 1 to 5 (lowest to highest) (table 8.2A).

THE EASINESS OF THE CHILD HANDLED BY THE INTERVIEWERS (COOPBAB). COOPBAB is the reciprocal of the mean of several components (ranged from 1 to 5 or lowest to highest) (table 8.3A).

Growth

ANTHROPOMETRIC INDICATORS (WAZ AND HAZ). Weight, height, and age data were collected as recommended by WHO. Birth dates were determined from birth certificates. Weights were taken to the nearest 0.1 kg using a hanging scale with a capacity of 25 kg. A wooden stadiometer built by the project was used to measure height in cm (2–6 years).

Raw weights and heights were converted to Z-scores (WAZ and

Table 8.2A **Percentage of babies scoring one (lowest) to five (highest) on five components of infant behaviour and affect (ELICBABY)**

Component	Percentage of babies with score				
	Lowest	Low	Average	High	Highest
Eagerness	5	19	24	42	11
Dull to gleam	1	23	27	40	9
Attractiveness	4	14	32	43	8
Attraction to child	6	17	40	31	6

Table 8.3A **Percentage of babies scoring one (lowest) to five (highest) on five components of ease of handling (COOPBAB)**

Component	Percentage of babies with score				
	Lowest	Low	Average	High	Highest
Angry	31	33	12	18	5
Irritable	20	31	24	20	6
Affective	18	36	18	23	5
Task orientated	13	37	16	28	6
Provocative	20	37	20	20	3

HAZ) of the NCHS–WHO standards using software provided by the United States Centers for Disease Control. Two centimetres were added to the standing heights of the children just below two years, whose measurements were treated by the CDC program as recumbent lengths. The means of WAZ and HAZ were -1.78 and -2.29, respectively.

Mental development
The Bayley mental development index (MDI) and Bayley physical development index (PDI) were used to construct these variables. The means of MDI and PDI were 92.3 and 103.6, respectively.

References

Aina, T.A., M. Zeitlin, K. Setiolane, and H. Armstrong. 1992. Phase I Survey Results: Positive Deviance in Nutrition Research Project, Lagos State, Nigeria." Draft Report to UNICEF.

Behrman, J.R., and B.L. Wolfe. 1984. "More Evidence on Nutrition Demand. Income Seems Overrated and Women's Schooling Underemphasized." *Journal of Development Economics* 14: 105–128.

————, and ————. 1987. "How Does Mother's Schooling Affect Family Health, Nutrition, Medical Care Usage, and Household Sanitation." *Journal of Development Economics* 36: 185–204.

Belsky, J. 1984. "The Determinants of Parenting: A Process Model." *Child Development* 55: 83–96.

————, R.M. Lerner, and G.B. Spanier. 1984. *The Child in the Family*. Reading: Addison-Wesley.

Bengston, V.L., and J. Robertson. 1985. *Grandparenthood: Traditional and Emergent Perspectives*. Beverly Hills, Calif.: Sage Publications.

Bentler, P.M. 1985. *Theory and Implementation of EQS: A Structural Equations Program*. Los Angeles: BMDP Statistical Software.

Bollen, K. 1989. *Structural Equations with Latent Variables*. New York: Wiley.

Bradley, R. 1989. "Home Measurement of Maternal Responsiveness." In: M.H. Bornstein, ed. *Maternal Responsiveness: Characteristics and Consequences, Volume 43*. New York: Jossey-Bass, pp. 63–74.

Bronfenbrenner, U., P. Moen, and J. Garbarino. 1984. "Child, Family, and Community." In: R. Park, ed. *Review of Child Development Research*. Chicago, Ill.: University of Chicago Press, pp. 283–328.

Caldwell, J.C., and P. Caldwell. 1977. "The Economic Rationale of High Fertility: An Investigation Illustrated with Nigerian Survey Data." *Population Studies* 31: 5–27.

Chomitz, V.R. 1992. "Diet of Javanese Preschool Children: Relationship to Household Environmental Factors and Stature." Unpublished doctoral dissertation, Tufts University School of Nutrition, Medford, Mass.

Colletta, N.D. 1991. "Module VI: Mental Health Problems and Emotional Needs of Young Children. Cross-cultural Child Development: A Training Course for Program Staff." Washington, DC: Christian Children's Fund.

Satoto, and N.D. Colletta. 1987. "Changing Caretaking Behaviors to Improve Child Growth and Development. An Action Research Proposal." Submitted to the Ford Foundation, New York and Jakarta (unpublished).

Engle, P.L. 1992. "Care and Nutrition: ICN Theme Paper." Report prepared for UNICEF.

Fischer, C.S. 1977. *Networks and Places: Social Relations in the Urban Setting*. New York: Free Press.

Grant, P.J. 1984. In: *The State of the World's Children*. New York: Oxford University Press for UNICEF, p. 3.

Heller, P., and W. Drake. 1979. "Malnutrition, Child Morbidity, and the Family Decision Process." *Journal of Development Economics* 6: 203–235.

Hoffman, L.W. 1988. "Crosscultural Differences in Child-rearing Goals." In: R.A. LeVine, P.M. Miller, and M.M. West, eds. *Parental Behaviors in Diverse Societies. New Directions for Child Development, No. 40*. San Francisco: Jossey-Bass, pp. 99–122.

Hwang, C.P., M.E. Lamb, and A. Broberg. 1989. "The Development of Social and Intellectual Competence in Swedish Preschoolers Raised at Home and in Out-Home Care Facilities." In: K. Kreppner and R.M. Lerner, eds. *Family Systems and Life-Span Development*. Hillsdale, NJ: Lawrence Erlbaum Associates, pp. 105–127.

International Encyclopedia of Social Sciences. 1968. D.L. Sells, ed. *International Encyclopedia of Social Sciences, Volume 3*. New York: Macmillan, p. 163.

Jöreskog, K.G., and D. Sörbom. 1989. *LISREL7: G Guide to the Program and Applications.* Chicago, Ill: SPSS.

Kohn, M.L. 1969. *Class and Conformity: A Study in Values.* Homewood, Ill.: Dorsey Press.

Kreppner, K. 1989. "Linking Infant Development-in-Context Research to the Investigation of Life-Span Family Development." In: K. Kreppner and R.M. Lerner, eds. *Family Systems and Life-Span Development.* Hillsdale, NJ: Lawrence Erlbaum Associates, pp. 33–64.

Landers, C. 1989. "A Psychobiological Study of Infant Development in South India." In: J.K. Nugent, B.M. Lester, and T.B. Brazelton, eds. *The Cultural Context of Infancy.* Norwood, NJ: Ablex, pp. 169–208.

LeVine, R.A., N. Klein, and C. Owen. 1967. "Father–Child Relationships and Changing Lifestyles in Ibadan, Nigeria." In: H. Miner, ed. *The City in Modern Africa.* New York: Praeger, pp. 215–255.

Lloyd, B.B. 1970. "Yoruba Mothers' Reports of Child-rearing, Some Theoretical and Methodological Considerations." In: P. Mayer, ed. *Socialization, The Approach from Social Anthropology.* New York: Tavistock Press, pp. 75–108.

Minturn, L., and W.W. Lambert. 1964. *Mothers of Six Cultures: Antecedents of Child Rearing.* New York: Wiley.

Morris, D. 1969. *The Human Zoo.* New York: McGraw-Hill.

Myers, R. 1992. *The Twelve Who Survive. Strengthening Programmes of Early Childhood Development in The Third World.* London: Routledge.

National Research Council. 1989. *Recommended Dietary Allowances.* 10th edn. Washington, DC: National Academy Press.

Olusanya, P.O. 1981. *Nursemaids and the Pill: A Study of Household Structure, Female Employment, and the Small Family Ideal in an African Metropolis. University of Ghana Population Studies, No. 9.* Lagos: Tyburn Enterprises.

Rohner, R.P. 1975. *They Love Me, They Love Me Not: A Worldwide Study of the Effects of Parental Acceptance and Rejection.* Washington, DC: Human Relations Area Files.

SAS Institute Inc. 1989. *SAS STAT User's Guide. Version 6, Vol. 1.* Cary, NC: Statistical Analysis Systems Institute.

Schneewind, K.A. 1989. "Contextual Approaches to Family Systems Research: The Macro–Micro Puzzle." In: K. Kreppner and R.M. Lerner, eds. *Family Systems and Lifespan Developments.* Hillsdale, NJ: Lawrence Erlbaum Associates, pp. 197–222.

Whiting, B.B., and J.W.M. Whiting. 1975. *Children in Six Cultures: A Psycho-Cultural Analysis.* Cambridge, Mass.: Harvard University Press.

Zeitlin, M., H. Ghassemi, and M. Mansour. 1990. *Positive Deviance in Child Nutrition: With Emphasis on Psychosocial and Behavioural Aspects and Implications for Development.* Tokyo: United Nations University Press.

———, C. Super, A. Beiser, G. Guldan, N. Ahmed, J. Zeitlin, M. Ahmed, and S. Sockalingam. 1988. *A Behavioral Study of Positive Deviance in Young Child Nutrition and Health in Rural Bangladesh,* Chapter 6. Report to the Officer of Health and the Asia and Near East Bureau of the Agency for International Development, Baltimore, Md.

9

Synthesis of concepts and research needs

Introduction

In chapters 1–8 we carried out the first two objectives of this document, to review the literature on research pertinent to the family in five disciplines and to formulate and test an integrated empirical model of family characteristics that determine child welfare and development. In this chapter we use the findings from the literature and our own analyses to propose and support a definition of family social wellness. We propose models for testing and using this definition for the design and evaluation of policies and programmes. Finally, we discuss research approaches and tools needed to support a family social health approach to development assistance.

Definition of well-functioning families or family social health

Viewed together, the family literature provides consistent criteria for defining family social health, wellness, or well-functioning that could be subdivided in a variety of ways. For the purposes of providing assistance to socio-economic development, we choose to group them under four dimensions that roughly correspond to four different domains of policy or intervention approaches. These dimensions also

238

show an approximate congruence with the four spheres of action designated by the Family in Development initiative of the Agency for International Development (AID): the family as an economic system, the family as a social and biological reproductive system, political choices and the family, and families at risk (Agency for International Development 1991).

1. *Family management*, including skills in accessing and managing resources needed to sustain the family under normal conditions and during crisis (food, money, shelter, transportation, health care, education, etc.), and skills in governance of the family as a co-operative unit (decision-making, bargaining, problem solving).
2. *Family caring capacity*, characterized by sensitive and loving transactions between family members and by adequate technical knowledge and caring skills in physical maintenance, nutrition, health, socialization, and education.
3. *Family beliefs, rules, and goals* including explicit and implicit ideals and values for the family itself, goals for individual members, resource-sharing rules, cultural rules and codes for family behaviour, perceptual frameworks, and cognitive interpretations.
4. *Family boundary maintenance*, or structural integrity, covering the formation and dissolution of reproductive partnerships, birth control, child custody and fostering, the launching of adult children, care arrangements for the elderly, temporary separation, and death.

These dimensions are embedded in the family's interactions with its ecological context, and must also be considered from the perspective of family stage in the life cycle (Walker and Crocker 1988). The international development assistance field should find the contextual considerations familiar, as far more attention already has been given to the contextual community level than to families themselves.

Importance of family social health in producing child growth and development

We used our data on families in Indonesia and Nigeria to create the empirical models (see ch. 8) that illustrate the importance of social health at the family level. These models support the above definition, although the studies were not designed to gather data explicitly on each dimension. Our data sets included many covariables of malnutrition and mental development (demographic, social, economic, attitudinal, and behavioural) and these covariables showed expected modest correlations with growth and cognitive test scores. We found that models using these variables to measure the quality of family functioning (social health) and to explore the effects of family social health on the children's overall development showed stronger and more meaningful associations than the one-on-one relationships. We interpret these findings as an indication that family-level interventions that improve the child's total condition are likely to be more effective than vertical programmes that influence only one aspect at a time.

Family management

Family management enables the family as a unit to acquire and manage resources consistent with its goals and cultural codes. We call this "management," rather than "coping," because psychologists use the term coping to refer to only one aspect of management, the response to crisis. The management dimension of family social health corresponds to the AID sphere of the family as an economic system. It includes McMaster's "basic task area" (see Epstein, Bishop, and Baldwin 1984): earning a living, day-to-day home economics, planning, and seeking to take advantage of social services and new business opportunities. Proactive, upwardly mobile management styles are associated with favourable child outcomes. Although our model data were not collected to test the family management dimension, a number of our academic and health care measures reflect its presence.

Caring capacity

This dimension, which corresponds to the family as a social and biological reproductive system, has a loving and fun-loving component and a micro-level competency component: these include knowing how to breast-feed, play peekaboo, soothe a crying child, be sensitively verbally responsive, tell a story, prepare oral rehydration therapy, and clean a skin puncture; knowing when to go to the doctor; knowing how to protect food and kitchen utensils from animals. It captures the capacity to enhance and celebrate living through micro-level transactions between domestic partners, their children, and others.

The affective aspect of caring capacity involves management at the micro-level, where the behavioural transactions between individuals cross the perceptual boundary from "doing" to "being," as in "being" empathetic, warm, and sensitively responsive. The technical aspect includes child stimulation, nutrition, health care, sanitation, family planning, and other teachable skills – the common topics of parent education programmes.

Beliefs, rules, and goals

The beliefs, rules, and goals of the socially healthy family provide a support structure for economic success for both parents and children. They facilitate resource sharing and forward planning, which benefit all members. They are rooted in society's concepts of the ideal family, in cultural value systems that draw support from the cultural contexts of the community and society. Concerns for these value systems at the societal level correspond to AID's sphere of political choices and the family.

These values and ideals have an altruistic and an artistic component, reflected, for example, in the Yoruba proverbs about parenting (ch. 7), in pictures of the Madonna and Child, as well as in pictures by Norman Rockwell. Cultural ideals for the family give meaning to life. The ability to fulfil them is a criterion for judging the success of life itself. Cultural periods remembered as golden ages have been defined by the quality of family life.

Importance of cultural paradigms, legal and social entitlements, and cognitive interpretations

Research literature across the social sciences shows that important determinants of family social health include cultural and religious ideals and values, individual beliefs, and the "fit" between these paradigms and the social conditions required for economic prosperity. These paradigms are expressed in family law, social welfare entitlement, family size limitation, parenting codes, cognitive interpretation of events, and in gender and age-specific conventions for intra-household resource and task allocation. Examples of evidence from the literature include:
1. *Sociology*: continuing dialectic between socio-economic conditions, values, laws, and lifestyle prescriptions; negative effect claimed for values of capitalist economy on social responsibility; positive effects of US medical establishment's diet and exercise prescriptions

on mortality indicators; dialectic process illustrated by current US debate over abortion.

2. *Anthropology*: many examples of resource allocation rules that negatively and positively affect categories of individuals. Observation that children in certain modernized cultures are less responsible and altruistic than children in more traditional societies.

3. *Household economics*: recognition that implicit cultural contracts and legal and institutional factors that determine the disposition of household assets, such as family laws regarding property rights and social entitlements, play a greater role in intra-household resource allocation than active bargaining among family members ("shoot-out at the family corral").

4. *Psychology*: the extreme resistance to change of male gender roles in dual-earner households in the United States where the wife earns as much as the husband but continues to perform most domestic tasks; the finding that the main determinant of why some families cope while others fall into crisis under similar stress is the meaning that the stressful event holds for the family and the individuals within it.

5. *Development assistance*: international assistance agencies historically have been careful to remain neutral in their approach to values in order to build consensus across cultures. Ideologies put forth by these agencies, such as Child Survival, have played a major role in shaping programmes and effecting evaluation indicators. With the worldwide movement towards deepening democratic reform, however, AID (1991) has recognized that cultural adjustment of legal and social structures is needed to reduce intra-family inequities.

The cultural renewal process: How paradigms change

The renewal process by which cultural value systems adapt to support socio-economic improvement also can be considered as a form of "cultural adjustment" that is needed in parallel to structural adjustment. Historically, cultural paradigms of the family change from within through a dialectic, self-corrective process. Opinion leaders within the culture formulate and voice these changes. Ideologies coalesce around political and economic forces and the mood of the times; they both respond to and are precognizant of socio-economic change. Certain orientations have deep cultural roots, as for example the 3,000-year-old Jewish tradition. Other social trends appear as chaotic as the weather. Cultural consensus continually reshapes from within.

Positive change in culture-wide codes, such as healthful diet changes in the United States, appear to occur when the local intelligentsia first develops and articulates the new codes through consensus building in professional circles and then through the media, social services, and legislation, with ongoing feedback via professional meetings and journals and mass communications.

Studies of changing parenting codes also reveal a self-regulating, adaptive process when underlying resources are sufficient to permit families to regenerate. The greater the cultural distance between the traditional and modern lifestyles, the greater the paradigm shift required. In many of the world's poorest countries, cultural renewal has not kept pace with social change because of the dearth of resources available to the intelligentsia, which must formulate and legitimize new codes. Such moral rearmament activities are trivialized and ring hollow when they are left solely to the propaganda wing of the government in power. Cultural reconstruction becomes deadlocked by conflict between social profitability for the culture as a whole and the survival needs of its individual families. Values supporting small family size, for example, cannot prevail as long as individual families cannot afford to limit the number of their children. Cultural renewal also is deadlocked by resistance to necessary reductions or downward adjustments of entitlement to groups who continue to hold power.

In the most seriously affected parts of the world, moral codes developed over millennia of social evolution have disappeared with the lifestyles they supported. The absence of adequate cultural renegotiation and regeneration by legitimate opinion leaders has produced social conditions resembling cultural wastelands, over which unprincipled profiteers, degenerate gangs, and religious fundamentalists vie for control. Chapter 10 suggests actions that may assist developing countries in cultural renewal.

Family boundary maintenance

Flexible boundary maintenance, adapting to changing life-cycle needs, is a characteristic of well-functioning family systems. Involuntary boundary problems occur during armed conflict, sudden death, migration to find paid employment, and extreme poverty that forces reproductive partners to abandon each other and their children. Pathological boundary crises include male abandonment and separation leading to female-headed households; extramarital or conflicted polygamous relationships; struggles over child custody, support, and fostering; contested inheritance and property rights; and predation by some family members on others. These pathologies often involve problems with boundaries between family members, reflected in violence, sexual abuse, and dysfunction involving substance abuse. Families classified "at risk" typically have boundary problems.

Proposed research model for measuring family social health

Instrument development for the evaluation of family support and parent education programmes is still in its infancy. Krauss (1988) reviewed more than a dozen measurement instruments that have attempted to assess family functioning. Use of these tools has resulted in inconclusive outcomes and generally has failed to establish hard links between programmes, family measures, and individual well-being. Nevertheless, these instruments provide a smorgasbord of concepts and items to be considered in future research.

The use of a family social health approach in programme design and evaluation calls for new modelling procedures that assess the following:
1. How family social health determines the demand for inputs provided by programmes;
2. The impact of those inputs on the family as a whole and on individual family members;
3. The effects of family social health on child outcomes under conditions of changing inputs.

This formulation draws on ideas expressed by Berman, Kendall, and Bhattacharyya (1994). The best ways of accomplishing this task require further discussion. Dunst and Trivette (1988), for example, use hierarchical regressions and canonical correlations for family systems analysis. We suggest the development of structural latent variable models similar to those presented in chapter 8, but which incorporate certain desirable features of regressions. The coefficients in the models in chapter 8 cannot be used to estimate effect sizes. These models were not designed to incorporate policy variables (e.g. government expenditure on education and other programmes created outside the family). The hybrid models that we propose would permit prediction of the impact of different levels of programme resources on targeted outcomes, but would continue to take into account the integrity and complexity of the family system. Such models would incorporate both supply and demand relationships. The UNICEF conceptual framework might serve as a starting point for conceptualizing analyses that test the effects of multiple existing vertical programmes on households and families.

The need for further research

The boundaries between the methods and orientations of the different social sciences increasingly overlap. This merging of disciplines with a redefinition of paradigms has been claimed to be a part of the trend towards "de-differentiation" in the post-modern era (Lash 1990). For policy-related work, disciplinary interests recede in importance as the topics of study spring into the foreground. The family is a topic that demands this blending and synthesis of methods. In fact, the family could prove to be the best single topic for inter-disciplinary methodological development, because within-disciplinary methods for family studies already are well articulated and explored, providing a tested menu of methods and results to contrast and compare.

Fields that are multidisciplinary in origin, such as international nutrition and food policy, may be at the forefront of disciplinary pluralism. The same nutrition-related theses are produced by academic departments of nutrition, epidemiology, international health, psychology, human development, human biology, sociology, anthropology, economics, and demography. Social scientists working in these already multidisciplinary fields may be more experienced and objective in bringing a cross-disciplinary perspective to the family than researchers based in disciplines with long-established family studies.

New greatly increased computing capacity invites statistical analysis plans that draw eclectically from the various disciplines and synthesize elements from them into increasingly comprehensive explanatory models. For example, endogeneity – bidirectional flow of causality previously modelled by econometricians – now can be taken into account in epidemiological models using packaged programs for simultaneous logistic regression. Conversely, the structural equation models that we find in psychological research can be adapted along econometric lines to permit cost-effectiveness estimates for varying development inputs, as we suggest above.

Antecedents of new, more inclusive modelling may be drawn from systems modelling in development studies that began in the early 1970s. The international nutrition planning movement provides a relevant example. In the second half of the 1970s, multidisciplinary research teams in institutions in both industrialized and developing countries designed elaborate cross-disciplinary conceptual frameworks. In the late 1970s and early 1980s, disenchantment with the mathematical modelling capabilities of the time, and failure to couple systems theories to action, swung the pendulum towards less formal and less quantitative approaches to operational research and evaluation, in which the systems relationships served as conceptual frameworks.

As the moment approaches when numerical methods will be able to keep pace with programmatic action, the attempt to quantify cross-disciplinary theory building re-emerges as a central priority. The current and coming generations of computers provide sufficient computing power for a quantum leap in statistical social science applications. These applications have the potential for creating portable computer field tools that remove many of the time lags and much of the guesswork from global monitoring and development assistance. Many of the component pieces and features that should be incorporated into these applications already are evident. What has fallen furthest behind is statistical programming. A new, well-publicized cross-disciplinary statistical programming agenda for the social sciences is critically needed to stimulate the creation of the needed software packages.

This call for theoretical and statistical research and development is applications driven. Computers of the new generation already are in our homes and overseas field offices, where their potential is underused. The pay-offs for such development work should be comparable to the increments in efficiency gained by moving from boat mail to airmail to fax to e-mail. We suggest that the following should be done:

1. Develop an intradisciplinary research team on the family to:
   (a) Evaluate cross-disciplinary findings and formulate new theories based on this evaluation.
   (b) Determine research agendas and data analysis needs.
2. Hold a meeting of statisticians serving these disciplines to define statistical research and computer software development to meet the needs of the research agenda. Work will be needed in the following areas:
   (a) Non-parametric, non-linear, and robust versions of all multivariate procedures, such as partial correlation, multiple regression, ANCOVA, MANOVA, to deal with data not nor-

mally distributed, or non-linear, and that may have problematic outliers. At present, statistical software for univariate analysis copes with these issues whereas software for multivariate analysis does not, with very few exceptions.

(b) Easy-to-use jackknifing procedures that permit accurate estimation from smaller samples (essential for field procedures too burdensome to conduct on very large samples).

(c) Flexible, multivariate repeat-measures programs – e.g. MANCOVA packages that permit individualized specification of needed covariate and other calculations.

(d) Better methods for dealing with statistical significance when conducting multiple tests on large sets of variables – e.g. more programs for specifying combined variable models for testing subsets of coefficients together (methods that do not demand data normality).

(e) Methods or rules for making multivariate models more robust in that the coefficients they produce need to become less sensitive to the entry or removal of individual variables. In the present state of the art in model building, the almost arbitrary addition or removal of individual variables from a large data set can create almost any outcome desired by the data analyst.

(f) Better programs for sequence recognition and for analysis of interactive systems.

(g) Better software for qualitative data analysis in formats that can be merged with quantitative data sets.

(h) Management information systems (MIS) applications that conduct more automatic data quality checks and that have built-in multivariate analysis programs, customized to the MIS data and robust against the effects of outliers.

References

Agency for International Development (AID). 1991. "Family and Development Progress Update, April 1991."

Berman, P., C. Kendall, and K. Bhattacharyya. 1994. "The Household Production of Health: Integrating Social Science Perspectives on Micro-level Health Determinants." *Social Science and Medicine* 38: 205–215.

Dunst, C.J., and C.M. Trivette. 1988. "Toward Experimental Evaluation of the Family, Infant and Preschool Program," In: H.B. Weiss and F.H. Jacobs, eds. *Evaluating Family Programs*. New York: Aldine de Gruyter, pp. 315–346.

Epstein, N.B., D.S. Bishop, and L.M. Baldwin. 1984. "McMaster Model of Family Functioning." In: D.H. Olson and P.M. Miller, eds. *Family Studies Review Yearbook, Volume 2*. New Delhi: Sage Publications.

Krauss, M.W. 1988. "Measures of Stress and Coping in Families." In: H.B. Weiss, and F.H. Jacobs, eds. *Evaluating Family Programs*. New York: Aldine de Gruyter, pp. 177–194.

Lash, S. 1990. "Modernity or Modernism? Weber and Contemporary Social Theory." In: *Sociology of Postmodernism*. London: Routledge, pp. 130–133.

Walker, D.K., and R.W. Crocker. 1988. "Measuring Family Systems Outcomes." In: H.B. Weiss and F.H. Jacobs, eds. *Evaluating Family Programs*. New York: Aldine de Gruyter, pp. 153–176.

10

Policy and programme recommendations

The recommendations in this chapter have the aim of improving family social health to strengthen the impact of high-quality family functioning on children and on national and global development. In most cases, this effort occurs in the context of other goals for vulnerable family members, such as child development, legal reform, micro-enterprise development, and agricultural production.

With respect to policy, we recommend that efforts to strengthen the family be built into different domains as diverse as income tax and pension regulations; inheritance law; industrial regulatory laws; education, health and agricultural policy; food subsidies; and other social entitlements for the poor.

In the design of services and interventions, we urge the continuing process of integrating vertical services into innovative child development programmes that strengthen families and benefit children at the primary care or grass-roots level.

Need to alleviate poverty

Family social health cannot be maintained below a certain resource threshold. Extreme poverty undermines each of its dimensions: management, care, beliefs/rules/goals, values, and boundary maintenance.

To strengthen family life, programmes that relieve poverty must also seek to develop the potential of families as an important force for promoting development. The household must be viewed as an "economic source" rather than as an "economic sink" in social and economic policy (Edwards 1979).

Need to support local family policy initiatives

Opinion leaders in developing countries need first to engage in assessment and analysis of the conditions of family life. They need to do this work within designated family initiatives and agencies analogous to AID's Family in Development initiative or to the US Government's Administration for Children, Youth, and Families (ACYF). As in industrialized countries, the seminal research and intellectual creativity supporting these activities must come primarily from universities.

Policy on the family is an extremely private matter from a cultural perspective. Almost by definition, it cannot be set by outside experts, regardless of their credentials in anthropology, law, or any number of other fields; it *must* be determined by local scholars, and cultural and legal authorities. For adequate policy formulation and national leadership, these must be both men and women of intellectual stature, with resources to formulate concepts, conduct research, and synthesize findings on the relevant issues. They must be enabled to provide the voices of leadership that guide their governments.

Although considerable development assistance has gone towards empowering the rural poor and urban underclasses through community development activities, external assistance for members of the élite to formulate public policy has sometimes been considered unnecessary. In theory, élite people hold the purse and the power themselves; in practice, those who control their countries' wealth are not the intellectuals who operate its policy institutes, write textbooks, or direct research. In recent years, structural adjustment policies have tended, in the name of cost savings, to reduce third world scholars, their institutions of higher learning, and government technical agencies to levels of destitution at which they no longer can fulfil their mission to provide the intellectual leadership for the formulation of national policy and programmes. In Nigeria, for example, 600 per cent inflation in recent years has not been counterbalanced by increases in the salaries of university professors. The failure of third world intellectuals to perform under impossible working conditions may be taken as further evidence of their dispensability.

Assessment, cultural renewal, and policy formation

A study by the United Nations (1987) indicates that very few governments have based their family policies and programmes on a clear understanding of the problems of local families. The laws adopted in newly emerging states often have been taken from the laws of previous European and other colonial powers, or other sources not sensitively attuned to actual needs. Yet family laws, and formal and traditional social entitlements, have profound effects on family and individual welfare (Folbre 1992).

Examination of the social evolution of child support illustrates the need to review these laws. All traditional family systems enforced paternal support and care for almost all children, as well as the participation of both biological parents together as a family unit in decision-making and care of their offspring. This enforcement often operated through rules that banned procreation outside marriage or assigned all children born of a mother as legal children of that mother's husband.

Where families and religious leaders no longer have the power to legislate these values, many children are unsupported by their fathers, and some are unsupported by either parent. Therefore, most industrialized countries have found that it no longer works to treat the support and socialization of children as a purely private issue. Government must step in to restore these supports through child entitlement policies (Bruce and Lloyd 1992).

According to Bruce and Lloyd (1992), from whom much of this section is adapted, "Who pays for the kids?" should be an explicit and fundamental issue of population and development policy, not a hazy afterthought. Assessment should focus on the conditions of families and the effects of existing laws and social welfare provisions on family functioning. Local scholars should assist governments in developing frameworks for understanding the interaction between families and the process of development. These frameworks should provide the basis for government policy formation on family issues and family-related research. The formulation of action agendas should be a part of this assessment and analysis process.

These agendas must be forward looking and flexible in orientation. According to the United Nations (1986, 7),

Families should be seen not so much as states-of-being but as states-of-becoming which are given to an enormous range of flexibility and adaptation not only during the life cycle of the family but also in a process of interaction with technology, values, social structures, etc. Unfortunately, there is not a great deal of literature on the process through which families in developing countries move and the isolated and cumulative effects of the family on development and vice versa.

The formal protection of children in many developing countries is now covered only indirectly under marital policies or in policies largely unknown and unimplemented. Developing countries must come to recognize that child entitlements are not just of sentimental importance, but are vital to long-term national development goals. In a process of cultural renewal, recasting timeless values in modern terms, they must articulate norms, procedures, and laws that entitle children directly to both parents' human and economic resources. Indeed, in most countries, the condition of the next generation's human capital will determine national success or failure in an increasingly unified world labour market. The establishment of child entitlements serves individual equity considerations as well as societal income distribution goals. These entitlements can create a serious counter-pressure to the tendency of gender and parental status to be key determinants of wealth and well-being.

There need to be explicit costs and economic expectations related to having children, and penalties for those who try to leave their responsibilities behind (Folbre 1992). The phrase "every child, a wanted child" should be complemented with the phrase "every child, a costly child." In most countries where child maintenance laws have been effectively implemented, there are dramatic results. In Australia, when child payments were deducted from non-resident father's wages, the proportion of fathers providing support to children went from under 45 per cent to over 70 per cent in 18 months. Where few fathers are absorbed into formal wage labour, the means of extracting child support payments are substantially reduced. A process should be set in place so that those members of the élite who guide and make policy are enabled to create these norms and begin to experience their meaning for themselves, thereby participating in the ongoing process of social construction called for in chapter 2 (pages 32–34).

Negative effects of existing policy structures

Assessment must identify existing negative outcomes of social change and development on families. Both intended and unintended outcomes need to be assessed. Assistance in one area should not be at the cost of impairing other functions of families, who must be seen in their ecological contexts. The types of negative factors to be identified include the following:

1. Persistence of male-dominated inheritance laws, and male access to resources under conditions in which large numbers of women and their children no longer enjoy the protection of male-headed households or receive financial support from husbands and fathers.
2. Negative effects on children that occur when the dissemination of new technologies or resources interferes with traditional child-care practices, school attendance, or food sources.
3. Family allowance programmes that make it necessary for the poorest families to continue to bear more children to obtain adequate resources for survival. One example is food supplementation programmes that provide food only for those families with children under five years of age.
4. Government interventions for children that involve professionals in ways that undermine the parents' capacity to care for their children in the future. This may occur because the professionals hold a negative perception that poor parents lack expertise and that children must be protected against harm from their parents' ignorance. This produces a negative impact on parents' confidence and ability to socialize their children. School curricula that make fun of local cultural "superstitions" are an example. "Policies often assume that families requiring assistance are somehow deficient or weak because of the inadequacies of the families and their members rather than because of structural inadequacies in the society or economy" (United Nations 1987, 43). Bureaucracies that serve their own convenience rather than that of their clients may inadvertently substitute for the family's function and capacity to care for its members, rather than serve them as backups. Hospital care of breast-fed infants without their mothers, so that the mother loses her breast milk and switches to bottle-feeding, is one example.

Unfortunately, some of the neediest families happily relinquish their duties. According to Becker (1992, 113), welfare recipients tend to be those least concerned about their children and least willing to help themselves. He proposed helping these families by giving them the "carrot and stick" to induce them to take better care of their children:

Families that look out for the children's interests should get additional payments. For example, benefits might be larger if the parents take children to regular health checkups, if the children have good school attendance records, if parents participate in school programs, or even if children can get good grades and perform well on achievement tests.

New social realities

Assessment and action must consider the policy implications of social changes presented in chapter 2. The effects of modernization on families usually are linked to rapidly changing technologies, shifts to a consumption orientation, and increasing social mobility with an emphasis on increasing individual achievement (Berger and Berger 1984; Dizard and Gadlin 1990). Despite positive impacts on such factors as health, survival, and education, there is a cost in terms of familial bonds. Falling fertility leads to few relatives in the next generation. Unrestrained independence of individuals, according to the United Nations (1987), contributes to the deterioration of family values in which "the young generation hardly believes anymore in values that call for the constitution and the preservation of family units" (United Nations 1987, 10). In the society where everyone is anonymous, many young people do not find security. This anonymity is associated with high levels of criminality, violence, and widespread abuse of alcohol and drugs (United Nations 1987).

As noted earlier, other effects of modernization that have shifted all aspects of the family life cycle include increasing numbers of single-parent families, increasing numbers of women in the labour force, and long lives for the elderly, who have fewer children to support them. The recent resurgence of family rhetoric in political debate is an indicator of the growing concern of national leaders to preserve families. There is no consensus, however, on how to deal with family problems. In the United States the slogan "back to family values" has been attacked by "whose values?" (Newsweek 1992).

Public familism

The concept

Negative changes can be reversed by social policies and programmes that support the dimensions of family social wellness. The caring di-

254

mension has been defined by Dizard and Gadlin (1990, 6) under the name of "familism" as the bonds of reciprocal and unconstrained material and emotional support between family members. Part of the task of protecting "familism" is to expand "public familism," defined as the aggregate of policies that help people to sustain their private lives (Dizard and Gadlin 1990, 204). Note that this does not mean that government programmes should *replace* responsibilities that rightfully should remain within the family, but, rather, they should protect an environment in which the family is able to carry out its functions. As an example, pension funds and social security systems that provide financial support for the elderly should serve to facilitate rather than to replace the emotional support and crisis management provided by their children. The challenge is how to provide these systems in ways that do not diminish long-standing traditions of mutual aid, love, and respect.

"Public familism" also refers to a public spirit of family interconnectedness and mutual responsibility that is able to counterbalance the social isolation associated with the decline of familism. Dizard and Gadlin (1990, 224) conclude,

If we can acknowledge our manifold dependencies, if we can see those dependencies as the links between our private lives and the larger social patterns our private lives constitute, we might then be able to forge a society in which autonomous individuals are capable of consciously shaping their own families and, in doing so, constitute a world in which "caring, sharing, and loving" are broadly incorporated into both public and private lives.

Policy makers must be conscious of the forces at play to be able to engage families in "mending the bridges" when traditional structures and values are eroded before new ones spontaneously fill their place. This mending must be done to maintain cultural continuity and national identity and to serve the goals of economic development.

The limits of public familism

American Public Radio on 15 July 1992 featured the story of a married couple confined to wheelchairs with severe cerebral palsy, a neurological birth defect that forces both partners to use computerized voice-synthesizing machines to speak understandably and that makes them unable to find employment. This couple gave birth to a normal baby girl. The state provides income and nursing care for the couple's personal needs, but has no provision for a round-the-clock

255

nanny to assist them with their child. The rights and obligations of the couple, the state, and the child all can be contested.

In cases where public services are required, structures capable of meeting the personal emotional needs of individuals do not evolve overnight. Most group structures that meet intensely personal needs, such as churches where individual members confess, pray, and witness together, or 12-step programmes that provide anonymous confession and social support, have evolved in the non-governmental sector of public life.

It is doubtful that the socialization and behaviour-control functions of the family can ever be taken over completely by the public domain. Psychiatric in-patient programmes, halfway houses, and other services cannot fully repair inadequate early socialization. Individual conscience develops within the family. Across societies the ultimate transmitters of right and wrong conduct are the parents, as supported by chapters 6 and 7 on Javanese and Yoruba family life. The success of marriage and family life is shaped by parents of the previous and present generations, not by government policy alone. Development of conscience depends upon the quality of parent–child relationships, such as the affection, nurturance, and support that a parent gives the child and the child's identification with the parents (Christiansen 1991). Our Yoruba model (ch. 8) shows that there is a strong reciprocal influence between affectionate and attentive mothering and co-operative personality of the child. The quality of emotional attachment developed in the first year of life determines the capacity for making strong bonds during adult life (Morris 1969). The treatment of children by parents not only is extremely important in its own right but also greatly influences the relations between the younger and the older generations (Drazen 1978).

The task of expanding "public familism" is far from clear. Social recognition of our reciprocal bonds of dependency in the public realm may be an end-point towards which societies of the information era are headed.

Confusion over the roles of organized religion, the government, non-governmental organizations, and the family

The role of organized religion versus secular agencies in reinforcing family values, and the definition of which obligations should remain in the family versus which should be public, are not obvious and may become even less clear in the future.

The role of organized religion

According to conservatives, the abandonment of religion, liberal values of self-indulgence, lax moral standards, and lack of family obligation threaten the conventional family. Dizard and Gadlin (1990) conclude, however, that there is no prospect that the values of the "good old days" will return. W.J. Doherty (personal communication 1992) observes that, in the post-modern information era, individuals are bombarded by the rhetoric and imagery of so many alternate value systems that the words and images of the various religions themselves become relative, and cannot be taken literally. Yet if moral values rooted in religion are the most powerful underpinning to unite the individual, family, and society, the attainment of public familism may be impossible without religion.

Berger and Berger (1984) propose that the earlier fabric of bourgeois society in the United States was characterized by balance, based on religion, between individualism and social responsibility, and between individual liberation and strong communal ties. Secularized "hyper-modernity" has lost this balance to "hyper-rationality" and "hyper-individualism" (Berger and Berger 1984, 118). Donohue (quoted in Christiansen 1991, 113) states similarly: "Intoxicated with rights, many Americans have lost interest in traditional concomitant responsibilities."

The role of organized religion in the preservation of the family must differ from country to country. There is no question that social and moral values are deeply rooted in religion. Yet many of these values are progressively reinterpreted in abstract and secular terms and reincorporated into the social sciences and social services in secular societies. A study by Mason (1978) of the cohort of 200 adult children of Christian missionaries serving in China from 1900 to 1949 illustrated the cross-generational transformation of religious beliefs into secular values. Few of these adults, who had spent their childhoods in China, entered church-related careers; most were pursuing social reform movements and social service professions similar to the educational, social welfare, and health-related services provided by the missionary communities of their childhoods. Most of the respondents considered themselves less religious than their parents and most showed a significant shift to liberal religions or to no religion. Secular Jews who no longer follow the strict dietary laws of traditional Judaism are prominent in the scientific nutrition profession in the United States as arbiters of the dietary rules that govern healthful diets.

257

The values transmitted through social services alone, however, may be too diluted to be compelling. Private and voluntary religious practice also may fail to fill the gap between the strength of values in religious versus secular societies. Many programmes, usually in developed countries, revolve around supports and services including child care, counselling, and addressing problems of individual shortcomings. Judging from the literature, family cohesion is not always as positively correlated with increased availability of services as was generally hoped. What may be the case is that the availability of these services has improved family cohesion by diminishing stress and tension levels against a backdrop of increasingly eroded values, technologies, and lifestyles, which in themselves result in increased levels of stress and tension (United Nations 1987). These observations strengthen the argument for cultural renewal and social construction in the direction of stronger moral or religious values.

Religious revival as part of cultural renewal

In most cases, a strong continuity of religious and cultural values appears to buffer a country against the negative effects of modernization. Therefore, to the extent possible, countries may wish to maintain or enhance the influence of religion on family life. On the negative side, many lives have been lost in wars waged in the name of religion, and burgeoning civil unrest in many parts of the world involves a resurgence of inward-looking isolationist forms of fundamentalism. Fundamentalist religious interpretations that exclude women from public life and educational opportunity cripple the next generation. This occurs because uneducated and secluded mothers cannot prepare their children for competition in modern labour markets. Women whose lives are confined to the home also can hardly be expected to bear only one or two children, when child-bearing is their main source of fulfilment. Therefore, the effects of religious revival on the family depend on the progressive or regressive nature of the values revived.

We believe that there are positive benefits for the family in the religious revival occurring among the younger generation in Indonesia, although this revival may be viewed as a counter-modernization movement. Government policy backs this movement by requiring all private and public schools to teach religious and moral values as part of the core curriculum, from the kindergarten to the university level. The government also preserves national moral values through censorship: forbidding Western-style beauty contests in which the contestants wear bathing suits; rigorously censoring Western movies with regard to explicit sexual activities and violence; and heavily supervising television programmes. For the westerners, this censorship would violate individual rights and civil liberty. Conversely, Western individualistic values are offensive to the communitarian Indonesian culture, for which the balance between individual and community interests is the fundamental value governing daily life. Chapter 6 described in detail how these values influence Javanese society.

Secular approaches

In some countries, secular social values appear to succeed in protecting children without requiring marriage or two-parent families. In Denmark, for example, fathers and stepfathers continue to invest in the child after divorce. Every man who lives with the child is socially bound to stay in contact with that child, whether he is the biological father, mother's friend, or legal stepfather. The pressure of secular public opinion does not allow men to avoid this responsibility (W.J. Doherty 1992, personal communication). In such settings, in which fragmented and permeable families are the norm, it may be important to accept pluralistic definitions of the family, to abandon the preoccupation with keeping both biological parents and their children together, and to refocus on bolstering the values and processes that will work in a broad variety of family types.

Slowing, speeding, or adjusting cultural change

Studies conducted by Aldous (1961), in West Africa, and Burch (1967), using data from India, Nicaragua, and the United States, showed that many traditional family support structures persisted to varying degrees in modern life. The extended family system appears to be re-created in the urban areas by the migrant family. Burch concluded that "the non-nuclear component of the family may not uniformly decrease in urban areas of developing countries. This fact calls for some modification of the prevailing views about the 'breakdown of the extended family' in the face of modernization" (Burch 1967, 363).

One may argue that the conditions of developing societies may be more typical of earlier stages of industrialized society as described by Hareven (1990). The major transition may not go further in the same directions experienced by the industrialized countries. Examples from Japan's experience with its capitalist system (Rozman 1991) and Korean immigrants in the United States, some of whom maintain their extended kinship orientation (*Wall Street Journal*, June 1992) and some of whom discard it as soon as they are able (American Public Radio, July 1992), provide conflicting evidence. Berger and Berger (1984) introduce the term "creative schizophrenia": "the individual in the modern urban-industrial situation can be modern at work, and traditional at home, alternating between these two worlds of his life in a manner that is not only quite comfortable but actually productive" (Berger and Berger 1984, 88). Growing breakdown of the family in the process of transition in developing countries also has been marked by extreme poverty and lack of access to employment and other opportunities.

The main issue is how to introduce innovations in traditional societies while bridging gaps and enhancing social balance; how to slow the clock socially with respect to important cultural values and to revitalize these values while speeding the clock technologically. Referring back to the end of chapter 2, we believe that the credibility of the notion of human progress may depend on both local and global initiatives to create a new vision of quality of life at the family level that is in harmony with environmental and economic solutions at the global level. As mentioned before, it is the task of intellectuals and leaders to analyse these issues and to make recommendations.

Seeking answers in post-modern industrial conditions and Asian examples

As noted in chapter 2, the economic focus of the twenty-first century, according to Thurow (1992, 45), will be on new technological process industries that can be located anywhere on the globe. This fact creates possibilities for economic viability in any country that can train a labour force to meet the demands of the process industries. Viability in the competition for new processes does not depend on creative autonomy, but on high mathematical and technical skills and a disciplined workforce. The mastery of these skills requires disciplined educational effort from a young age – effort that may be best sustained by cohesive family ties.

These global conditions may profoundly shift the emphasis of the global youth culture. The lure of thrill-seeking and autonomous consumerism could yield to tolerance for the detail and routine required by process work. To the extent that the industrialized countries redirect their own youth cultures towards the production of disciplined children and cohesive families, it may be easier for the élite of developing countries to follow suit.

Instead of looking to "the West" for trend-setters, developing countries that wish to industrialize while retaining hierarchical traditional values may be able to turn towards Japan and the "little dragons" of the Pacific Rim (Vogel 1992). Philosophies of early childhood education that prepare the children of these countries for process-orientated skills continue to place more value on respect for elders and authority structures than on self-expression and uninhibited inquisitiveness. Close participation of the family in the children's school experience has been identified as a factor leading to high academic achievement among Asian refugee children in the United States (Caplan, Choy, and Whitmore 1992).

Specific recommendations

The recommendations listed below should be viewed only as a starting point for in-country consideration.

Design of services and programmes

Multi-purpose community-based programmes strengthen Family Management and Family Care while also affecting Family Beliefs, Rules, and Goals and Boundary Maintenance. These programmes build on evidence that good social networks improve family management and family morale. Instrumental assistance, advice, informal monitoring, and approval from support group members, neighbours, and friends increase the accountability and initiative levels of families. Almost all community-based programmes organized by vertical agencies in areas such as health, nutrition, family planning, and micro-enterprise development, can be structured horizontally at the grass-roots level to produce these secondary benefits.

One example from the United States is the Family Resource Program, which in some communities provides a broad range of services for the family, including child care centres, community mental health centres, the Head Start Program, and health clinics, among others (Weissbourd and Emig 1989). An example from Indonesia is the *posyandu* (Integrated Health and Nutrition Programme), which covers maternal and child health and nutrition and family planning

261

services; India's Integrated Child Development Services (ICDS) is another example of a systematically developed package of child and family welfare services.

These developing-country programmes, however, have not yet widely incorporated child development activities or education that help families to cope with the problems of daily life. We recommend that more resources be directed to the following:

1. *Early childhood development education* that takes a two-generational approach, improving both present and future family conditions. These programmes are solidly based on evidence of benefits on school completion, employment, and other impact indicators of good management and good care. They promote child and adult development simultaneously by enhancing the family's management and child-care capacities and strengthening the interdependent relationships between the family and the community. Because of widespread parental interest in child development, it also may be easier to implement nutrition and health activities under the umbrella of total child development than independently.

2. *Family life education* that addresses the full range of issues of family management, goals and caring skills. It can provide an excellent forum for community mobilization to take on community projects.

3. *Family preservation* that provides counselling for families facing all kinds of crises in boundary maintenance. Often, short-term intensive caring by community elders and friends can avert separations that would have long-lasting negative effects on the family.

4. *Migrant assistance programmes* that help to integrate the families of new urban migrants who can successfully find employment, and that help to locate or create rural jobs for those who can be repatriated to their villages. The success of this type of programme depends on infrastructure development in rural areas.

Family and social legislation and social entitlements

Family laws and social entitlements have their greatest influence on Family Beliefs, Rules, and Goals and Family Boundary Maintenance, while also affecting Family Management and Family Care. According to the implications of threat-point analysis ch. 3), a lack of social obligation that fathers support their children operates as a strong economic incentive for the progressive family dissolution apparent throughout the developing world. According to Bruce and Lloyd (1992), this implies the need for the following:

1. *Responsibility and economic costs of children* to be located equitably between mothers and fathers by social norms, procedures, and laws.
2. *Child affiliation and child maintenance policies* to be explicit and widely understood and operated, irrespective of the child's birth circumstances or of the marital or sexual relationship of the parents.
3. *Joint husband–wife land and property titles* to be issued when settlement and irrigation schemes change customary land tenure to individual ownership, and in new low-income housing projects (Dey 1992).
4. *Incentives and programme features that reward father and two-parent participation* to be built into the design of public programmes for children. As examples:
   (a) emphasize messages for men and couples in family planning and related reproductive health efforts;
   (b) encourage fathers' participation in prenatal, delivery, and post-partum care programmes;
   (c) include men and couples as workers and provide messages for them in campaigns to improve early child health;
   (d) draw men into children's education through explicit registration and fee-payment procedures.

The support of developing-country universities and policy institutes

In order for developing regions to achieve cultural renewal, legal reform, and real representation in the policy debates of the "global village," substantive resources need to be transferred to developing-country institutions of higher learning, whether or not the government in power can be persuaded to provide matching funds. It is not possible to base relevant social construction on books and journals that are more than 20 years out of date, as is so often the case in the libraries of developing-country institutions. New forms of academic exchange with industrialized-country institutions can provide a collegial channel for cross-cultural work on family problems. Strengthening university systems is an evident pathway for strengthening the voice of local professionals, since many developing-country universities already are in place, where they serve both as the training

263

ground and research base for intellectual leadership. Collegial exchange fosters a two-way debate and permits resource transfer to be conducted in the spirit of academic freedom without offending national sensitivities. International social policy and research institutes also could be created following administrative models established by agricultural research institutes, and building on the experience of such institutions as the Institute of Nutrition for Central America and Panama (INCAP). Such efforts fail when the demand for counterpart funds is passed on to state universities or institutes that lack adequate operating resources.

References

Aldous, J. 1961. "Urbanization, the Extended Family and Kinship Ties in West Africa." *Social Forces* 41: 6–12.

Becker, G.S. 1992. "Revamp Welfare to Put Children First." *Business Week*, 30 March.

Berger, B., and P. Berger. 1984. *The War Over the Family: Capturing the Middle Ground*. Garden City, NY: Anchor Books.

Bruce, J., and C.B. Lloyd. 1992. "Beyond Female Headship: Family Research and Policy Issues for the 1990s." Paper presented at IFPRI–World Bank Conference on Intrahousehold Resource Allocation: Policies and Research Methods, 12–14 February 1992. IFPRI, Washington, DC.

Burch, T.K. 1967. "The Size and Structure of Families: A Comparative Analysis of Census Data." *American Sociological Review* 32(3).

Caplan, N., M.H. Choy, and J.K. Whitmore. 1992. "Indochinese Refugee Families and Academic Achievement." *Scientific American* 200(2): 36–42.

Christiansen, B.J., ed. 1991. *When Families Fail: The Social Cost*. New York: University Press of America.

Dey, J. 1992. "Gender Asymmetries in Intrahousehold Resource Allocation in Subsaharan Africa: Some Policy Implications for Land and Labour Productivity." Paper prepared for presentation at IFPRI–World Bank Conference on Intrahousehold Resource Allocation: Policies and Research Methods, 12–14 February 1992. IFPRI, Washington, DC.

Dizard, J.E., and H. Gadlin. 1990. *The Minimal Family*. Amherst: University of Massachusetts Press.

Drazen, A. 1978. "Government Debt, Human Capital, and Bequests in a Life-Cycle Model." *Journal of Political Economy* 86: 505–516.

Edwards, G. 1979. "Familiar Groups as Molecules of Society." In: D.P. Snyder, ed. *The Family in Post-Industrial America: Some Fundamental Perceptions for Public Policy Development*. AAAS Selected Symposium, Boulder, Colo.: Westview Press, pp. 63–104.

Folbre, N. 1992. "Rotten Kids, Bad Daddies, and Public Policy." Paper presented at IFPRI–World Bank Conference on Intrahousehold Resource Allocation: Policies and Research Methods, 12–14 February 1992, IFPRI, Washington, DC.

Hareven, T.K. 1990. "A Complex Relationship: Family Strategies and the Processes of Economic and Social Change." In: R. Friedland and A.F. Robertson, eds. *Beyond the Market Place*, New York: Aldine de Gruyter, pp. 215–244.

Mason, S.R. 1978. "Missionary Conscience and the Comprehension of Imperialism: A study of the Children of American Missionaries in China, 1900–1949." Unpublished Ph.D. thesis, Northern Illinois University, Dekalb, Ill.

Morris, D. 1969. *The Human Zoo*. New York: Wiley.

Rozman, G. 1991. "The East Asian Region in Comparative Perspective." In: G. Rozman, ed. *The East Asian Region: Confucian Heritage and Its Modern Adaptation*. Princeton, NJ: Princeton University Press.

Thurow, L.C. 1992. *Head to Head: The Coming Economic Battle among Japan, Europe, and America*. New York: William Morrow.

United Nations. 1986. *The Role of Family in the Development Process*. New York: United Nations.

———. 1987. *The Family: Strengthening the Family, Guidelines for the Design of Relevant Programmes*. New York: United Nations.

Vogel, E.F. 1992. *The Four Little Dragons: The Spread of Industrialization in East Asia*. Cambridge, Mass.: Harvard University Press.

Weissbourd, B., and C. Emig. 1989. "Early Childhood Programs for Children in Poverty: A Good Place to Start." In: G. Miller, ed. *Giving Children a Chance: The Case for More Effective National Policies*.

265

Contributors

Emmanuel D. Babatunde is an Associate Professor of Anthropology and the Director of the Honors Program at Lincoln University, Pennsylvania. His postgraduate studies at Oxford University were in Social Anthropology and led to a Ph.D. in the area of Family Values and Social Change, with particular reference to the impact of an oil boom on the notion of person among the Bini and Yoruba in modern-day Nigeria. He also has a Ph.D. in Comparative Multicultural Education from the Institute of Education, London University.

Dr. Babatunde has published extensively on development and social change, the patrilineal ideology and the status of women, the subtle use of cultural devices such as myths and social expectations to subordinate women, the changing trends in family interaction in Nigeria, and the cultural ritual activities in which women verbalize views unique to them in male-oriented cultures. He has served as a consultant and resource person to numerous national and international projects on the impact of culture on child nutrition, child welfare, food roads, and rural infrastructures, as well as the cultural impact on the moral development of children.

Dr. Babatunde is the Recipient of the 1995 Christian R. and Mary F. Linback Distinguished Teaching Award.

Nancy Colletta is a clinically trained developmental psychologist with a Ph.D. from Cornell University and an M.A. degree in early childhood education. She has worked in developing countries for 25 years. Her work has focused on designing programmes for preschool children both to optimize their development and to prepare them to function more adequately as they enter the formal school system.

Most of Dr. Colletta's fieldwork has been in Asia and includes designing a home-

266

based early intervention programme for poorly nourished preschoolers in Indonesia. That project, located in villages in Central Java, used a cartoon-based curriculum, written on a second-grade literacy level, and trained volunteers to help mothers provide adequate stimulation for their children. In an additional project, a developmental monitoring card, based on the growth-monitoring card, was designed to monitor child development in the first five years of life. The card lists developmentally sequenced milestones and simple interventions for parents to carry out each month. The sound psychometric properties of the card and its ease of use led to it being adopted for national use in Indonesia in 1993.

Working with the Christian Children's Fund and with UNICEF, Dr. Colletta recently conducted a 25-country child development training programme. The programme was designed for those individuals in each country (usually programme officers) who are in charge of designing child development programmes for preschoolers. The training package looked at child development needs in a cross-cultural context, linked children's needs to developmentally appropriate care, and considered developmental interventions of various levels of intensity and duration. Throughout, the emphasis of the training was on programme development and evaluation of programme outcomes. The training programme has been published as *Understanding Cross-cultural Child Development and Designing Programs for Children* (PACT, New York 1992).

David Garman is an Associate Professor of Economics and Deputy Chair of the Department of Economics at Tufts University. He received his Ph.D. in Economics from the University of Michigan in 1984 and has taught at Tufts since 1983.

His research interests centre on applications of econometrics, and he has worked on topics such as the impact of college attendance on earnings, and the flexibility of wage and price across US industries. His work has appeared in the *Journal of Money, Credit and Banking*, the *Journal of Industrial Economics*, *Industrial Relations*, the *Southern Economic Journal*, the *Quarterly Journal of Economics*, and the *American Economic Review*.

He has taught statistics and econometrics for many years, and has designed software that promotes the learning of statistical concepts through visualization.

Ellen Mara Kramer is a paediatric nutritionist with a background in anthropology. Over the past 15 years she has both worked directly in child nutrition programmes and participated in the review and evaluation of programmes. Currently, she works for a Tufts University project that is designing programmes for the Schools of the Twenty-First Century. Ms. Kramer holds an M.A. in Anthropology from Temple University, an M.S. in Nutritional Biochemistry from the Massachusetts Institute of Technology, and an M.S. in Maternal and Child Health from the Harvard School of Public Health. She is a registered dietitian.

Ratna Megawangi is a faculty member of the Department of Community Nutrition and Family Resources at IPB (Bogor Agricultural University, Indonesia). She received her Ph.D. from the School of Nutrition at Tufts University in 1991.

Since 1991, her research interests have focused on women and family. She has served as a principal investigator (PI) to two projects on "The Roles of Husbands in Promoting Family Wellness in Two Provinces" (1993–1994), and "An Evaluative Study on the Indonesian Family Welfare Program" (1994–1996), and as co-PI to an ongoing project on "Family in Transition" (1993–1996).

Dr. Megawangi also serves as a resource person to the Ministry of Population/ National Family Planning Coordinating Board, where she is a member of a National Working Group for Policies on Women. She is also a member of the IAC (In-country Advisory Committee) for Women's Studies in Indonesia.

Beside her academic work, she is also a columnist writing extensively on women and family issues in newspapers and journals in Indonesia.

Marian Frank Zeitlin is a Professor at the School of Nutrition, and a Senior Research Associate at the Eliot Pearson Child Study Department of Tufts University in Medford, Massachusetts. She also is a Visiting Professor in the Sociology Department of the University of Lagos, Nigeria. Dr. Zeitlin specializes in social science research related to nutrition and the design of nutrition, health, child and family development programmes. With a first degree in mathematics, she received her Ph.D. in International Nutrition Planning from the Massachusetts Institute of Technology. Her work on the family has grown out of a five-year, three-country project for UNICEF on positive deviance in nutrition and on psychological resilience, studying the characteristics that favour normal growth and development among children living in poverty. This project's main research finding was that well-developing children have socially healthy families. She has worked in 24 countries and has published three previous books and numerous book chapters and papers.